'These respected authors have written a comprehensive account of how to promote positive behaviour in the children they work with ... I highly recommend this book to all undergraduates and those new to teaching.'

Marilyn Fleer, Laureate Professor, Monash University, Australia

'The book makes a very valuable contribution to our understanding of behaviour, redresses unreasonable expectations and facilitates in-depth reflection and promotes a strengths-based approach to behaviour management.'

Mary Maloney, Mary Immaculate College, Limerick, Ireland

'O'Toole and Hayes have produced an extremely thought-provoking, comprehensive and accessible text on this most emotive and challenging of topics for educators – the behaviour of the children we work with.'

Jarlath O'Brien, *Times Educational Supplement* **behaviour columnist and author**

CW00819801

Supporting Positive Behaviour in Early Childhood Settings and Primary Schools

Sharing insights of various theoretical perspectives to help understand the complex root causes of children's behaviour, *Supporting Positive Behaviour in Early Childhood Settings and Primary Schools* highlights key responses that can encourage positive mental health, resilience and behaviour.

Drawing on a range of theoretical frameworks, this book:

- Translates theoretical insights into adaptable and practical responses
- Considers children's strengths and needs with regards to resilience and mental health
- Includes case studies, tasks and questions for reflection
- Identifies innovative practical strategies for supporting positive behaviour in educational settings

Combining theoretical perspectives on supporting positive behaviour, *Supporting Positive Behaviour in Early Childhood Settings and Primary Schools* is user-friendly and conceptually unified. It gives early childhood and primary students and teachers a clear understanding of what to do to facilitate positive behaviour and why to do it, encouraging true professionalism in education, and ensuring children learn and develop to their highest potential.

Leah O'Toole is a lecturer in Early Childhood Education with the Froebel Department of Primary and Early Childhood Education, Maynooth University, Ireland.

Nóirín Hayes is Visiting Professor at the School of Education, Trinity College Dublin, Ireland and Professor Emerita, Centre for Social and Educational Research, Technological University Dublin, Ireland.

Supporting Positive Behaviour in Early Childhood Settings and Primary Schools

Relationships, Reciprocity and Reflection

Leah O'Toole and Nóirín Hayes

Routledge
Taylor & Francis Group

LONDON AND NEW YORK

First published 2020
by Routledge
2 Park Square, Milton Park, Abingdon, Oxon, OX14 4RN

and by Routledge
52 Vanderbilt Avenue, New York, NY 10017

Routledge is an imprint of the Taylor & Francis Group, an informa business

British Library Cataloguing-in-Publication Data
A catalogue record for this book is available from the British Library

Library of Congress Cataloging-in-Publication Data
Names: O'Toole, Leah, 1977- author. | Hayes, Nóirín, author.
Title: Supporting positive behaviour in early childhood settings and primary schools : relationships, reciprocity, and reflection / Leah O'Toole and Nóirín Hayes.
Description: Abingdon, Oxon ; New York, NY : Routledge, 2020. | Includes bibliographical references and index. |
Identifiers: LCCN 2019035529 (print) | LCCN 2019035530 (ebook) | ISBN 9781138298064 (hardback) | ISBN 9781138298088 (paperback) | ISBN 9781315098845 (ebook)
Subjects: LCSH: Behavior modification. | Early childhood education.
Classification: LCC LB1060.2 .O86 2020 (print) | LCC LB1060.2 (ebook) | DDC 371.39/3–dc23
LC record available at https://lccn.loc.gov/2019035529
LC ebook record available at https://lccn.loc.gov/2019035530

ISBN: 978-1-138-29806-4 (hbk)
ISBN: 978-1-138-29808-8 (pbk)
ISBN: 978-1-315-09884-5 (ebk)

Typeset in Sabon
by Swales & Willis, Exeter, Devon, UK

Dedicated with all my love to James, Katie, Saidbhín and Cillian (Leah O'Toole)

And to my family and grandchildren May and Eli (Nóirín Hayes)

Contents

CHAPTER 1

Deconstructing authority, control and discipline

INTRODUCTION

Supporting positive behaviour by children is experienced as a challenging aspect of the work of many educators,[1] particularly in the early stages of their careers. It is tempting to look for quick solutions to behaviour 'management' in educational settings, and there are many 'how-to' guides available, offering strategies that purport to be useful in any circumstance. It is easy to see how an educator struggling with issues of behaviour would cling to such ideas in the hope of finding a way to create enough order for children to be able to learn. It must also be acknowledged that working with children who exhibit challenging behaviour can be very stressful, so any approach that offers hope of reducing that stress is attractive.

However, understanding children's behaviour is a complex task. Like all human beings, children have many reasons for behaving as they do, some based on internal factors such as individual dispositions, unmet needs like hunger, or fear and anxiety, and some based on external factors such as inappropriate disciplinary expectations, educational structures and sociocultural mismatches between home and educational settings (Bronfenbrenner and Morris, 2006). Educators are often disappointed when a strategy that offered a 'sure-fire' solution with one child or group of children fails to work with another child or group of children. Unfortunately there is no 'one-size-fits-all' solution to support positive behaviour because every child, group of children, educator and educational setting brings different strengths, challenges and viewpoints to the dynamic interaction that happens between them each day.

Many books on children's behaviour focus on 'management', offering practical strategies without a theoretical lens through which to critique them. Such approaches to understanding behaviour may lead to an emphasis on controlling children, rather than meeting their social and emotional needs to support them to behave positively in educational settings. True professionalism requires an understanding of both *what* to do and *why* it should be done (Olson and Bruner, 1996). Therefore this book aims to give insights on why children behave as they do, and as a result of that understanding, how to formulate appropriate responses on a moment-to-moment, child-to-child basis. Recent work in psychology, sociology and education has shown that such understanding of children's behaviour is best supported through a multi-theoretical, cross-disciplinary approach (Hayes, O'Toole and Halpenny, 2017). No one theory, discipline or strategy provides all the answers.

The aim of this book, therefore, is to share the insights of a variety of theoretical perspectives with educators to support them in their understanding of the complex root causes of children's behaviour. However, the book is not solely theoretical, but rather espouses the idea that the whole point of teaching educators about theory is for them to use it as a lens through which to improve their practice. Through this understanding, the book aims to facilitate development of appropriate responses that may encourage children's positive behaviour in educational settings. It uses a variety of approaches, including case studies, tasks and stimulus questions for reflection to facilitate in readers the development of innovative and effective practical strategies for supporting positive behaviour in educational settings for children from birth until the end of their primary school years.

WHAT IS 'CHALLENGING' BEHAVIOUR?

A variety of terms are often used regarding children's behaviour and we choose in this book to focus on supporting positive behaviour rather than 'managing challenging behaviour' because the language we use can frame our view of what it is we are trying to achieve. When we focus on 'management', we may view children almost as circus animals to be trained or controlled, whereas when we think about support, we understand that children, like adults, are human beings who may need a little assistance every so often to be their best selves (O'Brien, 2018). Nevertheless, it is useful to begin with a reflection on the kinds of behaviours that challenge you personally in the educational setting in which you work. Providing a definition of 'challenging' behaviour is difficult, because perceptions of the appropriateness of behaviour can change based on the context in which it takes place. Consider the experience of the little girl in the following vignette:

> Farida has been attending her local preschool for eight months now. It took her a little while to settle in and learn how her teacher Jane would like her to behave, but she now feels very comfortable here. Today the children are doing some painting. Farida decides her painting would be improved by adding the sun to the sky, so she gets up from the painting table, goes to the cupboard where the paint is kept, chooses some yellow paint and brings it back to the table. 'Well done, Farida, for being so independent', Jane tells her.
>
> Four months later, Farida has left preschool and started in 'big school'. Today the class are painting and again Farida decides to get some paint

to enhance her picture. She leaves her table, and goes to the art cupboard. 'Sit down Farida', says her teacher Ms Farrell. 'That's very naughty, you can't be wandering around the classroom. I have twenty-five other children to work with. You must work independently.'

Source: Hypothetical scenario developed from the points made by Brooker (2008) regarding the use of the term 'independence' at preschool and primary school levels

There is much evidence that expectations of children with regards to their behaviour can change significantly between educational levels (O'Kane, 2015). The meanings imbued by educators at different educational levels or by parents may not match, even though similar language is used. For example, Brooker (2008) notes that at preschool, 'independence' tends to mean the child choosing his[2] own activities, whereas at primary level, 'independence' tends to mean the ability to follow instruction and stay on-task (a task chosen by adults) without intervention. In some ways these skills are actually diametrically opposed, in spite of being given the same label of 'independence', and if adults are unsure what behaviours they want from children, it is little wonder that children sometimes struggle to know how to behave in educational settings.

Even within one educational sector, individual educators may have differing expectations. Consider how a very traditional educator might experience the behaviour of the children (and indeed the educator) in this description of a 'constructivist' classroom provided by Applefield, Huber and Moallem (2000, p. 16):

Ms. Blake's ninth grade classroom can be distinguished from other classrooms both in looks and sounds. Upon walking down the corridors we hear from the classroom at the end of the hallway an array of voices and sounds like buzzing, chattering, an occasional 'I got it' and sometimes expressions of frustration. Upon entering the classroom, we see clusters of students working with various objects. In fact, if it were not for the age of Ms. Blake, it would be hard to identify who the teacher is in this classroom. Ms. Blake is talking with one of the groups near the doorway and says, 'Why did you select that arrangement and place the bulb there? Will it work if attached in another way? Talk about it in your group and I will get back to you shortly.' She then moves to the next group, sits down with them and watches as students continue working with batteries and bulbs in the center of their cluster. They don't seem to notice Ms. Blake and keep on talking with each other. She is smiling as she observes them.

Applefield et al. (2000) make the point that with preconceived notions of ordered, systematic and quiet classrooms, it would be easy to think that Ms Blake had lost control, and that noisy children who are not paying attention to the teacher are misbehaving. However, this, they argue, misses the point that in fact the educator has created a community of learners, engaged in deep, self-directed learning.

Each educator has his own perception of what constitutes 'challenging behaviour'. For one person, noise may be unacceptable, whereas for another, noise is considered an integral part of the learning process. For some educators, it is vitally important that children line up properly in a school yard, for others table manners at lunchtime are crucial, and for yet others what matters is neat writing in a copy book. As human beings we all have our 'pet hates' that may not bother another person quite so much. As children move up through educational systems, from day care to preschool, to primary school, and also between rooms in early educational settings and classes within primary schools, it is quite a difficult task for them to figure out which are the crucial areas of behaviour for the specific adult they will be spending time with this year. Educators are of course entitled to maintain their own personal standards, so long as there is an understanding that 'standards' do not always match across contexts, and if some children need support in understanding what is expected of them, it does not necessarily represent misbehaviour.

REFLECTION

How would you define 'challenging behaviour'? What are your own 'non-negotiables' in terms of behaviour within your educational setting? How might your expectations differ from those experienced by children before now? How might you need to support them to understand what you expect of them? Are there any of your expectations that, on reflection, are not appropriate or reasonable?

EXPERIENCES OF DISCIPLINE AND THE IDEA OF 'REPRODUCTION'

In reflecting on the meaning of 'challenging behaviour', educators must also consider their own experiences of discipline in childhood, because it may be that as human beings we are programmed to reproduce what we know, even if that leads to inappropriate practice.

We all have different ideas about what kinds of behaviour might challenge us. We also all have different experiences of discipline, and different ideas of what is appropriate. In some classic sociological work on how educators are formed, Lortie (1975) identified the concept of an 'apprenticeship of observation', whereby the experiences of educators in colleges of education have little impact when compared with the implicit learning that occurs while sitting in classrooms as students. In other words, educators are likely to teach in the ways that they were taught, without much critical analysis of whether or not these are the best methods.

Similarly, and more specifically related to children's behaviour, Toshalis (2010) shows how student educators reproduce the kinds of discipline they experienced themselves. He maintains that colleges of education often keep rigid control of their students, and student educators are not supported to attempt creative practices that run the risk of something going wrong. The message given to student educators, according to Toshalis, is that resistance is more costly than compliance, and it is acceptable to allow oneself to be controlled from 'above', so long as one maintains control over those 'below' – the children. Reproduction of disciplinary approaches may be appropriate when one's own experiences of discipline have been good, but what about where unfair, discriminatory or even abusive practices have been in place? Common sense might indicate that such educators would be more likely to aspire to fairness, having experienced unfairness themselves, but there is extensive psychological research dating back decades to show that in fact, human beings tend to recreate what they know, even in circumstances that they themselves experienced as difficult.

For example, Chapter 3 notes the work of Albert Bandura (1977) on social learning theory, which shows how children tend to imitate the actions of adults, even where those actions are aggressive or violent. Alternatively, children with gentle adult models tend to behave gently. This has been used to explain findings such as those of Baldry (2003) that children who witness violence in the home are more likely to bully other children. Chapter 4 describes the insights of attachment theory, whereby an 'internal working model' (IWM) of relationships is developed based on experiences within early relationships. This internal working model directs our behaviour within all future relationships, and dictates what we expect from them, so that in later childhood and in adulthood we tend to recreate friendships, romantic relationships and other interactions that mirror the dynamics of those early relationships, even if they were characterised by violence, neglect or distress. Chapter 8 draws on the work of Bourdieu (1997) to show how reproduction can even work at a broader cultural and societal level, and educators can be complicit in ensuring that certain groups of children are excluded from educational success, often based on valuing certain behaviours, devaluing others, and responding to children differentially as a result. These understandings can contextualise the findings of Toshalis (2010) that without regular reflective practice and critical examination of their own schooling experiences, educators are likely to perpetuate destructive trends in discipline that were modelled to them. Take a moment to reflect on the approaches to discipline that were modelled to you in your education to date:

REFLECTION

Bring to mind an example of discipline experienced in your childhood that you felt was fair, either involving a parent or an educator. What behaviour on your behalf was being addressed? How did the adult respond? How did you feel during and after the interaction? What effect did it have on your subsequent behaviour? What elements of that approach would you like to reproduce in your own efforts as an educator to support children's positive behaviour?

Bring to mind an example of discipline that you felt was unfair, either from a parent or an educator. What behaviour on your behalf was being addressed? How did the adult respond? How did you feel during and after the interaction? What effect did it have on your subsequent behaviour? What elements of that approach should you ensure not to reproduce in your own efforts as an educator to support children's positive behaviour?

Considering our own experiences in retrospect requires a commitment to reflective practice and critical analysis. Educational systems generate complicity, and both students and educators unconsciously collaborate to maintain status quo. Those who benefit most from the system, such as those who have progressed through educational systems to sufficient standard to become educators themselves, are disciplined into believing in their own merit, and that they 'deserve' that outcome. Those who benefit least, such as those who leave school early or who do not reach their academic potential, are disciplined into believing that this is due to a flaw in them rather than any flaw in the system (Bourdieu, 1991). Equally, there may be a tendency to sanitise our memories of discipline. For example, Bower and Knutson (1996) found that people who experienced a specific form of physical discipline as a child were less likely to label that form of discipline as abusive.

Toshalis (2010) has also shown how educators often resort to punitive disciplinary approaches when efforts at engagement of children are unsuccessful. Educators can become so focused on maintaining discipline that they act against any sign of creativity or independence of spirit, defaulting to discipline as a way of coping with what they perceive to be challenging or off-task behaviour. They may focus more on discouraging misbehaviour than on promoting learning or inspiring engagement. This book aims to give readers the opportunity to step outside their own disciplinary history and fears about 'losing control', in order to mindfully decide how they would like to approach the promotion of positive behaviour in the children they work with.

AUTHORITY AND CONTROL

Educators are often in a unique position in their experiences of authority, control and discipline. On the one hand, in their work with children, they are often considered as the adult to hold the role of 'power', notwithstanding recent moves towards recognition of the agency of the child (Hayes et al., 2017). On the other hand, particularly in the early stages of their career, educators may work within relatively rigid structures that require them to conform to institutional norms (Toshalis, 2010). There is much evidence from classic work in social psychology that being in positions of authority may bring out the worst of human nature (Zimbardo, 1971), but that equally obedience in the absence of proactive, critical analysis of such institutional norms can have devastating effects (Milgram, 1965).

The Stanford Prison Experiments

In 1971, Philip Zimbardo and his colleagues in Stanford University designed a study that aimed to investigate the psychology of prison life that has since become known as an infamous and disturbing insight into the corrupting nature of power. A group of students were randomly assigned as guards or prisoners in a mock prison, and on the morning that the experiment began, the students allocated as prisoners were 'arrested' at their homes and brought to the 'prison' in the basement of Stanford University. There, they were fingerprinted, strip-searched, blindfolded and taken to their cells. Uniforms and identification numbers were used to make 'prisoners' feel anonymous. 'Guards' were also given uniforms, mirrored sunglasses, whistles and billy clubs. Within an astonishingly short period of time, the guards began to resort to extreme measures to assert their authority over the prisoners, including sleep deprivation through 'counts' in the early hours, physical punishments, and a variety of humiliations designed to dehumanise the prisoners and break their spirit (Zimbardo, Maslach and Haney, 2000). Following a prisoner rebellion protesting these methods on the second day of the experiment, the guards (who, remember, were really young students playing a role) stripped the prisoners naked, took their beds, placed the 'ringleaders' into solitary confinement and escalated their harassment of all other prisoners. In order to break the solidarity between 'prisoners', they set up a system of privileges, whereby those who were most compliant could gain rewards such as food, a comfortable bed and the opportunity to wash. The experiment had to be ended after only six days because the guards became so sadistic and the prisoners became so depressed and even physically and mentally ill (Zimbardo et al., 2000). Readers may wish to visit www.prisonexp.org/ to find out more about the Stanford Prison Experiments.

In reflecting on this infamous experiment in later years, Zimbardo noted that even he became so immersed in his role as prison warden that he lost all sight of the original purpose of the experiment, and almost forgot that he was a social psychologist supposedly studying a social phenomenon (Zimbardo et al., 2000). The damage inflicted on participants of this research was extensive, and

Zimbardo's work has been vigorously criticised on ethical grounds (Perry, 2012). In defending the research, Zimbardo stated that:

> The value of the Stanford Prison Experiment (SPE) resides in demonstrating the evil that good people can be readily induced into doing to other good people within the context of socially approved roles, rules, and norms, a legitimizing ideology, and institutional support that transcends individual agency.
>
> (Zimbardo et al., 2000, p. 193)

The relevance of this research to education thus becomes clear – educational settings provide such socially approved roles (educator), rules and norms (disciplinary policy and practice), legitimising ideology (the importance of education), and institutional support (educational systems) that may, in the absence of reflective practice and critical consciousness, cause otherwise good, kind adults to treat children in appalling ways. While physical discipline is now illegal in many countries, it still persists in some, and even where it is illegal, some 'borderline' practices persist, such as forcing children to stand in one position for long periods of time. Through an international human rights lens, this is known as the 'stress position' and has been identified as a form of torture (Sussman, 2005). Educational settings sometimes also use humiliation as a punishment, through approaches that publicly shame a child. Objecting to such practices within an institutional setting is not always easy, as illustrated by the work of Zimbardo's high-school classmate, Stanley Milgram, in his classic work on human processes of obedience.

The Milgram experiments

Stanley Milgram designed his infamous studies of compliance and obedience in the wake of the Nuremberg trials after World War II.[3] Here, many Nazi soldiers had maintained that they were simply following orders in carrying out some of the most gruesome and inhumane acts of the Holocaust. Milgram wondered whether there was something inherent in the German psyche that led ordinary people to behave so abhorrently, or whether anybody in similar circumstances might do the same. From 1961 to 1962, he conducted over twenty experiments designed to investigate this, and invited participants to take part in a study that they thought was about the processes of memory and learning (Perry, 2012).

In the most famous variation of the experiment, when a participant arrived at the laboratory, he was greeted by a man in a white coat who looked the very picture of authority, and a person purporting to be another participant who was in fact a member of the research team. He was told that one participant would be randomly assigned as the teacher and another would be assigned as the learner, but the draw was rigged so that the real participant was always the teacher, and the accomplice was always the learner (Milgram, 1965). The participant was told that his job was to teach the learner a list of word associations and punish him by administering an electric shock when a mistake was made. The learner was brought to a room and, in the presence of the participant, seemingly strapped to a device that would administer the electric shocks. The participant was then brought to another room and given control of the 'shock generator'. The shock generator, which of course was not actually functional, contained thirty voltage levels ranging from 15 to 450 volts with designations ranging from 'slight shock' to 'danger: severe shock' (Milgram, 1965, p. 128). The 'teacher' was instructed to increase the voltage level each time the 'learner' made a mistake in the word pairings. Milgram found that in spite of cries of pain, demands to stop the experiment and more ominously, sudden silence from the next room, two-thirds of people would continue to administer the electric shocks at increasing voltage levels simply because the 'experimenter' told them to. In other words, the majority of people were willing to electrocute and potentially murder another human being simply because someone in authority had told them to do so.

Perry (2012) provides a fascinating history of the Milgram experiments in her book *Behind the Shock Machine*. She highlights the unethical nature of these experiments, which in many cases left their participants traumatised and carrying crippling guilt for the rest of their lives. They would not be replicated today in any reputable scientific setting, although they have been replicated for entertainment purposes through reality television (Perry, 2012). Perry critiques the traditional view of the Milgram experiments as an insight into the effects of authority in normal settings, highlighting the extensive lengths that Milgram went to in order to create circumstances in which participants were most likely to obey. Nevertheless, the Milgram experiments are still discussed and deconstructed even in modern psychology because, like the Stanford Prison Experiment, they highlighted 'the evil that good people can be readily induced into doing to other good people' (Zimbardo et al., 2000, p. 193) given the right (or rather the wrong) contexts. Understanding the power of contextual factors to overcome our internal moral compasses, it is not hard to imagine a student or newly qualified educator engaging in abusive or inappropriate disciplinary measures in an educational setting, simply because a principal or more senior educator tells him to. Awareness of these processes can help us to interrupt them, and ensure that our personal moral compass on appropriate support for positive behaviour for children is not overcome by negative institutional norms.

In particular, it is worth noting that in over half of the variations of Milgram's experiments, more than 60% of people disobeyed the experimenter (Perry, 2012). Clues as to why can be drawn from the specific contexts developed within each variation. Interestingly, Milgram (1965) ran a version of the experiment whereby an additional complicit researcher pretended to be a participant, and in this version, the second researcher was also allocated as a 'teacher'. He would object to the experimenter's encouragement to continue to shock the 'learner' and refuse to continue. Milgram found that this effectively freed the participant from obedience to the experimenter, and thirty-six of the forty participants refused to continue, whereas in the original variation without such 'moral support' only fourteen of the forty participants resisted the pressure to conform. This highlights the power of one voice to free others to express concern about abusive practice. If we transfer this to the educational setting, we see how an objection to inappropriate disciplinary practices by one educator may free his colleagues from the binds of conformity, allowing them to also resist inappropriate institutional norms. Again, this highlights the importance of a conscious, reflective and critical analysis of what constitutes 'challenging' behaviour and what are the best, and worst, ways to respond to it.

CONCLUSION

This introductory chapter has offered an opportunity to deconstruct ideas of discipline, authority and control, while also encouraging readers to reflect on their own previous experiences in order to become conscious of potential processes of reproduction that may or may not be appropriate. It aims to support educators to step outside automatic responses, and to identify the need for reflective practice in supporting children to behave positively. The following chapters continue this exploration of children's behaviour, identifying its causes and suggesting potential solutions for dealing with difficult behavioural situations, drawing on a variety of insights from theory, research and practice.

In Chapter 2, an 'authoritative' approach to promoting positive behaviour is explored. Educators often wonder about the most appropriate and effective interaction style for supporting positive behaviour, and often feel compelled to choose between strict approaches to discipline based on control and 'zero tolerance', and relationship-based approaches that emphasise care but perhaps neglect boundaries for children. This chapter introduces Diana Baumrind's (1971) concept of authoritative parenting which has in recent years been translated into the concept of authoritative teaching (Gregory et al., 2010). The central argument of this approach is that rather than creating a dichotomy between 'structure' (boundaries, clear rules) and 'support' (a sense of belonging, care and self-direction), children need both.

Much contemporary work on supporting positive behaviour in educational settings draws on classic behaviourist concepts, developed by psychologists such as Watson and Rayner (1920) and Skinner (1953). The key ideas within this approach are introduced in Chapter 3. Behaviourists believe that all behaviour is learned through association and reinforcement and so can be unlearned or reshaped through judicious application of reward and consequence. This chapter will support readers to understand how children's behaviour can be shaped through control of the educational environment, including triggers preceding behaviour and consequences that follow it. Importantly, however, this chapter will also explore critiques of behaviourist theory, since many guidelines for educators that use this conceptual lens fail to declare their theoretical foundations, and so often disguise their limitations. These limitations are deconstructed in detail in this chapter.

Chapter 4 examines children's behaviour through a relational lens, drawing on psychoanalysis (Freud, 1955) attachment theory (Bowlby, 1969, 1973, 1980,

1988) and Ryle and Kerr's (2002) Cognitive Analytic Therapy. Readers will be supported, through theoretical exploration and case studies, to understand that behaviour may be influenced by the emotional life of the child. Key concepts include 'internalising' behaviour, whereby the emotions are directed inwards leading to withdrawal and/or self-damaging behaviours; 'externalising' behaviours, whereby emotions are directed outwards, leading to aggression and violence; 'hypervigilance', whereby a child who has experienced trauma is constantly on the alert for danger, and may see it even when it does not exist, leading to inappropriate 'fight or flight' responses; and 'catharsis', or achievement of emotional release to avoid misdirection of energy into challenging behaviour. The dynamic nature of relationships will also be explored, highlighting the role of the 'internal working model' and 'reciprocal roles' of both children and educators.

A humanist perspective is investigated in Chapter 5, and this foregrounds the idea that a child's behaviour is a manifestation of a complex inner world, so that approaching the development of positive behaviour solely from the adult's perspective shows only half the reality. Such approaches emphasise the capacity of all human beings, including children, to develop positively, and frame negative behaviour as a form of communication and a coping strategy in a world perceived by the child as hostile (Rogers, 1995). In supporting children's positive behaviour, humanists emphasise self-direction rather than coercion, genuineness, empathy and unconditional positive regard (Freiberg and Lamb, 2009). This approach is also sometimes known as 'person-centred' or 'student-centred'.

Chapter 6 will help readers to understand how simple biological considerations such as hunger or tiredness can impact on children's behaviour, and to identify simple interventions based on this knowledge that can prevent episodes of negative behaviour from occurring. Readers will also be introduced to the concept of 'executive function' and how children's brain development over time can have implications for their behaviour through the development of skills such as impulse control and self-regulation. Children's biological need for movement and play will also be emphasised, along with a strong caution for educators to avoid mistaking an inability to sit still for misbehaviour. Temperament will be considered as an influence on behaviour, and some additional physical and sensory needs will be considered. The chapter introduces the 'biopsychosocial' model (Engel, 1977) as one means of understanding the complex and integrated way in which biology interacts with psychological and social factors to influence behaviour.

Chapter 7 introduces the reader to the work of Urie Bronfenbrenner, the principal architect of bioecological theory. He argues that it is impossible to understand a child's behaviour unless we consider the context in which it occurs. In its most recent iteration (Bronfenbrenner and Morris, 2006) the bioecological model of human development identifies *process* factors (such as relationships between children and adults), *person* factors (such as temperament), *context* factors (such as classroom climate) and *time* factors (such as the child's age) that must be understood in interaction with each other to explain behaviour. In this chapter, readers will be supported to use Bronfenbrenner's Process–Person–Context–Time (PPCT) model to draw together the learning from previous chapters, deconstruct the root causes of specific examples of children's behaviour and identify potential responses.

Developing the ideas introduced in Chapter 7, Chapter 8 further interrogates the influence of culture on behaviour, and on perceptions of that behaviour. Through the lens of sociocultural theory, we see that many beliefs and practices relevant to children's behaviour vary across cultures – norms of behaviour, images of children and their competence and responsibilities, beliefs regarding the appropriateness of various forms of discipline, and ideas on how relationships between adults and children should be conducted. When there are differences between home and educational settings regarding beliefs and practices, a child can be seen as misbehaving when his behaviour would be acceptable in a different context. This applies to socioeconomic considerations as well as those based on language, ethnicity and religion (Bourdieu, 1997). Since culture is in many ways invisible when we are immersed within it, educators' attempts to support children to behave positively are often guided by biases and assumptions of which the educator is unconscious. This chapter will support readers to deconstruct their own class-based, cultural and linguistic 'taken-for-granted' assumptions, with a view to analysing how they could, if unchallenged, potentially contribute to or trigger children's behaviour within educational settings.

While the various approaches to supporting positive behaviour outlined in this book must necessarily be presented in a linear format for ease of comprehension, Chapters 6 and 7 show how, in reality, children's behaviour is not straightforward but rather is messy and complicated, with many factors combining and interacting to influence outcomes (Hayes et al., 2017). Therefore, in real-life situations, educators need to draw on a variety of theoretical perspectives incorporating a wide range of practical solutions in supporting positive behaviour. Chapter 9 allows the reader to synthesise the theoretical ideas presented in previous chapters by applying them to the practical example of countering bullying in educational settings. Various issues related to bullying among children will be presented in this chapter, including definitions and categories of bullying (physical, relational, cyber, homophobic, etc.) and warning signs that bullying may be taking place. The chapter then proceeds to analyse how the approaches and understandings outlined in previous chapters might be adapted to counter bullying in the educational setting.

In the final chapter, Chapter 10, key points of learning are identified to support children's positive behaviour. Previous chapters present a range of theoretical and practical approaches, some of which may even seem contradictory to novice readers. This chapter will support readers to come to terms with these tensions, helping them to identify their own personal theories of children's behaviour, and also articulating some common threads that weave through all or most of the theories and practices explored in this book. Such common threads include the importance of warm and caring relationships between adults and children in supporting positive behaviour, the need to understand children's experiences, perspectives and agency to develop appropriate responses, and the power of positive support for good behaviour as opposed to a focus on punishment for negative behaviour.

NOTES

1 There are a variety of terms used in research and practice to describe adults who work with children in educational settings, including 'teacher', 'preschool teacher', 'early years practitioner' and 'early childhood educator' to name a few. This book uses the term 'educator' to refer to adults working with children at both early years and primary level. The term 'educational settings' is used to refer to schools, preschools and other early years educational contexts. The book is aimed at educators working with children from birth to the end of their primary school years.

2 The reader should note that male and female pronouns are used in alternate chapters throughout this book in order to facilitate a gender-balanced approach. In this chapter we begin with male pronouns, chapter two will use female pronouns, and so on.

3 Milgram's documentary on these experiments entitled 'Obedience' is available here: https://video.search.yahoo.com/search/video?fr=mcafee&p=milgram+documentary+obedience#id=1&vid=ed1752a79dfe795bc6ebb8d392bf7282&action=click

CHAPTER 2

An authoritative approach to promoting positive behaviour

INTRODUCTION

Chapter 1 highlighted the importance of reflective practice when supporting positive behaviour in educational settings. This can be challenging, because when we attempt to step outside our automatic responses, and question our methods, sometimes we are left unsure about the most appropriate and effective approaches. King and Kitchener (1994, 2002) refer to this as the quasi-reflective stage of reflective thinking, and show how educators can sometimes be immobilised by a sense that if all their implicit 'taken-for-granted' knowledge is no longer reliable, how can they ever know with certainty how to act in an educational setting? With regard to children's behaviour, educators often feel compelled to choose between strict approaches to discipline based on control and 'zero tolerance', and relationship-based approaches that emphasise care but perhaps neglect boundaries for children. Consider the experience of this student educator:

> I suppose when I started on placement I had in my head that I wanted the children to like me. I got into teaching in the first place because I loved my teachers in primary school, especially my second class teacher. I remember she was just so kind, and she always made you feel like she wanted you there in the classroom. She never shouted at us, and I went in thinking that's the kind of teacher I want to be. Well, did I get a shock! There was one little guy in the class who just wouldn't sit still, he'd be walking around the classroom all morning. I'd ask him to sit down and he'd laugh in my face. Another girl repeatedly threw herself on the floor, and there were another two girls who just spent all day distracting the other children and being aggressive towards them. I tried being kind and gentle and asking them to consider other children's feelings and all I got were smiles and giggles in return. The class teacher and my school placement supervisor told me I had to be stricter to maintain order in the classroom so after that I decided to be scary! If any of them put a toe out of line I shouted at them. I ordered the little guy

walking around to sit down immediately or he'd be sent to the principal's office, and I did have to send him a few times. And that approach was an even worse disaster than the 'softly-softly'! Some children rebelled and got even more challenging, and then one day I was shouting at this little girl for something, I can't even remember what she did, and she burst into tears. She was sobbing, and I realised she was shaking and I thought 'Oh no! What am I doing?! She's six years old!' I'm very worried about my next placement. The 'please like me' approach really doesn't work but the 'be afraid of me' approach doesn't either!

Source: Reproduced with the permission of an undergraduate student educator

This student discovered what many other educational practitioners, researchers and theorists have also noted: a child's world needs to be stable, consistent and predictable. If her routine is chaotic, with no established rules, a child will find it hard to cope. However, if the rules are too rigid with no room for flexibility, or if adults are aggressive and frightening, this can have many negative effects also (Bronfenbrenner and Morris, 2006), and is of course ethically indefensible. In recent decades, those studying children's behaviour have realised that rather than creating a dichotomy between 'structure' (boundaries, clear rules) and 'support' (a sense of belonging, care and self-direction), children need both (Hayes et al., 2017). In an educational setting characterised by excessive strictness and aggression from adults, or in a chaotic educational setting characterised by a lack of boundaries or support for positive behaviour, children tend to behave badly. Balance between structure and support is required (Gregory et al., 2010). Much of this understanding originated with Diana Baumrind's (1971) concept of authoritative parenting which has since been translated into the concept of authoritative teaching (Gregory et al., 2010).

BAUMRIND'S PARENTING STYLES

Baumrind developed her theories by observing interactions between preschool-aged children and their mothers. She found that the most effective parenting styles were characterised by appropriate levels of structure and direction to promote positive behaviour, but that this was balanced with acceptance of the child, a strong emotional connection, and granting autonomy to encourage self-reliance in an age-appropriate way. Using this framework, Baumrind identified 'styles' of parenting that are still referred to in modern psychology, and she called them authoritarian, permissive, neglectful and authoritative.

Authoritarian parents focus on controlling children. They do not allow children to make any decisions for themselves and they do not allow any independence of thought or behaviour. They are not accepting of children's individual needs or differences and so are often rejecting of children. They expect children to accept their judgement unquestioningly – 'Because I said so!' Children with authoritarian parents often show anxiety and unhappiness, low self-esteem, hostility, aggression, dependency, lack of interest in the environment, getting overwhelmed by challenging tasks, and poor academic performance (Hayes et al., 2017). Consider the behaviour of the child in this vignette. Think about how experience of an authoritarian parent might have contributed to it:

Today the children are working with lots of different materials to create an image of their 'dream home'. 'It could be up in the clouds, or under the sea', says their educator, Bisi. 'I'm going to put a slide instead of stairs in mine!' shouts Alannah. 'Good idea!' says Bisi. 'Mine has a stable for nunicorns', says Keith. 'Do you mean unicorns?' smiles Bisi. 'Great idea. Use your imagination everyone'.

After a while, as the children are working on their dream homes, Bisi notices that one little girl is just looking at the other children and the materials without creating anything herself. 'Are you okay, Mia?' Bisi asks. 'Are you not making your dream home?' 'I don't know how to do it right', says Mia quietly. 'But it doesn't have to be "right" Mia, it's just about your imagination, your ideas', says Bisi. She makes some suggestions for what Mia could do ('What about a tree in the garden?') and Mia implements them but seems to find it very difficult to come up with any ideas of her own.

Source: Author observation in an early years setting

When a child experiences authoritarian parenting, self-expression and independence are often suppressed. In an educational setting, children of authoritarian parents may find it difficult to engage in self-directed work, because they have so little experience of deciding on their own actions, and are accustomed to adults telling them what to do. In this vignette, Mia wanted to know how to do the task 'right', with the 'right' way defined by the adult rather than by herself. Such children may need the support of warm, responsive educators when engaging in creative tasks, in order to understand that there are no definitively right or wrong answers, and that mistakes or alternative ideas to those of the adult are not only tolerated but encouraged as part of the creative process. This may help to avoid more extensive negative behaviour – Baumrind found that authoritarian parenting could lead to both withdrawn behaviours and defiant behaviours.

On the other hand, permissive parenting can also have negative effects. Permissive parents exercise little control over their children and allow them to make many decisions for themselves when they are not yet ready to do so. Some permissive parents observed by Baumrind were warm, accepting and overindulgent, and were permissive because they believed that children should be allowed to decide for themselves, or because they believed it was a sign of love to allow children to do what they wished without censure. Some permissive parents felt unable to control their child and so gave up. Some were emotionally detached, or so overwhelmed by their own life stresses that they had little time or energy for interacting with their children. This style of parenting can lead to child neglect. Just as extreme authoritarian control of children can be linked with negative outcomes for children, the other extreme of permissive or neglectful disorganisation within parent–child relationships has been linked with poor outcomes for children also. For example, research has identified impulsivity, disobedience and rebellion (Berk, 2009), along with dependence on adults, less persistence on tasks, poor academic achievement, and anti-social behaviour including bullying (Gregory et al., 2010). Consider the thoughts of this teacher in a primary school reception class:

Some of them are so much more lenient on the child. We would bring them out at home time; some of them are with the parents and are fine, other children are climbing the walls or the garden trees. We wouldn't let them do it. If we brought them for a walk or something and they did that they would be in trouble whereas the parents just seem to let them … There are parents and the child could be running amok and they'd be saying 'He's grand' and you're thinking 'No, he's not!'

Source: O'Toole (2016, p. 260)

It can be particularly difficult for children who experience permissive or neglectful parenting at home to settle into educational settings, because they are not accustomed to rules, boundaries or structure, and they may react badly to them, at least initially. Children of permissive or neglectful parents may provide some of the most challenging experiences to educators, and may require patient, supportive and consistent educators to gently but firmly enforce boundaries. If a child has never experienced rules before, it can take some time for her to understand how they apply. The behaviourist approaches described in Chapter 3 may be particularly useful for establishing boundaries and rules with a child who has little experience of them.

The most successful parenting style identified by Baumrind was the 'authoritative' style. Such parents apply appropriate structure and boundaries for children, but they also show love and acceptance, and allow enough freedom and autonomy for children to develop and learn without becoming overwhelmed. They are warm, attentive and emotionally fulfilling but maintain firm and reasonable control, encouraging self-regulation, emotional expressiveness, communication and, where possible, joint decision making. They create environments that are neither too fluid nor too rigid (Bronfenbrenner and Morris, 2006). These approaches to parenting have been linked with children's positive mood, self-regulation, task persistence, cooperativeness, high self-esteem, responsiveness to parental views, social and moral maturity, and favourable academic performance (Berk, 2009). Note how the father in this vignette ensures that boundaries are maintained to the benefit of the child, but does so in a warm and loving manner:

> Two-year-old Siobhán does not want to go to sleep even though it is well past her bedtime. She has gotten up and come into the sitting room to her father. Her father says he understands that sometimes it is hard to go to sleep, but we all need to rest our bodies and our brains. In spite of protests from Siobhán, he brings her back upstairs, tucks her in and offers to sing her a lullaby to help her sleep.
>
> Source: Author observation

In this case, a permissive parent would not enforce a bedtime for the child at all, but rather would be more likely to allow the child to choose when to go to bed. A neglectful parent would also be unlikely to create boundaries around sleep times, and may not even provide an appropriate sleep space for the child at all. Such a child's sleep could also be interrupted by adults' celebrations, arguments or other needs. Sleep disturbance can have very negative consequences for children in terms of development generally, but more specifically in terms of educational outcomes, since research has identified the link between lack of sleep and cognitive difficulties for children (Bub, Buckhalt, and El-Sheikh, 2011). An authoritarian parent, on the other hand, would be likely to respond aggressively to a child getting out of bed. Bedtime would be rigidly enforced through shouting or even physical restraint, regardless of circumstances, and this could have very negative implications also, because in future a child may not get out of bed to seek help even when it is very much needed due to illness, fear or some other genuine need.

This type of experience could also impact on educational outcomes therefore, since appropriate help-seeking from adults is important to support children's learning and development (Hayes et al., 2017). In this vignette, Siobhán's father ensures that boundaries and rules are maintained, and a simple protest from the child is not enough to deter that in the absence of a good reason for her to be awake. However, he also shows understanding and support for the child in noting that it can be hard to sleep sometimes and offering a strategy to help her sleep, the lullaby. Baumrind's original work, supported by much subsequent research, would predict that experiences of authoritative parenting such as this support children's future self-regulation, responsiveness and positive behaviour in educational settings and beyond (Bronfenbrenner and Morris, 2006).

An intercultural interpretation of Baumrind's parenting styles

One criticism of Baumrind's work is that it may be culturally specific (Chao, 2000, 2001). Hayes et al. (2017) argue that these concepts have value only when viewed through the lens of cultural diversity, and we must not reduce 'good parenting' to checklists and simplistic formulas, as there are many ways to be a good parent. For example, the extent of 'autonomy granting' deemed appropriate varies across contexts and cultures. Belsky (1984) has presented a model of parenting that shows the multiple determinants of parental functioning. What this means is that the behaviour of individual parents depends on many factors, such as the contextual supports and stress they experience, and their own psychological well-being. There are a multitude of influences on parenting styles and on children's behaviour more generally.[1]

Nevertheless, Baumrind's work may still offer a useful conceptualisation of parenting across many settings, contexts and cultures (Hayes et al., 2017; Larzelere, Morris and Harrist, 2013). Authoritative parenting is sometimes simplified into two aspects that seem to contribute to its effectiveness (Gregory et al., 2010): 'support' (parental warmth, acceptance and involvement) and 'structure' (strictness and close supervision as reflected in parental monitoring and limit-setting). This is useful when thinking about parenting across contexts – children need both to know that they are loved (as shown in culturally and individually specific ways) but also what the (culturally specific) rules and boundaries are (O'Toole, 2016). It is also useful in conceptualising approaches to supporting positive behaviour that appear to work well in educational settings – children need to know what the rules in school are but also that they are valued and welcome there.

AUTHORITATIVE APPROACHES IN EDUCATIONAL SETTINGS

The idea of 'styles' of supporting positive behaviour makes sense within educational settings, and this conceptualisation can help us understand interactions between children and educators, as well as those between children and parents. In educational settings, the identification of behaviour-based interactions as authoritarian, permissive, neglectful or authoritative can be useful in helping us to decide upon the most appropriate approaches in a given situation. Authoritarian educators tend to focus on strict discipline that runs the risk of being perceived as unfair by children. They use punitive disciplinary consequences like suspension and expulsion, and 'zero-tolerance' sanctions for even minor violations of rules, with little or no consideration for the circumstances of behaviour, or the child's intentions. On the surface, it may seem fair to treat all children the same and to apply the rules regardless of circumstance or intention, but consider the three children in this vignette. Do you believe that the consequences should be the same for all?

> ### Rule #1: Gentle hands and gentle feet
>
> Two-year-old Lola is playing with a doll. She is putting the doll on the table and covering her with a blanket, saying 'Night, night'. She sees that another child, Sienna, has a similar doll and decides she would like to have both. She walks up to Sienna, and tries to take the doll, but Sienna holds onto it and says 'No, mine'. Lola kicks her and takes the doll.
>
> Nine-year-old James is nervous. One of the other boys in the class, Jaden, has said that he will beat James up at lunch time and it is now time to go out to the school yard. The last time Jaden said that, he tore James's jumper and James got in trouble with his mother. He decides not to wait for the attack, but instead walks straight up to Jaden and kicks him hard in the leg.
>
> Eleven-year-old Eileen is angry. It is art time and one of the other girls in the class, Sandra, is trying to use the red easel. Everyone knows that the red one is Eileen's favourite and that she does her best drawings on it. That easel is hers, and Sandra knows it. Eileen marches over to Sandra and kicks her, telling her to pick another easel straight away or else.
>
> Sources: Author observations in educational settings

In each case in the vignette, it is important that the educator addresses the behaviour – remember, authoritative approaches do not disregard the rules, but rather enforce boundaries in a supportive, individually tailored way. However, while the behaviour is the same in each case – kicking – there are differing circumstances and intentions underpinning each incident. In understanding Lola's behaviour, we may note that there are two points of inappropriate behaviour: physical aggression and an inability to share. On the other hand, we must also note Lola's age, two, and understand that self-regulation of anger, and behaviours such as sharing or waiting, are very challenging for a child of this age (Cole et al., 2011). Lola may need support to behave better in future. Her educator must ensure that Lola understands that kicking is not allowed, and that she must learn to share. However, these boundaries must be enforced within the understanding that two-year-olds can find this very difficult. Her educator might like to model appropriate behaviour ('May I have that doll please Sienna? You're playing with it? Okay, I'll wait my turn'), reward Lola any time she sees her sharing,[2] and intervene any time she shows aggressive behaviour ('No Lola, we do not kick each other here').

James's behaviour (again, kicking) is the same as Lola's but the circumstances and intentions behind it are very different. On the one hand, at the age of nine, James is likely to be better able than Lola to understand why kicking is not allowed and to come up with an alternative strategy. On the other hand, James is clearly being bullied by Jaden, and their educator would need to take this into account when deciding how to respond.[3] In this case, the educator might decide to speak to both children separately, and perhaps to also involve parents. She might draw on the anti-bullying policy of the educational setting and apply its penalties to Jaden, while letting James know that she understands why he kicked in this case but hopes never to see that behaviour again. She must support James with the trauma and fear he has clearly been experiencing, and she might also decide to do some whole-class work on bullying to support all children to behave appropriately.

In Eileen's case, unlike Lola, she is potentially old enough to understand that everyone must share resources within an educational setting, that kicking is not appropriate behaviour, and to come up with alternative strategies to deal with her frustration. Of the three scenarios, Eileen's may require the strictest response and the most severe consequences. Nevertheless, there may be underlying reasons for Eileen's aggression that the educator might need to consider. The educator in this case might like to impose sanctions through, for example, loss of privileges or lack of access to the red easel for a specific length of time, discuss the incident with Eileen to identify her perspective on why she behaved as she did, and support Eileen to develop an alternative strategy to manage frustration such as the use of a squeezy ball or breathing techniques. Eileen may also be required to come up with a way to make up to Sandra for her aggression.[4]

An authoritarian educator treats all children the same and takes a zero-tolerance approach to enforcing the rules regardless of the reasons for behaviour. As we can see from these examples, however, a uniform approach that disregards intention and circumstance can lead to injustice and perpetuate issues such as bullying. Laursen (2003, p. 78) describes a distressing example of how a zero-tolerance approach directed educators towards the patently wrong response to a child in need of support:

> Recently Jessica, a 13-year-old girl, was expelled from a school system because she brought a bread knife to school. Upon arriving at school, she told a teacher that she had the knife in her locker. Subsequently Jessica explained that she brought the knife to school because her mom was suicidal and had been cutting herself on the previous night. She said 'I took the knife so she wouldn't use it to kill herself. That's the only thing I knew to do.'

Equally, educators often blame the children in their classes when they struggle to find teaching methods that engage them. As highlighted in Chapter 1, educators may resort to authoritarian styles because they are fearful of losing control, and they may not have the skills to engage children more appropriately. Authoritarian educators tend to focus more on discouraging misbehaviour than on promoting learning or inspiring engagement (Toshalis, 2010). This can cause alienation from the system that results in negative behaviour, disengagement and poor academic performance from children (Downes and Maunsell, 2007).

On the other hand, permissive educators who tolerate a wide range of behaviour and misbehaviour risk a level of disorder that means children's learning is inhibited (Gregory et al., 2010). Following Baumrind's conceptualisation, permissive educators may be indulgent or neglectful. Where educators are over-indulgent and fail to offer direction to children, the children's learning is limited. While child-directed learning is desirable, and, particularly in the early years, emergent approaches to curriculum are highly effective, in order to maximise learning, educators must also offer opportunities to extend learning (Hayes et al., 2017). A permissive educator tends to allow children to do what they want rather than what might be educationally or behaviourally appropriate. Where educators are disengaged or neglectful, consequences can also be negative for the children they teach; for example, Chapter 9 shows that one of the biggest risk factors for bullying within an educational setting is for adults to disregard its signs and fail to engage with it (O'Moore, 2010). Authoritative educators, on the other hand, meet children's developmental needs with structure that includes establishing clear rules, monitoring behaviour and enforcing rules consistently, but they also support children with warmth and encouragement (Gregory et al., 2010). As Baumrind (1996) describes it:

> Within the authoritative model, behavioural compliance and psychological autonomy are viewed not as mutually exclusive but rather as interdependent objectives: Children are encouraged to respond habitually in pro-social ways *and* to reason autonomously about moral problems *and* to respect adult authorities *and* to learn how to think independently.
>
> (p. 405)

Therefore children's autonomy and an emergent approach to curriculum are not inconsistent with an authoritative approach. Authoritative educators aim for a 'middle ground' that allows for consistent, firm, but fair implementation of rules, while also ensuring the kinds of environments where children can express their creativity and their emotional needs are met. Such educational styles have been linked to better academic performance and engagement, more positive, mutually supportive atmospheres in individual classrooms and at broader school level, more pro-social behaviour, stronger self-efficacy beliefs and higher self-esteem in children (Gregory et al., 2010). Emotional support from teachers is also linked to lower levels of bullying and victimisation in educational settings – if children feel that their educator is caring and concerned they are more likely to seek help when they are bullied, and when children seek help, bullying is reduced and educational settings are safer (O'Moore, 2010). Children require both structure and support from educators. Through this authoritative lens, discipline and support for emotional expression are not seen as being in opposition to each other, but rather as two co-existing, equally important aspects of good education. Consider the examples of structure and support evident in the following vignette, drawn from the authors' experience of the San Miniato approach to early education in Tuscany, Italy:

It is lunchtime and the preschool children (aged two to five years) are sitting outside at three tables. An adult brings the food out on a trolley and one child from each table helps to distribute the plates. Each child takes her turn to ladle some pasta onto her own plate, and when everyone is finished, one child from each table helps the adults to gather up the plates, and another helps to distribute the next course. As they eat, adults and children chat and laugh together. When a little boy gets up to go and play in the playhouse, an educator gently takes his hand and leads him back to the table, reminding him that he can play after lunch but not during it. When a little girl falls asleep, another educator lifts her and takes her quietly into the sleeping area, taking care not to wake her. When two children begin to argue, another educator talks to them both and supports them to find a resolution. As the lunch draws to a close, all of the children help to load up the trolley with plates, and then go inside to play.

Source: Author observation in an early years setting

An authoritative approach to supporting positive behaviour is evident in this example, drawing on concepts of both structure and support. Boundaries are maintained with children in that table manners are expected and facilitated and all children are expected to contribute to the smooth running of the lunchtime routine, tidying up dishes and sharing out food. Educators intervene when the little boy tries to wander off, and when the two children argue, but the interventions are gentle and supportive rather than punitive. When the little girl falls asleep, the educator is respectful and understanding of the two-year-old's developmental need for sleep regardless of the inconvenience of the moment! She supports her by bringing her to a comfortable resting place. Thus, a mixture of structure and support facilitates a happy, relaxed lunchtime experience for both adults and children.

An important point to make is that like parenting, education does not happen in a vacuum. Baumrind showed how adults influence children, but children also influence adults (Hayes et al., 2017). For example, if an educator is firm but warm, children tend to comply with what she says, and when they comply, educators are likely to be firm but warm in future. However, when educators discipline with harshness and impatience, children tend to rebel and resist, and because this is stressful for educators, they become harsher and more impatient, increasing their use of punishment. There are bi-directional influences between adults and children – each influences the other (Hayes et al., 2017). Equally, there are broader influences on dynamics in educational settings, such as culture, language, socioeconomic class and poverty, so disciplinary styles may vary with context. Nevertheless, many psychologists believe that with appropriate sup port, most adults have the capacity to create positive contexts for children's learning, development and behaviour (Hayes et al., 2017). A reflection on our style of interaction to date may be the first step to implementation of an appropriate authoritative style.

REFLECTION

What style do you display in your interactions with children? Do you need to develop more structure and guidance for children, having had perhaps too 'permissive' a style of interaction to date? Do you need to be more emotionally supportive to children? Are your expectations unreasonable, perhaps leading to too 'authoritarian' a style of interaction? Think about specific examples of your interactions with children that did not go the way you might have liked – what might an 'authoritative' adult have done in those circumstances?

(Hayes et al., 2017, p. 37)

CONCLUSION: AUTHORITATIVE EDUCATION IN ACTION

The theoretical concept of authoritative discipline is very useful in supporting educators to understand that a choice between boundaries and emotional support is not only unnecessary, it is counterproductive. Children need both to support positive behaviour. However, implementing an authoritative approach in reality can be challenging, and requires constant refinement and reflection. Some examples of challenging situations have been given in this chapter, along with suggestions for how an authoritative educator might respond. Consider the following vignettes and develop a hypothetical authoritative response, keeping in mind that the educator must *both* enforce rules and boundaries *and* offer emotional support and understanding to the children involved:

Three-year-old Gabriel has just joined your preschool. All of the other children seem to be able to sit down in the lunch area at snack time and eat their food, but Gabriel continuously walks around the room, dropping food everywhere. He also takes the other children's food, upsetting them and leading to arguments.

Ten-year-old Jenny comes to school repeatedly without her homework done. You have spoken to her mother, but she told you that she doesn't believe in weighing children down with homework, and that if Jenny chooses not to do it, she won't force her.

Seven-year-old Paula is a bright child who understands lessons quickly and bores easily. As a result, she is 'acting the clown' in class and distracting other children. She is also undermining you in the classroom by saying rude things to you in front of the other children.

There are many potential responses to these scenarios that could be considered 'authoritative' so long as they feature both structure and support. The coming chapters explore specific approaches that may facilitate both of these elements. For example, Chapter 3 on behaviourism will show specific approaches drawn from the concept of 'reinforcement' that can allow an educator to create structure, boundaries and clear rules. Chapter 4 will develop a relational understanding of the impact of emotion on behaviour, and how children can be supported to express emotion appropriately and so behave positively. Chapter 5 will emphasise access to children's own perspectives, and how children can be supported to regulate their own behaviour through a humanist approach. Chapter 6 will identify the importance of supporting a child's biological needs and understanding how these fit with behaviour. Throughout the latter part of the book (Chapters 7 to 10), all of these ideas can be combined within the framework of an authoritative approach to help the reader understand how to apply such an approach in practice.

Key concepts within this chapter for educational practice

1   Educators should not feel compelled to choose between clear boundaries and relationship-based, emotional care. Children need both structure and support, and behaviour tends to be more positive when both are in place.
2   Rules are culturally specific, as are methods of demonstrating love and care. Educators should be aware of this in developing their approaches to supporting positive behaviour.

NOTES

1 Chapter 8 explores behaviour from an intercultural and diversity perspective.
2 See Chapter 3 on Behaviourism for the theoretical underpinnings of these approaches and practical ideas on how to specifically use rewards. See Chapter 6 to further explore the impact of development on impulse control and self-regulation.
3 See Chapter 9 to explore the causes, warning signs and appropriate responses to bullying.
4 See Chapter 4 for ideas on how to identify underlying causes of emotional outbursts (to the extent that is appropriate in an educational setting), and develop strategies for emotional release. See Chapter 5 for ideas on how to access children's perspectives on events, and restorative approaches.

CHAPTER 3

Behaviourist perspectives and strategies for positive behaviour

INTRODUCTION

Much contemporary work on supporting positive behaviour in educational settings draws on classic behaviourist concepts, developed by psychologists such as Watson and Rayner (1920) and Skinner (1953). The key ideas within this approach to understanding children's behaviour relate to learning through association and learning through reinforcement. Behaviourists believe that all behaviour is learned and so can be unlearned or reshaped through judicious application of association and consequence. This chapter will support readers to understand how children's behaviour can be influenced through control of the educational environment, including triggers preceding behaviour and consequences that follow it.

However, this chapter will also explore critiques of behaviourist theory (sometimes referred to as 'learning theory'), since many guidelines for educators that use this conceptual lens fail to declare their theoretical foundations, and so often disguise their limitations. Behaviourist techniques are often used in educational settings without sufficient attention to questions of why they may or may not be appropriate in a particular situation. Readers will be supported to critically engage with behaviourist approaches on topics such as the positivity of a perspective that believes there is no such thing as a 'bad' child but rather sees potential in all children to behave well, and the practicality and clear direction and support that behaviourism gives to educators. However, this chapter will also problematise the sole focus on control of children as opposed to understanding their internal, emotional reality; extinction of behaviour on removal of reinforcement; and the potential dangers of an approach that seeks to simply shape behaviours rather than understand their cause from a child-protection perspective. A more up-to-date construction of children as agentic and as rights-holders will also be contrasted with the behaviourist image of the child as a subject to be controlled by an adult educator.

BEHAVIOURISM

The focus of the behaviourist approach is, as the name suggests, on overt, observable and measurable behaviour, rather than thoughts, feelings or internal processes of learning (Ertmer and Newby, 2013). The behaviourist approach is based on the theory that an individual's overt and observable behaviour is the result of that individual's learning. In other words, behaviour is learned, and so the implication is that negative behaviour can be unlearned (Woolard, 2010). The behaviourist definition of learning states that learning results in a change in behaviour; to determine whether learning has occurred we should therefore abandon the examination of inaccessible and unobservable mental events in favour of directly observable behaviours (Tennant, 2002). Some well-known behaviourist theorists have influenced many of the approaches widely used in educational settings in the present day. Here we describe the work of Ivan Pavlov, John Watson and B. F. Skinner, and give examples of how their key concepts are often used in education today.

Pavlov

The early 20th century saw an increase in research into learning as a behaviour, exploring how and where learning occurs and how it can be sustained. Much of the early work involved experiments with animals and included the experiments carried out by Ivan Pavlov (1849–1936) a Russian psychologist who, through his studies, recognised that dog behaviour could be manipulated to respond to different stimuli by careful alignment of the stimuli with rewarding events, such as feeding (Pavlov, 1927). Initially, in experiments designed to study digestion, he had observed that dogs changed their behaviour over time, learning to anticipate the arrival of food in association with the presence of preceding stimulus such as a bowl; on seeing the bowl the dogs began salivating even before the food was produced. To test this observation further Pavlov paired unrelated stimuli, such as bell sounds, with the food, and observed that the dogs also salivated to this association, indicating that they had learned that the bell sounds signalled the arrival of food. Pavlov called this process of changing behaviour in association with paired stimuli 'conditioning'. This type of conditioning is known as 'classical conditioning' and is part of everyday learning. For instance, children are not born with a fear of needles, but fear of injections can develop from association with previous negative experience of, in this case, pain. Likewise, students are not born fearing tests and examinations but test anxiety can develop from association with previous negative experiences (Stewart, 2012). Pavlov's observations on classical conditioning serve as the basis for current behaviourist learning theories.

Watson

Pavlov's work was recognised internationally, and in the United States was taken up by psychologists such as John Watson (1878–1958) and B. F. Skinner (1904–1990) to see how Pavlov's principles of learning and behaviour might apply to humans. Watson proposed that the process of classical conditioning was able to explain all aspects of human psychology. He argued that behaviour was simply down to a pattern of a stimulus and response impacting on a 'blank slate' or *tabula rasa*. He argued that individual differences in behaviour were merely a reflection of differential individual experiences, all of which could be manipulated and managed. In this regard he is remembered for the quote below:

> Give me a dozen healthy infants, well-formed, and my own specified world to bring them up in and I'll guarantee to take any one at random and train him to become any type of specialist I might select – doctor, lawyer, artist, merchant-chief and, yes, even beggar-man and thief, regardless of his talents, penchants, tendencies, abilities, vocations and the race of his ancestors.
>
> (Watson, 1924, p. 104)

This is an ambitious claim and one that could never, ethically, be tested. However, in one of the most infamously unethical experiments of all time, Watson and his colleague Rayner (1920) worked with a child called 'Little Albert'. They conditioned fear responses in Albert by pairing loud noises with furry objects so that over time, Albert showed fear of furry objects even without any loud noise. Behaviourists believe that this showed how children learn through association just as animals do. Consider how classical conditioning is successfully used (in much more ethical ways!) in these modern-day educational settings to support children's positive behaviour:

Every morning in Highfield Primary School, before it is time to go into class the children play together in the school yard while the parents talk together. When the bell rings, the children go and get their school bags from their parents, line up and get ready to go into class.

In Ana's room in Sticky Fingers Preschool, when it is time for children to transition from messy play to snack time, Ana sings the clean up song: 'Clean up, clean up, one two three. I help you and you help me'. When the children hear the song, they begin to put away the materials, and sing along while they wash their hands and get ready for their snack.

Source: Author observation in practice

In the primary school yard, the stimulus of the bell causes the conditioned response in the children of lining up and moving towards the classroom. The teachers may have to intervene with a small number of children to keep them on track, but for the most part, behaviourist principles of associative learning ensure that behaviour remains positive, and the transition from yard to class is smooth. Equally, preschool teacher Ana has employed behaviourist associative learning techniques to facilitate smooth transitions in her early years setting. The stimulus of the 'clean up song' prompts the conditioned response of cleaning up in the children, and this helps them move in a stress-free manner from one activity to the next. This is important, because research has identified such microtransitions as potential flash points for difficulties and distress for children and educators alike in educational settings (O'Kane, 2015), but this may be avoided through careful and consistent use of behaviourist techniques.

Skinner

Moving beyond the work of Pavlov, and Watson's interpretation of it, B. F. Skinner believed that learning occurred through more complex relationships with the environment than through the simple pairing of stimuli (Woolard, 2010). Also working with animals in laboratory settings he developed experiments that required pigeons and rats to perform tasks that would then be rewarded or not. By modifying tasks and using series of positive and negative consequences, he demonstrated how certain behaviours could be *shaped* and *reinforced* towards targeted, planned outcomes. These experiments established another major principle of learning referred to as instrumental conditioning or 'operant conditioning', that is, changing behaviour through operating on the environment. Using this technique, some of the animals in his laboratories were trained to perform complex tasks; for example, pigeons playing ping-pong, or distinguishing between different coloured lights. Much of Skinner's original archived video and audio footage of these experiments is publicly available through the B. F. Skinner Foundation here: www.bfskinner.org/.

Skinner is often referred to as the father of operant conditioning, and his work is frequently cited in connection with this topic (Skinner, 1938, 1953). He built his analysis on observable behaviour and its equally observable consequences, rejecting any role for inner or mental states (Woolard, 2010). The focus of behavioural approaches is on the overt, observable and measurable behaviour, rather than thoughts or feelings. Behaviour is seen as learned, and by extension inappropriate behaviour can be unlearned. Skinner studied the relationship between a stimulus in the environment (S) and a response in the animal (R), proposing what became known as the S-R theory of learning. He established from his research with various animals, including humans, that the best conditions for learning to occur were those where reinforcement (or reward) was given intermittently rather than at every response (Ferster and Skinner, 1957). Skinner identified three types of responses, or operants, that can follow behaviour:

> *Reinforcers* – responses from the environment that increase the probability of a behaviour being repeated. Reinforcers strengthen behaviour. An example of a reinforcer in an educational setting is when an educator gives a child a sticker for good behaviour.

> *Punishers* – responses from the environment that decrease the probability of a behaviour being repeated. Punishment weakens behaviour. The word

'punishment' is used here in a very particular manner and does not imply anything physical. An example from an educational setting might be when a child is not allowed to take part in a fun activity due to undesired behaviour.

Ineffective – responses from the environment that neither increase nor decrease the probability of a behaviour being repeated.

Reinforcers increase the probability of a behaviour occurring and can be either positive or negative. **Positive** reinforcement is the **addition** of pleasant stimulus; for instance, where a teacher praises desired behaviour the behaviour should increase. With **negative** reinforcement we see the **removal** of unpleasant stimulus leading to an increase in the given behaviour; for instance, where a teacher stops chastising a child when he works quietly it is predicted that he will continue to work quietly. Punishment, leading to the decrease in probability of a behaviour occurring, can also be either positive or negative. **Positive** punishment refers to the **addition** of unpleasant stimulus. For instance, where a child is required to observe a period of detention for a particular behaviour, that behaviour may decrease. In **negative** punishment, there is the **removal** of a pleasant stimulus leading to a decrease in behaviour as, for instance, when a child is excluded from a 'treat' activity for the particular behaviour. In operant conditioning the reduction or disappearance of behaviour is often referred to as the 'extinction' of that behaviour through judicious use of reinforcement or punishment. Extinction can also happen if a particular unwanted behaviour is ignored; that is, where the behaviour is neither reinforced nor punished.

EXTRINSIC MOTIVATION

According to Mischel (1971) all behaviourist approaches have as a common aim the direct modification of observable behaviours, which have been identified as in need of change. These strategies address factors maintaining problems (the current behaviours) and are not interested in the underlying, perhaps internal, *causes* of problems. In the behaviourist perspective, the interest is in the effect external events may have on an individual. The consequences of an action will impact on subsequent actions. Such consequences may be considered as a reward or a punishment and, consequences are seen to determine whether or not a person will repeat the behaviour that led to the consequences (Woolard, 2010). Taking this approach, the motivation to carry out various tasks or behave in particular ways is understood as external to the individual and under the control of the reward and punishment that is dispensed, or of the person dispensing those rewards or punishments, usually the educator. Hence this view of learning is based on what is called external or extrinsic motivation. This means that children are actually not interested in the activity itself, but rather care about the gain they can achieve, for example in the form of praise or a good grade. The cause of the act or behaviour may be localised outside the pupil, and those who are learning are seen as 'passive recipients or "empty jars" to be filled with knowledge'

(Postholm, 2013, p. 396). Equally, in his book *Beyond Freedom and Dignity*, Skinner (1972) argued that there is no such thing as morality, goodness or free will, but rather all humans, including children, behave as they do because they have been conditioned to do so. The implication of this for the educational setting is that, from a behaviourist perspective, children will never behave well because they understand that it is the right thing to do. Rather, it is the job of the educator to shape their behaviour towards the desired and approved or valued behaviour through judicious application of association and consequence. There is no such thing as a 'good' or a 'bad' child; all children can behave well if shaped and reinforced to do so.

REFLECTION

How 'free' are we as human beings? Do we make our own decisions and behave the way we do through free will? Was Skinner correct in his opinion that as human beings we only ever behave prosocially in order to achieve some reward, even if that reward is just to feel good about ourselves? Can you think of any truly altruistic act that you have engaged in, simply because it was the right thing to do, with no positive outcome for yourself?

This remains a controversial proposition, but in ethical terms it promotes an interesting perspective that may allow educators to separate children from their behaviour in stressful situations. There is no doubt that when a child engages in repeated behaviours, such as aggressive behaviours, that are experienced as challenging by an educator, it can lead to significant stress, particularly for newly qualified educators (Toshalis, 2010). In these circumstances, it may be useful to take Skinner's philosophical stance that there is no such thing as a 'bad' child, but rather 'bad' behaviour; each child's behaviour is the result of the sum of a complex mix of stimulus and response, and any human who had experienced this particular mix would be likely to behave similarly. While removing the emotion from behaviour is certainly problematic (see below for a detailed critique) it can be very useful as a means of temporarily allowing an educator to take a step back from the stressful situation to address the disruptive or difficult behaviour.

A MOVE AWAY FROM PUNISHMENT IN EDUCATIONAL SETTINGS

Perhaps one of Skinner's greatest legacies is the understanding he brought to education of the terrible damage that a focus on punishment could cause in children's learning and development. Skinner (1968) asserted that formal education was failing to teach children because it was usually based on 'aversive control', and in many countries this was certainly true. For example, corporal punishment was only banned in Irish schools in 1982, and it only became a criminal offence in 1996. Prior to this, physical assault of children as a disciplinary measure was not only legal but relatively commonplace in educational settings, an idea that may be shocking and abhorrent to modern educators. Nevertheless, some focus on punishment in educational settings remains in the present day through the use of approaches such as time out, writing lines or going to detention. However, according to Murdoch and Barker (1991), punishment is not effective and has many potentially serious side effects. Those identified include increased emotional responding, avoidance of the punisher, imitation of the use of punishment and modelling of aggression, passivity and withdrawal, decreased quality of relationship with the punishing agent, and hence decreasing the effectiveness of the punishing agent over time.

Drawing on his own research, Skinner (1968) favoured a positive approach to teaching, and argued that teachers failed to shape their pupils' learning because lessons and assessments were designed to identify what children do not know and cannot do rather than to emphasise what they do know and are able to learn. His work led him, and others, to emphasise the role of the teacher in managing observable behaviour as the key factor in successful education and classroom management and to ignore the less measurable internal process that might impact on learning. He attacked the use of what he considered to be pre-scientific terms such as 'attitudes', 'initiatives' and 'alienation' to explain human development by, he complained, 'almost everyone who is concerned with human affairs' (1972, p. 9).

Skinner's perspective assumes that it is possible and appropriate to train and shape children using the principles of reinforcement to the point that maladaptive or inappropriate behaviours are reduced or disappear altogether and/or there is an increase in adaptive or positively valued behaviours. The aim is to shape the child's behaviour within an 'if–then' linear interpretation of authority and control. Central to the efficacy of the behavioural approach is the principle that rules and consequences for behaviour are explicitly stated, taught and understood. His behaviourist approach has been framed in terms of five learning principles (Wubbels, 2011). The first principle states that positive reinforcement will strengthen behaviour by applying a stimulus (or reward) following the desired behaviour. The second principle, called negative reinforcement, removes a (usually negatively experienced) stimulus in return for the desired student behaviour. For example, an educator might not assign homework if students complete their tasks in class on time. The third principle, extinction, may occur when a reinforcer declines or disappears. With time, the disruptive student behaviour will usually also gradually decline. Educators who ignore attention-getting children's behaviour are implementing the extinction principle. The fourth principle refers to a situation where a reinforcer is withdrawn. If, for example, students have not been given homework, they may receive an additional assignment if they do not complete their tasks on time (in other words, freedom from homework is withdrawn). Finally, the most controversial principle is punishment, in which educators present aversive consequences. In general, this principle is used as a last resort and only for severe student misbehaviour.

APPLYING BEHAVIOURISM IN PRACTICE

While appearing to be very clear-cut in theory, in practice applying this approach requires a great deal of skill, not least in knowing when it is not appropriate. For instance, adults may not always determine correctly what constitutes a pleasant or an unpleasant stimulus. The removal of a child from the classroom as a punishment for, let us say, disruptive behaviour may in fact be a pleasant experience for the child who finds the class boring, dull or too challenging, and may thus have little or no impact on, or even increase, the behaviour the teacher wishes to decrease. Likewise, praising a shy child in front of the whole class group may in fact be an unpleasant experience and in effect function as a punishment rather than as a reinforcement of a given behaviour.

Gage and Berliner (1998) maintain that if an educator wants to know what a good reinforcer for a child will be he should look at how that child spends his time when nobody is telling him what to do. If a child spends every spare minute playing football, then a sport-related reward would be an effective reinforcer. If a child spends all his free time socialising and chatting, a socially based reward would work. Gage and Berliner (1998, p. 338) also provide a questionnaire that allows educators to identify an appropriate system of reinforcement for each child:

- The things I do for fun are …
- The type of present I would most like to receive is …
- My hobbies are …
- The types of things I like to do with other people are …
- I feel good when …
- I spend money every week on …
- If I had $100,000 I would …
- Of all the things I do every day I would most hate to give up …
- I am happiest when …

Based on the principles of behaviourism, several programmes for behaviour modification aimed at shaping desired student behaviour and translating successful laboratory approaches to the classroom have been developed, based around the careful use of association and reinforcement. Application of behaviourist techniques in educational situations typically distinguish between procedures that will increase desired behaviour and those procedures aimed at decreasing undesired behaviour (Brophy, 2006). Such techniques include simple praise, consistent feedback, clearly structured reward systems and non-punitive discipline. To be effective in classrooms such programmes must be fit for purpose, appropriate to the development levels of the children and be provided in a consistent and clear manner. Furthermore, all rules and consequences must be explicitly stated for understanding, and must be implemented consistently.

One of the simplest approaches to encouraging good behaviour is the prudent use of praise and approval for preferred behaviour. However, the praise has to be clearly associated with a given behaviour and must be meaningful for the child to respond to it. Children like to be praised; however, a general or passing comment that the child is being 'good' will have little impact if 'being good' is not clearly associated with a specific behaviour. This is particularly the case with younger children. Without consistent and clear associations between the praise and behaviour, the child is provided with no incentive to continue the desired behaviour. Lipoff (2012) suggests that when specific praise is provided, such as 'I like the way you explained the answer to that question', the child's behaviour is positively acknowledged and encouraged. The child feels supported and motivated in a nurturing way.

Behaviourist principles are not necessarily targeted at individual children. To encourage and sustain desired behaviour within classroom groups, educators can model the type of behaviour expected within particular contexts. If, for instance, an educator wants noise levels to lower, it is more effective to use a quiet voice to gain and maintain attention than to call out loudly an order to 'Be Quiet!' Not all children in a group can be expected to behave in exactly the same way, and knowing children well can allow the use of different techniques with different children. In such situations it is important to be fair, and to be seen to be fair, in terms of expectations. There will also be situations where one or two children seem to take up most of the educator's attention and it takes a skilful adult to remember to praise the children who are presenting desired behaviour while also challenging those whose behaviours may be disrupting the learning environment and those children who are behaving well. Communication and feedback is an important dimension of successful behaviourist approaches. The choice of rewards is important, so that they are relevant and also can be offered consistently. Rewards can be decided in partnership with children, and this may be more effective than adult-selected rewards, as it gives the children a sense of ownership and responsibility. If a child has behaved well, for instance worked diligently at a given task, and is not praised or rewarded, he is not likely to be motivated to continue with such behaviour and may well lose interest. However, if praise is given too regularly it will lose its impact, and this is where the skill of the educator in developing a strategy of intermittent reinforcement is so important and more effective (Ferster and Skinner, 1957).

While these generalised approaches across educational settings can be useful, more structured strategies based on behaviourist principles are also often applied. These include token economies, shaping ('successive approximation'), chaining, behaviour contracts and ABC (antecedent-behaviour-consequence) analysis. These systems can be used either with individual children or in groups.

Token economies

The concept of a token economy is often credited to Cohen and his colleagues (e.g. Cohen and Filipczak, 1971; Cohen, Filipczak and Bis, 1965), who developed the approach while working with institutionalised boys. He set up a system whereby academic achievement as measured by regular tests could be used to buy points that could be exchanged for goods, services and special privileges. Cohen achieved results that at the time were unprecedented, and academic standards improved significantly. Students also became less disruptive, attended classes more regularly and improved on many other behavioural measures.

Many modern-day educators develop similar approaches in educational settings, whereby children are awarded points of some form for positive behaviour, and the points can be saved up for some future reward. The points often take the form of a fun item that is appealing to small children, such as a sticker, marble or stamp, and when enough have been collected, the child or children can choose a more tangible reward like a prize or an experience like watching a film. Depending on the format and the rewards chosen, this format may work best with younger children in early years settings or the junior classes of primary schools. However, with younger children there needs to be a fairly immediate connection between the token earned and the reward received – it is difficult for four- or five-year-olds to work out that a special treat on Friday connects back to the token they earned on Tuesday for completing a particular task. With older children, the credit accumulation system is possible; for instance, a child must collect five points in order to receive a reward. Using this approach one can shape children's behaviour towards the desired behaviour the educator wants them to exhibit.

Shaping/successive approximation

Often, if a child is really struggling with behaviour, an educator attempting to use positive reinforcement can despair when it seems as though there is no opportunity to offer reward as there is simply no positive behaviour in evidence! With careful observation of the specific child over time the approach known as shaping or successive approximation (Murdoch and Barker, 1991) may be used. Here, the educator begins by first reinforcing any action that even vaguely resembles the behaviour he is trying to increase, even if the performance appears accidental. For example, if the educator hopes to support the development of social behaviour in a child, he might first reward him for standing beside another child, even if that is coincidental. Once that behaviour is well embedded and happening regularly, the educator only reinforces behaviours that are a little closer to target behaviours. For example, he might begin to reinforce this child when he looks at the other child. Using the methodology of successive approximation, he then only rewards successively closer steps. For example, he might begin to reward the child when he responds to communication from another child. When that behaviour is well established, he might then only reinforce the child when he initiates communication. Put simply, successive approximation involves gradually shaping the child's behaviour, bringing it from accidental occurrences of similar behaviour to elements of the desired behaviour the educator wants to see, through various steps to the performance of the target behaviour, through the use of reinforcement.

Chaining

A related approach is the idea of chaining (Murdoch and Barker, 1991). This is where two or more responses are required in the correct sequence for reinforcement to be delivered. Chains are quite simple at first, and are then built up step by step until the child is able to perform long sequences of behaviours to obtain the reward. For example, to encourage independent dressing skills, the child might first be reinforced for going to get his coat at the end of the day, then for learning to put arms in, then for learning to button the coat, etc. In other words, children need to chain a few different behaviours together in order to be rewarded. Time periods could also be chained together in order to achieve rewards in this way, so that initially a child may need to behave a certain way for a shorter period of time to achieve a reward, but as that becomes embedded, longer time periods may be chained on.

Behaviour contracts

A behaviour contract refers to a negotiated agreement between the educator and the child, often including parents, clearly stating expectations for behaviour, what the reward (reinforcement) will be if the child meets those expectations, and what the consequences will be if the child breaks the contract (Bowman-Perrott, Burke, de Marin, Zhang and Davis, 2015). Generally behaviour contracts are used when there is a serious and persistent behavioural difficulty, but it should be a collaborative approach with the child rather than one directed entirely by the educator. It is most likely to be successful if the educator asks the child to make suggestions as to what would be an appropriate reward or reinforcement for sticking to the contract, and what the consequences should be for failure to comply. This may be more appropriate for primary than early years level.

It is important for contracts to name *specific* behaviours to be changed, so for example rather than indicating that 'Jane will behave appropriately in class', it should specify that 'Jane will speak in a low voice rather than shouting'. It is best to focus on one or two behaviours at a time rather than many, and the consequences and reinforcers need to be thought out very clearly so that they are meaningful and effective. Negotiation and individualisation are important, and behaviour contracts should be time-limited with an agreed review date. Teacher and student should sit down together and review the contract together to see whether it has been working for both. There is evidence that behaviour contracts can be very successful in reducing negative behaviour, although perhaps less so in increasing positive behaviour (Bowman-Perrott et al., 2015).

Time out

Time out is one of those punishment techniques that Bruner (1996) identified as part of 'folk pedagogy', by which he meant strategies used in teaching that had no basis in evidence but rather emerged as part of culture-based beliefs. It has been identified with the behaviourist tradition and is a strategy used in Applied Behavioural Analysis [ABA]. Although originally designed for use in cases of extreme and sometimes dangerously disruptive behaviour, time out has come to be used in educational settings, often with a time-out prop such as a chair in the classroom (Prochner and Hwang, 2008). A child who misbehaves or is disruptive is removed from the reinforcing context of the behaviour and required to sit on a particular chair or stand in a particular place for a given length of time. The efficacy of persistent use of time out in early childhood for minor misbehaviours is suspect, and

Prochner and Hwang (2008, p. 521) note that ABA experts, in 2005, warned against using the strategy in regular classrooms at all.

ABC analysis

Skilled application of behavioural principles in classroom situations requires careful observation and analysis and can be thought of in terms of the Antecedent-Behaviour-Consequences (ABC) steps of behaviourism: Antecedent – observation of the situations leading up to a particular behaviour; Behaviour – an accurate description and understanding of the behaviour under examination; and Consequences – careful consideration of the consequences. With careful and consistent application of this ABC approach adults are more likely to develop effective behavioural strategies. Consider how the ABC approach helped this teacher to identify what was sustaining a negative behavioural dynamic in his classroom.

Six-year-old Jessica was having a difficult time in David's classroom. Her behaviour was becoming increasingly difficult to cope with for everyone involved: the teacher David, the other children in her class and Jessica herself. David decided to spend a week doing an ABC analysis to see what might be triggering Jessica's behaviour (antecedents), what behaviours were problematic and what could be lived with, and what consequences might actually be sustaining the behaviour. After a week he had a better idea of how to proceed:

Antecedents: In observing Jessica's behaviour over the course of a week, David has noticed that there are a number of common occurrences before incidences of negative behaviour that may be acting as triggers for Jessica. Firstly, Jessica is often angry just before the first break of the morning, and so hunger might be a difficulty for her. Secondly, Jessica often disrupts lessons that are structured using group work. Does she find it hard to concentrate when there is noise or when lessons are more child-directed than adult-directed? Lastly, David noticed that Jessica tends to become disruptive during maths lessons.

Behaviour: Of the specific behaviours noted by David, some that he has experienced as challenging are indeed problematic – for example, angry outbursts and aggression towards other children. However, on reflection, he realises that some of the behaviour he has been thinking of as Jessica being 'fidgety' occurs after prolonged periods of inactivity due to the structure of his lessons, and may in fact be an understandable reaction of a typically developing child's need for movement.

Consequence: During group work, Jessica often makes jokes and disrupts the other children. She is rewarded by laughter and attention from the other children. During maths lessons, Jessica is often angry and acts out. In order to allow other children to have quiet space to learn, David sometimes sends Jessica to the principal's office. On reflection he realises this rewards Jessica with the removal of the maths lesson she does not like.

As a result of an ABC analysis an educator can make a plan to remove any triggers for negative behaviours where possible, reframe any behaviours that may on reflection in fact be reasonable, and ensure that any consequences of behaviour are likely to reinforce positive behaviour and extinguish undesired behaviour. In this case, David could for example ensure that Jessica has a snack early in the morning to eliminate the trigger of hunger, scaffold her social learning through the use of pair work initially, working back up to larger group work eventually, review his lesson structures to incorporate more active methodologies and ensure that children are not expected to sit still for long periods of time, and try to differentiate his maths lessons for Jessica to ensure that the tasks are at appropriate level of challenge for her.

THE CHALLENGES OF BEHAVIOURISM: MAKING IT WORK IN PRACTICE

Despite its many critics, behaviourism has had some positive effects on education. Such positive influences can be seen in the emphasis on careful planning for certain learners, such as those with additional learning needs, and the use of praise as a reward for learning rather than criticism for perceived failure. Indeed, the ubiquitous use of stars, star charts and bonuses as rewards for appropriate behaviour in classrooms and early years settings is further evidence of the powerful legacy of behaviourism in education. This may be because it gives the adult a clear toolkit for 'managing' behaviour with careful planning and consistent reward/punishment regimes.

Some practical challenges that these strategies present for educators include the need for consistency that they require. Primary school classrooms and early years settings are busy and complex places and often finding the time to notice and reward a specific behaviour on a fair and consistent basis is very challenging. It can be difficult for educators in real-life situations to maintain the strict adherence to programmes that is required for them to work. Equally, educators are sometimes less than skilful in choosing behaviours to target and how to target them. When we are unclear in what exactly we want a child to do, try to tackle too many behaviours at once, or aim for behaviour that is not developmentally achievable, we set a child up for failure and a programme will break down. As already noted, reinforcers that are not of value to the child will not be effective, but also a reinforcer that may be effective at the beginning of a programme could lose its value and effectiveness over time as boredom sets in, so educators should periodically change their approaches when using behaviourist methods if they are to work best. However, all of these issues are merely operational, and there are difficulties with behaviourist methods and philosophies that run much deeper than this.

PROBLEMS WITH BEHAVIOURISM AS A FRAMEWORK FOR EDUCATION

Approaches such as token economies, ABC analysis, behaviour contracts and ABA are used extensively in education to this day due to their accessibility and effectiveness, and are often recommended as strategies without their behaviourist roots being explored. However, there are many problems with behaviourism conceptually and ethically, and the theory and approaches associated with it are shared in this book with a view to allowing readers to make reflective, critical, theoretically informed decisions on whether to use them or not.

Conceptual challenges to behaviourism

Despite the powerful impact and scientific patina of the behaviourist approach there were challenges to its views even from researchers within the field, particularly regarding the degree to which such an approach addressed the complexity of human development. In their work on animal behaviour, for instance, Pribram and others in the 1960s (Miller, Galanter and Pribram, 1960), reported observations that helped to convince him that external reinforcement was neither a necessary nor sufficient condition for learning. He found that under certain circumstances animals would continue to behave in a manner ostensibly controlled by reinforcement even when there was no reinforcement or where the animal was satiated and there was no value to the reinforcement. The implication of his work is that the activity itself held some intrinsic or internal interest for the animal beyond simply responding to external or extrinsic environmental factors.

Albert Bandura (1977) also challenged the simple S-R model of learning. He developed the social learning theory, which modified the S-R model to capture the more complex learning of the human, to take account of the cognitive processes involved in learning and to recognise the role of the social in learning. Through his studies he identified the powerful nature of observational learning and the role of modelling in the learning process. In the famous 'Bobo doll studies' he showed how children tend to imitate the aggressive or violent actions of adults, even without reward, whereas children with gentle adult models tend to behave gently. Bandura later retitled his theory the social cognitive theory (1986) to reflect the growing understanding of social influences on cognitive development. While emphasising social influences on learning, Bandura continued the behaviourist tradition of viewing the child as passive in the learning process; in this approach the child is seen to learn the behaviours and roles observed through internalisation rather than through active participation and transformation.

A third challenge to behaviourism came from information processing theories. This area of study arose from the developments in computing and information processing (Cullen, 2001; Hilgard, 1996; Wood, 1988). Research focused on the acquisition and use of different cognitive (thinking) processes. This approach to learning has given rise to the very active research area of artificial intelligence using computer-based simulations of the human mind to shed light on learning processes. From this field of study new terms such as 'plans' and 'strategies' emerged to describe the cognitive activity guiding human behaviour. However, the information processing metaphor for the mind is limited. Bruner (1996) characterised the approach as one where unambiguous information about the world is inscribed, sorted, stored, collated, retrieved and generally managed by a computational device. As far as human information processing goes, however, Bruner points out that the process of knowing is often 'messier' and more fraught with ambiguity than this view allows. He argues that education is not just concerned with well-managed information processing. Neither is it simply a matter of applying learning theories to the classroom nor using the results of subject-centred achievement testing. Education is, he contends, a more complex pursuit.

Ethical and philosophical challenges to behaviourism

Arguably more important than conceptual or academic arguments about theoretical principles are the ethical arguments against too much reliance on behavioural principles, and fundamental philosophical concerns about what learning is, what education is for, and how we view children and childhood. For instance, an over-emphasis on directing and controlling learning through an external reward and punishment system may undermine the intrinsic motivation within a child to direct their own learning. While there is no doubt that rewards can be used effectively, particularly with younger children, presumably when the child is in an environment where rewards are no longer administered, targeted behaviour will be extinguished, so no long-term internalisation of positive behaviour or moral development can be expected using this approach. In behaviourism it is also not considered necessary to create a learning environment that nurtures in individual children a sense that they can enjoy and sustain learning for its own sake both within and outside a structured educational setting. The problem is that behaviourism does not provide sufficient information with which to begin to consider and respond to the complexity of learning and behaviour or the processes involved in students' emerging understanding of concepts, skills and self-knowledge. The behaviourist approach to learning has been criticised for considering humans as mere respondents performing under the control of the laws of nature, which are accessible to discovery through carefully designed research rather than learning. In education, behaviourists characterise the child as passive, developing as a function of the environment, and the adult educator as the primary source of knowledge, the resource manager and the agent for socialising the young child.

Shaping children's behaviour is a powerful strategy and can be used to encourage the development of new behaviours through positive reinforcement of successive approximations to target behaviour. However, this has to be carefully used, and it takes skill to recognise when, for instance, to determine that closer approximations to the desired behaviour can be ignored as the previous one has been firmly established. If too large a step is expected of the learner at once, the behaviour may break down and shaping may have to resume at the point where the learner has repeated demonstrated success. It is also important to ensure that reinforcement is delivered immediately, contingent upon the desired response, since delays can result in a randomly occurring behaviour being reinforced and conditioned.

Another difficulty identified with the behavioural approach is achieving a fair reward system, and it may very easily appear inconsistent or contradictory if mismanaged. For instance, in determining whether rewards are for effort or for achievement there are in fact problems associated with both. For instance, effort is subject to interpretation and often fails to take account of differences in work quality. Rewarding achievement alone can create a situation that undermines the efforts and morale of the less able. While certainly effective in influencing behaviour in the short term, the value and effectiveness of basing teaching on the promise of prizes and rewards alongside a threat of punishment has been questioned (Abramson, 2013; Roache and Lewis, 2011). For instance, it could be seen as a form of manipulation where children change their behaviour patterns for the wrong reasons, either because there is something in it for them or they fear punishment. Such behaviour changes are more likely to be performance than learning.

Ethically speaking, the very effectiveness of behaviourist methodologies in shaping children's behaviours may be worth a critical appraisal since, in naïve hands, these tools can be used to encourage children to behave in a manner that may not be in their own best interests.

When Issy was three years old she developed very 'fussy' eating habits. A previously healthy little girl, she would refuse her meals, and previously enjoyed foods were suddenly on the no-go list. Every so often she would complain of tummy aches, but knowing that food can often become a battleground between wilful toddlers and their weary parents, her parents decided to introduce a star chart. Each time Issy ate her meals, she would get a sticker on her chart. When she had a certain amount of stickers collected, she could earn a treat of her choice – a trip to the zoo, a new small toy, whatever. The system worked a treat, and Issy ate. But she also complained more and more of tummy aches. She got thinner and more unhealthy. By the time she was diagnosed with coeliac disease, she was really unwell. The parents had inadvertently used positive reinforcement to shape Issy's behaviour and had gotten her to eat gluten-filled food that was making her sick.

While this is an extreme example of the use of reinforcement to the detriment of a child (albeit accidentally!), it is very possible for well-meaning educators to inadvertently use behaviourist principles to shape children's behaviour towards inappropriate aims, or miss an important child-protection issue that is being communicated by the child's behaviour. Just because we can do something does not mean we should. Consider Little Albert's treatment by Watson! Spooner and Browder (2003) state that asking questions that can be answered only empirically, as demanded by the behaviourist approach, can be restrictive if this is the only source of knowledge. They cite the example of approaches to the 'management' of so-called problem behaviours of students with severe disabilities from the 1960s to the 1980s which focused on punitive rather than educative procedures, due to the application of knowledge about what produced data-based effects, as opposed to asking moral and ethical questions about why students were protesting their contexts. When psychologists and educators were looking only at behaviour modification that could produce quantifiable results, instead of considering *why* people were exhibiting so called 'challenging behaviour', the research conducted largely missed important avenues of inquiry. Once these questions began to be asked, researchers were empowered to investigate whole new areas, such as the functions of challenging behaviour as communication.

For example, Chapter 6 explores how young children have a biological need for movement and play, and yet traditionally many educators may have used behaviourist reinforcement to encourage children to sit still for prolonged periods in order to facilitate arguably inappropriate inactive pedagogical methodologies. Images and constructs of children and how they ought to behave change and develop across time and space (Sorin and Galloway, 2006; Woodhead, 2006), and behaviourist ideas were developed at a time when children were expected to be 'seen and not heard'. According to Nowak-Łojewska, O'Toole, Regan, and Ferreira (2019), a new perspective on children emerged with the almost universal ratification of the United Nations Convention on the Rights of the Child (UNCRC, 1989), and more modern conceptions of children as human beings with agency and rights rather than humans-in-waiting, drawing on the work of researchers like James and Prout (1990) and Dahlberg, Moss and Pence (2013).

CONCLUSION

Most educators now feel an instinctive sense of discomfort at the idea of controlling children, and instead prefer to work towards self-regulation, self-directed learning and development of positive behaviour in a manner that respects the child's personhood and rights. A crucial consideration is the need to take account of the *experience* of children in an educational setting and not simply the desire of an educator to 'manage' behaviour. Educators must ask themselves whether they aim for very well-behaved little 'cookie-cutter' children who exhibit little personality, curiosity or self-directed learning, or whether perhaps a little chaos is a price worth paying for genuine engagement!

More contemporary approaches to encouraging good behaviour use behavioural principles in parallel with an understanding that learning and behaviour are socially and culturally embedded, and that children are human beings, and not laboratory rats or pigeons to be trained. Educators have a major influence on student learning; their personal qualities and relations with their students are central factors affecting student motivation and achievement (Postholme, 2013; Stronge, Ward and Grant, 2011). The following chapters offer alternative perspectives on behaviour that may be used in conjunction with behaviourist approaches, or as an alternative to them.

Key concepts within this chapter for educational practice

1   Children's behaviour can be shaped using reinforcement and association.
2   Educators should reflect very strongly on how and even whether to use these approaches because there are many methodological and ethical concerns with them.

CHAPTER 4

Psychodynamic and relational perspectives and strategies for positive behaviour

INTRODUCTION

Chapter 3 explored behaviourist approaches to supporting positive behaviour, and concluded that while behaviourism provides educators with some interesting and effective tools, it falls short on a number of levels. Firstly, many educators are uncomfortable with the controlling nature of behaviourism; the adult decides on the types of behaviour desired, often without regard for individual differences or cultural factors, and shapes children towards that behaviour without any effort to draw out their potential, or to help them understand appropriate behaviour. Equally, a behaviourist approach may not get to the root of the problem, since it fails to recognise that often behaviour is a way for children to communicate distress. An authoritative approach requires both structure and support, and with a sole emphasis on controlling behaviour we may lose a valuable opportunity to support children when they need it.

This chapter will examine children's behaviour through an alternative, psychodynamic and relational lens, largely drawing on psychoanalysis (Freud, 1955), attachment theory (Ainsworth, Blehar, Waters, and Wall, 1978; Bowlby, 1969; Main and Solomon, 1986) and Cognitive Analytic Therapy (CAT) (Ryle and Kerr, 2002). Readers will be supported, through theoretical exploration and case studies, to understand that behaviour may be influenced by the emotional life of the child, the relationships within and outside the educational setting, and our own behaviour as adults. Key concepts include 'internalising' behaviour, whereby emotions are directed inwards leading to withdrawal and/or self-damaging behaviours; 'externalising' behaviours, whereby emotions are directed outwards, leading to aggression and violence; 'hypervigilance', whereby a child who has experienced trauma is constantly on the alert for danger, and may see it even when it does not exist, leading to inappropriate 'fight or flight' responses; and 'catharsis', or achievement of emotional release to avoid misdirection of energy into challenging behaviour. The dynamic nature of relationships and their impact on behaviour will also be explored, with the understanding that adults too are influenced by their early relationships, 'internal working models' and 'reciprocal roles'.

The chapter will also explore appropriate responses to these understandings of the underlying causes of children's behaviour. In particular, it will foreground the importance of secure attachment both in the home and in the educational setting. It will highlight the particularly important role played by educators as a 'secondary attachment' figure. Using a relational lens, specific approaches to supporting positive behaviour will be identified.

PSYCHOANALYSIS

Sigmund Freud (1856–1939) is considered the 'father of psychoanalysis', and some argue that his work permanently changed our understanding of the human psyche (Askay and Farquhar, 2011; Storr, 2001). Freud[1] emphasised the idea of the 'unconscious mind'. These are parts of the mind that are active and can influence our emotions and actions, but are not accessible either to ourselves or onlookers. According to Freud, the contents of the unconscious mind consist of desires or wishes based on primary physical instincts. They are focused on immediate satisfaction and so are often out of step with the more conscious elements of the mind, which have many other considerations – social etiquette, time-constraints, self-image and so forth. Freud maintained that these unconscious elements are often of a sexual or destructive nature, and this would indicate that where people generally, and in this case children, behave inappropriately it is because these unconscious urges have been allowed to gain the upper hand.

While many of Freud's ideas have been subject to extensive criticism, particularly by feminist psychologists who note the paternalistic and even misogynistic nature of many of his concepts (Balsam, 2013), the findings of research on the brain support the idea that not all areas of brain activity are accessible to the conscious human being. For example, Freud theorised that when we experience a trauma, the memories of this trauma may be stored out of our consciousness as a defence mechanism so that we do not have to recall the painful memory. This is known as 'repression'. The idea of memories existing unremembered and hidden within our brains is supported by the work of distinguished neurosurgeon Wilder Penfield, who showed that by applying a mild electric shock to certain areas of the brain, patients could relive experiences and access memories that were previously inaccessible. His 'Montreal procedure' 'ushered in a new era of neuroscience understanding by demonstrating that stimulation of specific brain areas could evoke emotions and allow one to recall precise personal experiences that had long been forgotten, including sensations, sounds, and smells' (Ladino, Rizvi and Téllez-Zenteno, 2018, p. 151). In other words, the memories still existed in the patients' unconscious minds even though they could not remember them consciously.

In a psychodynamic focus on children's behaviour, Freud's emphasis on emotional expression as opposed to repression is important. According to Freud, if emotions (especially painful emotions) are not expressed, they become buried in the unconscious mind; they are 'repressed' (Askay and Farquhar, 2011). These emotions do not just disappear, however. They are like a river that is dammed and so flows around and over the blockage. Repressed emotions resurface in various ways. Sometimes this displacement of emotion can have a positive outcome, when energies are focused on the creation of art, inventions, or anything that serves a higher cultural or socially useful purpose. This is known as 'sublimation'. Displacement of emotion sometimes has neutral effects, such as forgetting names and words, misreading and slips of the tongue (Freud, 1901). Freud maintains that such 'mistakes' are really not mistakes at all, but rather are an indication of what is really on our mind.

However, according to Freud, displacement often leads to negative outcomes, including negative behaviour and physical illness. Freud began his work initially with patients, mainly women, whom he referred to as 'neurotic' and 'hysterical'. His method was based on the assumption that hysteria was the product of a psychological trauma which had been repressed by the patient. The treatment consisted of the use of psychoanalysis to help the patient recall the trauma with the accompaniment and so dispersal of emotions (Storr, 2001). This purging of emotions or relief of emotional tension is known as 'catharsis'. In other words, bringing repressed thoughts and feelings into the conscious mind frees the patient from them. While this might sound radical, and perhaps even a little strange, contemporary research on the association between stress and experiences such as burnout (Maslach and Leiter, 2017) and cardiovascular disease (Schnall, Dobson and Landsbergis, 2017) shows that the idea of a mind–body link might not be so strange after all.

HOW PSYCHOANLAYSIS EXPLAINS NEGATIVE BEHAVIOUR IN EDUCATIONAL SETTINGS

One form of 'displacement' identified by Freud was aggression and antisocial behaviour. A psychoanalytic explanation of a child's misbehaviour in an educational setting would be that some unacknowledged stress, pain or trauma is being channelled into negative behaviour. Thus a child's behaviour is seen as a form of communication to adults that something is wrong, and the child needs support to resolve her emotional trauma in order to be able to behave well again (NEPS, 2007). Negative behaviour often stems from unmet need (O'Brien, 2018). Thus, psychodynamic approaches would argue that behaviourist methods of solely managing and controlling behaviours act as agents of repression, forcing the emotions to be ignored and making the situation worse. Rather, children must be supported to express their emotions in a safe and appropriate way. Psychodynamic approaches to supporting positive behaviour predict that as avenues for emotional expression increase in educational settings, incidents of aggressive or inappropriate behaviour should decrease.

Another psychoanalytic process of which educators should be aware is 'transference'. Freud (1905) described emotional reactions (both hostile and affectionate) to a therapist, which are not based on the actual situation but rather on the client's relationship with her parents. He maintained that the client unconsciously 'transferred' the feeling she had for her parent to the therapist, and believed in her conscious mind that she felt the same way about her. Equally, psychodynamic understandings of the relationships between educators and children incorporate the idea that children's feelings towards their educators are often based on their feelings towards their parents. Many educators have experienced the 'Freudian' slip of a child calling them 'Mammy' or 'Daddy'!

Therefore, while many of Freud's early ideas on the impact of sexuality are no longer widely considered valid, he did provide us with important concepts for understanding children's behaviour in educational settings – concepts such as the unconscious mind, repression, displacement, catharsis and transference.

TASK

Identify some ways in which children in your educational setting can be supported to express their emotions appropriately, so that they are less likely to be 'displaced' into negative behaviour. Be creative: think about the role of visual art, drama, music, oral expression, play, writing for older children, etc. You will find some ideas later in the chapter.

ATTACHMENT THEORY

Attachment theory is heavily influenced by psychoanalysis, and its central argument is that the bond or attachment formed by an infant with the primary care-giver forms the basis of all future relationships, and of psychological well-being for the rest of the individual's life. The theory states that this bond also has a highly significant influence on a child's current and future behaviour. Modern attachment theorists build on the early work of John Bowlby (1969), who maintained that the growing child needs to develop a sense of trust, and later a growing autonomy and sense of independence. Attachment theorists tell us that trust, security, confidence and optimism (as opposed to distrust, insecurity, inadequacy and pessimism) are developed by infants when they experience affection, care and the reasonably prompt satisfaction of their needs.

When babies are hungry, in pain, fatigued, or feeling threat or anxiety, they cry. Bowlby saw this as an innate instinct that babies have to call their care-giver to them, and ensure the care-giver is close by to meet their needs. This instinct may have developed as an evolutionary response to encourage adults to take care of their young, dependent offspring. When the distance between the baby and the care-giver is too great, the baby experiences separation anxiety and the evolutionary urge to close the distance between herself and the care-giver is engaged, leading to a 'separation protest' from the baby (Riley, 2011). This gives us the beginnings of an attachment-based understanding of children's behaviour that may be interpreted as negative – from our earliest days we understand that when feeling anxious, protest behaviours like crying, kicking and making noise are likely to bring a response from an adult who will hopefully help us manage that anxiety (Riley, 2011). Later in childhood and in life, however, when a child is feeling anxious, an evolutionary response may kick in, whereby she acts out in an attempt to draw the adult to her, but this is interpreted as misbehaviour and has the opposite effect, or the attention that it does draw is negative.

Bowlby thought that a parent's response to distress during infancy forms the basis of attachment between infant and parent. If parents respond consistently and warmly, the baby learns to trust that when she is in need, her parent will always be there, and secure attachment is formed. If parents consistently fail to respond to the infant's need, in situations such as abuse or neglect, the baby learns that adults are at best unreliable and at worst scary, and the baby develops an insecure attachment to the parent. Another key attachment theorist is Mary Ainsworth, and with her colleagues (Ainsworth et al., 1978) she identified two categories of insecure attachment – 'insecure-ambivalent/resistant' and 'insecure-avoidant'. Main and Solomon (1986) later identified a 'disorganised' category of insecure attachment.

Insecure-ambivalent children respond to anxiety by crying and acting aggressively; they 'externalise' their emotions. Insecure-avoidant children on the other hand respond to anxiety by withdrawing from the world and turning away from the adult. Such children may appear on the surface to be calm and appear less distressed behaviourally (Smith, Woodhouse, Clark and Skowron, 2016), but research has shown that when indicators of stress like cortisol (stress hormone) levels are measured, insecure-avoidant children actually show higher levels of distress during separation than securely attached children (Zelenko et al., 2005); they 'internalise' their emotions. In situations of extreme abuse or neglect, or when a child experiences a traumatic separation in early childhood, such as the death of a parent, she may develop a disorganised response to anxiety, whereby no clear strategy exists to manage her emotions, and the child may become 'frozen' (Bowlby, 2007).

While the early attachment theorists like Bowlby and Ainsworth believed that only the mother could be the attachment figure for a baby, we now know that babies and children can form attachments with a number of important adults (Duschinsky, Van Ijzendoorn, Foster, Reijman and Lionetti, 2018). Ideas of mother–infant attachment formation are sometimes misused for political reasons to argue against women's right to work outside the home (Belsky, 1988). Equally, families take many different forms, and fathers in particular have been shown to be just as important attachment figures for children (Berk, 2015). Nowadays, when most psychologists use the phrase 'primary care-giver', they mean the person who takes care of the child the most. Educators represent some of the most important non-familial attachment figures in children's lives (Hayes et al., 2017).

THE IMPACT OF ATTACHMENT ON BEHAVIOUR IN EDUCATIONAL SETTINGS: THE INTERNAL WORKING MODEL

As children grow older, their attachment becomes less reliant on being physically beside their parent and more dependent on the relationship's abstract qualities, such as affection and trust. Securely attached children become more confident to be without their parent for longer periods of time. A phrase that is often used in attachment theory is that attachment provides 'a secure base from which to explore the world' – in other words, securely attached children can confidently go out into the world because they know that their parent will still be there for them when they return (Hayes et al., 2017). The quality of attachment becomes 'internalised' as the child grows older – a baby needs to be physically beside her parent to feel secure, but as she grows within loving relationships, she develops the understanding that she is loved and safe regardless of whether her parent is physically beside her, and a securely attached older child or adult is confident for longer and longer periods without physical proximity to the primary care-giver because she carries with her an internal representation of that relationship to sustain her. In attachment theory, this is known as an 'internal working model' (IWM) of the relationship with the attachment figure.

Importantly, the IWM forms the basis of the child's concept of 'self' ('I am loved and lovable' or 'I am unloved and unlovable'), and provides foundation and direction to future relationships, such as those formed with both adults and other children in educational settings (Hayes et al., 2017). When a child expects the world to be comforting and supportive, she approaches new relationships with this expectation, and so securely attached children tend to behave well and invite future supportive relationships. On the other hand, when a child expects the world to be dangerous and unsupportive, she equally approaches new relationships with this expectation; through defensiveness and fear, she may misbehave and reduce the chances of forming positive relationships in the future (Bowlby, 1973). This process of interaction between the child's traits and her experiences, and its influence on the person she becomes, is known as 'internalisation'. The most up-to-date understandings of the neuropsychological bases for internalisation of attachment experiences through the impact of the stress hormone cortisol (Balbernie, 2007; De Bellis, 2005) and the anti-stress hormones opioids and oxytocin (O'Connor, 2013) on brain structures offer support for attachment theory. Gerhardt (2004) puts it more simply when she tells us that love matters, because affection shapes a baby's brain.[2] Attachment Theory predicts that relationships and patterns of interaction established with parents in early childhood will impact on relationships and behaviour later on, and it would seem that research supports this prediction. The Harvard-based Center on the Developing Child (CDC, 2007) include this as one of their 'key principles' of child development, indicating that:

> Early experiences affect the development of brain architecture, which provides the foundation for all future learning, behaviour and health. Just as a weak foundation compromises the quality and strength of a house, adverse experiences early in life can impair brain architecture, with negative effects lasting into adulthood.
>
> (www.developingchild.harvard.edu)

There is extensive evidence of the impact of early attachment on children's later emotional and behavioural development. Attachment to the mother at twelve months has been found to correlate with curiosity and problem solving at age two, social confidence at age three and empathy and independence at age five, as well as lack of behaviour problems at age six (Berk, 2009). In other words, security of attachment may predict the kinds of behaviours that are seen in early years settings and primary schools. Sroufe's (2005) longitudinal study found that pre-schoolers who were securely attached as babies were rated by their teachers as higher in self-esteem, social competence and empathy than their insecurely attached counterparts. At age eleven, children also had better relationships with peers, closer friendships and better social skills (Sroufe, 2005), and there is even evidence that security of attachment in childhood is related to quality of friendships and romantic relationships in adulthood (Feeney and Noller, 1990) as well as parenting skills with one's own children (Van IJzendoorn, 1995). However, it is important to note that more up-to-date studies of attachment have found that Bowlby and Ainsworth's original ideas on the impact of the first three years of life were not quite accurate. They argued that security of attachment was 'set in stone' by the age of three, and could not be changed beyond this point. In more recent years we have come to understand that while early attachment experiences are highly influential, attachment style can be fluid across the life-course, depending on the availability of 'emotionally corrective experiences' (Taylor, Rietzschel, Danquah and Berry, 2015). This gives hope to educators working with children who have experienced a less than ideal start in life that all is not lost. Promising research avenues have developed in recent decades on children's resilience and the effect that 'one good adult' such as a warm, attuned, responsive educator can have on children's trajectories and life chances (e.g. Brohl, 2007). While the first three years are hugely important, 'neuroplasticity' means that experience still shapes the brain even in older children and adults (Duschinsky et al., 2018), so we must not give up on children in educational settings once they pass the age of three! Equally, recent work has emphasised the importance of considering contextual and cultural influences on attachment (Van Ijzendoorn and Sagi-Schwartz, 2008).[3] It is very important for educators not to judge parents or diagnose children's attachment style since, as O'Connor (2013, p. 9) points out:

> It is true that poverty and deprivation don't automatically lead to poor attachment – far from it, in fact. But we must never underestimate the impact of difficult circumstances on the physical and mental health of parents and the direct impact this can have on their capacity to be responsive to their children.

HOW ATTACHMENT THEORY EXPLAINS CHALLENGING BEHAVIOUR IN EDUCATIONAL SETTINGS

The beginning of our understanding of the links between attachment and behaviour date back to Bowlby's (1944) work 'Forty-four Juvenile Thieves: Their Character and their Home-life'. In this article, Bowlby identified how difficulties or significant separations in mother–child relationships or emotional traumas during the first decade of life could predict negative behavioural patterns that lasted well into later childhood and even into adulthood. This work is a product of the time it was written, and some of the language used in it would not be considered acceptable today. For example, Bowlby refers to children as young as nine years old in this way: 'Some are normal human beings ... whilst others have been unstable characters or hardened criminals for a number of years' (p. 6). A psychologist would not, or certainly should not, write about children in this manner nowadays. Nevertheless, Bowlby's early work offers important insights on the links between the emotional lives of children and their behaviour.

Separation anxiety may be sparked in children when they are under stress, even when they are older or have established a secure IWM, so that under normal circumstances they do not have to be physically close to their parent to feel secure. Have you noticed how a child who falls over while playing often runs back to her parent or educator for comfort before going back to play? Bowlby would explain this by saying that a stressful situation (the fall) caused the child to seek her 'secure base' (the parent/educator) for comfort, and that once that comfort has been achieved she can go and 'explore the world' again. Educational experiences in childhood provide many potentially stressful situations even for the most secure children. For example, international literature has highlighted the challenge presented to children by transitioning from preschool to primary school (Hayes et al., 2017). Day-to-day interactions with other children and with adults could be potential sources of stress to children, as could engagement with activities, lessons or tasks experienced as difficult. Attachment theorists believe that when children experience anxiety, the evolutionary instinct to 'protest' is sparked and they may misbehave as a result.

REFLECTION

What can you do help reduce 'separation anxiety' for babies and children? How can you help them begin to trust that they are safe in the educational setting? What systems in crèches, preschools and other early years settings might contribute to separation anxiety without this being realised?

What about older children in primary schools? How might you recognise anxiety that could be masquerading as negative behaviour? What kinds of experiences during the school day might provoke anxiety-based responses in children? Many of these may not be recognised as such. How can you predict and plan for helping children to manage their anxiety in these situations?

These processes of anxiety leading to misbehaviour may be particularly acute in a child who is insecurely attached or who has suffered a trauma. A child whose emotional needs have not been met comes to view the world as 'comfortless and unpredictable; and they respond either by shrinking from it or doing battle with it' (Bowlby, 1973, p. 208). A neglectful or abusive parent may inhibit curiosity in the child – she is afraid to go and 'explore the world' because she does not trust that the parent will still be there when she gets back – perhaps leading to withdrawn behaviour in the educational setting. Thus, anxiety can lead to withdrawn behaviour when insecurity is directed inwards (psychologists call this 'internalising'). Alternatively, such negative early experiences may provoke feelings of 'hypervigilance' (always being on alert for danger, even when it does not really exist), leading to aggression, poor impulse control, prolonged emotional dependency, difficulty relating to other children, hostility, isolation and non-compliance (Riley, 2011). According to Erickson, Sroufe and Egeland (1985, p. 162), 'Such a child ... carries an underlying anger that he or she has not learned to express directly'. Thus, we may see violent behaviour when insecurity is directed outwards (psychologists call this 'externalising'). Consider how attachment theory would explain what is happening in this vignette:

Jamie has recently been taken into care because his father was behaving violently at home. In school today, the class are learning a dance to go with the rhyme 'head, shoulders, knees and toes'. When his teacher takes his hands to show him how to place them on his head, Jamie kicks her and runs to hide under the table.

Source: author observation in a primary school reception class

Hayes et al. (2017, p. 35)

In this vignette, through experience of violence at home, Jamie has developed an IWM that tells him to be very careful when adults raise their hands. His hypervigilance has detected a threat to his well-being where in fact none exists. An educator informed by attachment theory understands that the 'fight or flight' instinct has been engaged, and Jamie has acted to defend himself. Such an educator might make efforts to reassure the child that he is in fact safe in school, and to establish a secure base from which he can explore his learning. An educator who was unaware of attachment theory however, would be likely to punish Jamie for what appears to be unprovoked aggressive behaviour, and through escalating aggression and fear, actually contribute to future negative behaviour by the child.

THE INTERNAL WORKING MODEL OF THE EDUCATOR, COGNITIVE ANALYTIC THERAPY (CAT) AND THE RECIPROCAL ROLE

It is important to note that educators' own attachment styles and internal working models may also impact on the relationships they form with children (Riley, 2011). As could be expected, research has shown that teachers who themselves possess a secure attachment style are best placed to provide a secure base for children – 'Teachers are best able to serve students when they themselves have been adequately served' (Sergiovanni, 2005, p. 101). In particular, Riley (2011) explores how the attachment styles of both teachers and children can impact on disciplinary interactions. In interpreting the behaviour of children, teachers can also internalise, externalise or be hypervigilant. They can misinterpret innocuous behaviour by children as a threat to them or their authority and react inappropriately – consider the discussion in Chapter 1 of the tendency of novice teachers to resort to inappropriately harsh disciplinary measures due to fear of losing control. This could be framed as hypervigilance. Educators may also engage in 'transference' in their relationships with children – as adults we must be aware that our reactions to children are not always based on the traits of the children themselves, but sometimes are directed by our own unconscious processes based on our previous relationships (Riley, 2011). As such, relationships between adults and children in educational settings may, like all human relationships, be based on what Ryle (1998, p. 307) calls the reciprocal 'dance'. The temperament, previous experience of relationships, culture and expectations of both parties can influence the outcomes of interactions. For example, a child with a highly critical father may interpret a teacher's constructive criticism as an aggressive insult, and so react badly, leading to the teacher, who after all was only trying to help, to in turn react badly, and so on. Alternatively, if it is the teacher who grew up with a critical father, she might interpret a child asking a question as a criticism of her explanation, again leading to a negative cycle of interaction. It is easy to see how such incidents of transference can escalate into incidents of negative behaviour (from both child and adult) unless an educator is theoretically informed.

The work of Ryle and Kerr (2002) on Cognitive Analytic Therapy (CAT) further develops the idea of an IWM into a more nuanced conceptualisation known as Reciprocal Roles. The concepts and tools of CAT have recently been applied to education for the first time (Nowak-Łojewska, O'Toole, Regan and Ferreira, 2019; Regan, 2019), proposing a radically relational understanding of children's behaviour. CAT proposes a therapeutic framework focused on reciprocity in relationships and the replaying of relational patterns established early in life.

> In CAT the 'Self' is understood as fundamentally relationally-constituted: early relationships are dynamic two-way processes in which the child is an active participant; these early relationships provide the child with an internal working model of relationships (reciprocal roles), which then influence how she is in future relationships (with others and herself) and how she anticipates other people will be with her.
>
> (Nowak-Łojewska et al., 2019)

The basic unit for understanding and describing the dynamic nature of relationships in CAT (other to self, self to other, self to self) is the 'reciprocal role'. Rather than broad categories of secure or insecure attachment, the concept of reciprocal roles acknowledges that we inhabit many different roles in many different circumstances, and these are dynamic and responsive to the behaviour of others we encounter. According to the Association of Cognitive Analytic Therapy (ACAT) (n.d.), the idea of reciprocal roles highlights the fundamental importance of how we relate to each other, showing how we tend to treat people the way we anticipate they will treat us, and how, from the way others relate to us, we learn how to relate to ourselves. For example, if a child in an educational setting is fearful of the educator and expects aggression or attack, she can become defensive and become either fearful or ready to fight back. This is the reciprocal role: Attacking–Defensive (ACAT, n.d.).

The THRIECE[4] (Teaching for Holistic Relational and Inclusive Early Childhood Education) project is the first to apply the learning and tools of CAT to the educational sphere. It aims to support educators to reflect on the dynamic nature of the ongoing relationship with a child, a parent or the system, and on their role in this relational dynamic. One interesting outcome has been to support the development of approaches to supporting positive behaviour through a radically relational lens (Regan, 2019). Consider the reflections of some of the educators participating in the THRIECE project on how a relational understanding has supported them to work with children's behaviour, particularly in terms of the concept of a reciprocal role and their own part in the behavioural dynamic.

'We have taken on some of the key words, we would think about relationships more…. The reciprocal roles … I have started to think a lot more about that … why is this impacting on me and where is it coming from?'

'I don't think I would have ever thought as deeply about that before, … had the language or thought about the relationships and how they were causing it to happen or how they were making me think it out'

'Identifying the feeling in yourself first …'

'It's helped me with the way I think before I react to his [child's] actions … [reflecting relationally] it's like you "hover" over it and I've had time then to think about things before something happens in class with him because he would do the same things on a weekly basis'

RELATIONAL APPROACHES TO SUPPORTING POSITIVE BEHAVIOUR

Thus we can see that understandings of behaviour informed by psychodynamic and relational theories would lead to very different responses from educators from those informed by behaviourism. Rather than approaches aimed at controlling children through reinforcement, relationally informed educators aim to promote security and emotional expression. This is achieved through the relationship between the adult and the child, providing a secure base from which learning can happen, and developing creative methods to promote emotional expression and prevent repression from leading to displacement and negative outcomes.

The adult as secure base

Perhaps the central recommendation for an educator attempting to use a relational approach to supporting positive behaviour is a focus on the role of the adult in providing a 'secure base' for children in the educational setting. Supporting children to manage separation anxiety is highly important for all children, but crucial for those who may have insecure attachments with their primary care-givers, or those who have suffered a trauma that may impact on their IWM and sense of safety (Geddes, 2006). A calm atmosphere where educators are engaged in their practice and attuned to children may mitigate the difficulties that might arise from attachment issues (Hayes et al., 2017). Consider the experience of this early childhood educator who took her time in developing the secondary attachment with a little girl in her educational setting:[5]

You always walked in and headed straight for the paint. It was your favourite thing to do. Appearing so independent, you were only two and were able to get your apron, paper and paint by yourself.

Then garden time would arrive. I would hear you say 'I don't want to go to the big garden.' Your expression was clear, I was able to follow your lead. We stayed inside listening to your stories all about the pictures you had painted.

As you moved from the toddler room to the preschool room this was harder to facilitate. At garden time we would get your raingear on and everyone would go to the garden together. You loved the giant sand tray. However, if I was out of view you began to cry, calling me back to you.

I would make my way over to you and try to lift you into my arms. You would gently hit or push me away shouting 'NO, NO'. Even though I heard those words 'NO' I knew what you really wanted and needed was to feel safe. I stayed beside you, gently rubbing your back saying 'I'm here, you're not ready yet but I'm here.' As time went on and our bond became stronger you started to trust me, allowing me to comfort you in my arms, resting your head on my shoulder.

It is really difficult for you to ask for help, although you appear so independent and confident. Our bond has grown so much in the time you have been with me. I will always remember the day you came back after the Christmas break and jumped into my arms. I knew you finally really trusted me to take care of you. It took over a year but strong bonds are not created overnight.

Freud, Bowlby and Ryle show us that the relationship formed between a child and her educator may be very much dependent on the original relationship that she formed as a baby with her primary care-giver, through the process of transference and the power of the IWM and reciprocal roles. In this case, the attachment-informed, relational educator's awareness of the processes at play in an insecure-avoidant attachment allowed the educator to see that although the little girl was on the surface telling her to go away, she really needed her to be gently available to her. As Bronfenbrenner and Morris (2006) describe it, teachers and early childhood educators are often partners with children in the development of relationships whose prototype lies in the parent–child relationship. This is supported by the work of John Bowlby's son Richard Bowlby (2007), who identifies the importance of developing a 'secondary attachment' while the child is in non-parental day care. There is evidence that this idea may also be applicable to later educational settings, and Riley (2011) offers an extensive analysis of the student–teacher relationship through the lens of attachment theory, in which teachers can potentially provide children with a 'secure base' from which to explore their learning. As this educator has shown, however, for some children attachment-informed approaches require time, patience and understanding that behaviour that may seem on the surface to be negative or provocative, could in fact be a 'separation protest', crying out to draw you nearer.

Establishment of a 'secure base'

It is not always easy to know how to begin to establish a secure base with children, and by the very nature of insecure attachment, children with an IWM based on fear and anxiety may resist attempts by adults to form warm, supportive relationships (Riley, 2011). Here John Cryan, a primary school teacher in Dublin, Ireland, describes his approaches to relationship building with children. Are there any of these ideas that could be adapted for the educational setting in which you work?

Start first thing. For a child to learn effectively and behave well she should feel loved, wanted, valued, safe, confident and happy. In order to achieve that and create a positive atmosphere you must start first thing in the morning. Greet each child in the morning by name, and ensure they greet you and establish eye contact. Tell them you missed them if they were out and welcome them back. Teach the children about social niceties such as accepting compliments, reacting to birthday greetings, reacting to greetings such as 'Have a great weekend!' For some children, actively teaching them how to engage socially is so important.

Make encouragement a constant part of your day. Make a big deal of improvements, however small. Compliment the children in a group who have worked well, and try to transmit a positive outlook. Tell the class on a regular basis that you think they are brilliant. Tell them you love coming in to work. Children will usually perform to our beliefs and expectations. If you tell them they are brilliant, they will be brilliant. Act surprised at bad behaviour.

Change! As a teacher we have to be willing to change ourselves and not expect small children to make all the changes. Think about your systems and methodologies and what effects they might inadvertently be having on children's behaviour and their connection to you. Think about how you use your voice – as a man I have to realise that a booming voice might be scary for some children. Be clear in the instructions you give and be flexible, be open. Be able to say you're sorry and admit when you're wrong because this models to children how to manage mistakes and to look on mistakes as an opportunity to learn. This creates a safe space for learning – a 'secure base'. Encourage guesses, get things wrong on purpose yourself.

Humour and laughter are essential, as is emotional expression. Help children to recognise and identify all emotions, and understand that all emotions are normal. Use approaches like discussion, letters, cards, diaries, a comment box. I have a monster called William Worry and children can write their worries and post them into his mouth. I have a Quiet Zone where children can go to take a moment to reflect and be calm. Adults have a place to go when they need a break; so should our pupils.

Link with parents. Be positive, open, friendly, warm. Together you can create space for children to learn, grow and be happy, and in my experience if you can achieve that, positive behaviour follows.

Play

Another approach to promote positive behaviour that is emphasised within relational and psychodynamic approaches is play. Play can create an emotionally positive and supportive environment for children to learn and express themselves (Hayes et al., 2017). Mosley and Sonnet (2006) maintain that a prime method of doing this at primary level is through games. They believe that if educators bring a group together and nurture a sense of belonging at the beginning of a lesson, this will encourage better behaviour throughout the day, because children are starting on a bright note. This introduction could be done at the start of the day, the start of a morning or afternoon session, or the beginning of a particular lesson or activity. If children feel positive about themselves, they are less anxious about the challenges ahead, and more likely to behave well (Mosley and Sonnet, 2006). In early childhood settings play is infused throughout many pedagogical approaches and is seen as the primary mode through which learning occurs (Brennan, 2012). Play therapy has been shown to be very effective in dealing with a wide range of mental health and behavioural problems in children, even with those children who have experienced significant trauma or who have been diagnosed with various behavioural disorders (Cochran, Cochran, Nordling, McAdam and Miller 2010; Hayes, 2019). Play can be used in a very planned way to promote positive behaviour, and Mosley and Sonnet's (2006) book *101 Games for Better Behaviour* is useful for practical ideas. Particularly useful in the context of psychodynamic approaches are games to promote catharsis, or a release of emotional energy.

Emotional expression

The key idea to be understood with regards to play and expression of emotion is that when children are provided with appropriate means to release their energies, their difficulties are less likely to emerge as negative behaviour. Formal curricula at primary level also offer many opportunities for such catharsis. For example, when studying history, a goal may be empathy with historical figures ('How do you think Neville Chamberlain felt when he stepped off the plane and declared "We have peace in our time"? What about later, when he realised that Hitler in fact could not be appeased? Have you ever felt … ?'). Literacy lessons may aim to support creative writing, putting words on feelings, emotional development in language, and the capacity to express emotion. Drama allows for role-play and expression of emotion in a 'safe' setting because children can talk about feelings without them being personalised. Art can equally give children of all ages the opportunity to express their emotions. According to Boyer (2016), children in early childhood classrooms may represent their emotions in personally expressive ways through art, journalling, or free play using symbolic tools like crayons or clay, paper and pencil, or blocks and miniature figurines. Of course it is important to note that if such expression raises a traumatic or stressful issue with which you do not feel equipped to engage, do seek support from your principal or manager, or speak to the child's parents (Boyer, 2016).

It is important to be aware of the emotional life of children in every aspect of teaching. Negative behaviour can be a method of communicating the child's frustrations, and if we can improve the child's ability to communicate in more appropriate ways, we can reduce the negative behaviour. In Freudian terms, when we focus on getting rid of frustration in order to improve behaviour we are encouraging catharsis to support emotional development.

Emotional literacy

One of the most important modes of supporting emotional expression for children, and in fact for all human beings, is through language. According to Rose, Weinert and Ebert (2018), a wide range of studies have confirmed relations between children's language and different aspects of socioemotional competence. Babies have a special responsiveness to speech, and this encourages parents to talk to their baby, with obvious effects on social development and bonding (Berk, 2009; 2015). In learning through language in the educational setting, the child can come to a better understanding of self and relationships with others. Through the process of expressing thoughts and feelings the child can clarify concepts and explore emotions. Language, and writing in particular for older children, can greatly contribute to the child's cognitive, emotional and imaginative development through expression of

CASE STUDY

This picture shows three-year-old Saidbhín's response to having night-mares – she drew herself surrounded by her family, all encircled by a protective bubble, keeping out the swirling nightmare on the left. The artistic expression of fear achieved catharsis for Saidbhín and led to a reduction in nightmares. How might you support catharsis through art in the children you work with, with a view to avoiding negative behaviours based on fear and anxiety?

FIGURE 4.1 Emotional expression through art.

Author experience[6]

feelings, instincts and reactions, thus contributing to positive behaviour through healthy expression of emotion. Children should be encouraged to explore everyday experiences and feelings through talk, writing, play and drama, in order to facilitate understanding of emotion. This also allows children to give order to their feelings and reactions to people and events, and it may also act as a preventer of negative behaviour because it interrupts the process of a build-up of negative emotion that may cause difficulties in behaviour. In Freudian terms, it allows for catharsis.

Mosley and Sonnet (2006) also provide some games and activities to promote emotional literacy. For example, the activity 'It's not really funny' provides a picture to act as a prompt for discussion. The educator can ask children to describe what is happening in the picture, ask them to explain how each child might be feeling, ask the children to think about times they were unintentionally unkind. How did they realise that the person was upset? What could they have done differently? How could they make it up to the person? The educator can focus on the need to think about our behaviour beforehand, the language for a variety of emotions, building empathy, and mutually supportive relationships.

CONCLUSION

A psychodynamically informed, relational approach to supporting positive behaviour in educational settings provides a radically different perspective than that provided by behaviourism. This emphasises the importance of the argument put forward by this book: our responses to children's behaviour are determined by the 'theories', formal or informal, articulated or unacknowledged, that guide our understanding of why children behave as they do. An ill-informed understanding of the causes of children's behaviour could lead to at best ineffective responses, and at worst to damaging responses from educators. Through a relational lens, the responsibility of an educator, and the most effective approach to supporting positive behaviour, is to create a safe space in which children can learn, develop and behave to their best potential.

Key concepts within this chapter for educational practice

- Negative behaviour can be caused by displacement of emotion. This means that repression of emotion can be a cause of 'challenging' behaviour, but if children can be supported to express emotion appropriately through 'catharsis', positive behaviours may be supported.
- Relationships between children and their primary care-givers in early childhood provide a blueprint for future relationships and sense of self. Attachment theorists refer to 'internal working models' and Cognitive Analytic Therapists refer to 'reciprocal roles'. The central idea is that humans (children and adults) make predictions, not always accurately, about people and environments based on these blueprints, and this directs our behaviour, so undesirable or difficult behaviour can be sparked by anxiety, fear and hypervigilance.
- From a relational perspective, providing a warm relationship in which a child can feel safe and experience a 'secure base' is the best way an educator can support positive behaviour in an educational setting.

NOTES

1 *The Complete Psychological Works of Sigmund Freud* was published in 1955 and has been reissued many times since. You may wish to directly consult Freud's original work for more detail on the concepts discussed here, including the unconscious mind, repression, sublimation and catharsis.
2 See Chapter 6 for further exploration of the biological bases of behaviour and how they may be impacted by children's experiences.
3 If you would like to read up-to-date work related to attachment theory, you may be interested in the Minnesota Longitudinal Study which has been following the development of a group of children since 1975. You can access their findings here: www.cehd. umn.edu/icd/research/parent-child/
4 THRIECE is an international project funded by Erasmus+ involving educators at early years, primary and university level across three countries: Ireland, Poland and Portugal. It offers

online training modules for educators on holistic, relational and inclusive education, and the relational module offers training on using the insights and tools of CAT in educational settings. If you would like to access these modules, you can do so through www.mie.ie/en/Research/Teaching_for_Holistic_Relational_and_Inclusive_Early_Childhood_Education_THRIECE_/

5 This vignette is published with sincere thanks from the authors to the highly relational early childhood educator who wrote it, but asked not to be named in order to protect the anonymity of the little girl in question.

6 Saidbhín is the first author's daughter and she generously allowed us to use this picture as the cover art for our book Hayes, N., O'Toole, L. and Halpenny (2017). *Introducing Bronfenbrenner: A Guide for Practitioners and Students in Early Years Education.* London: Routledge.

CHAPTER 5

Humanist perspectives and strategies for positive behaviour

INTRODUCTION

A humanist perspective foregrounds the idea that a child's behaviour is a manifestation of a complex inner world, and approaching the development of positive behaviour solely from the adult's perspective shows only half the reality. Such an approach emphasises the capacity of all human beings, including children, to develop positively, and, like the psychodynamic, relational approaches explored in Chapter 4, it frames negative behaviour as a form of communication of unmet need, and a coping strategy in a world perceived by the child as hostile. In supporting children's positive behaviour, humanists emphasise genuineness, empathy, unconditional positive regard and self-direction rather than coercion. These approaches are sometimes called 'person-centred' after the person-centred therapy developed by Carl Rogers, or 'student-centred' after the educational approaches that Rogers adapted from his therapeutic methods.

Further developing relationship-based approaches to supporting positive behaviour in Chapter 4, this chapter will encourage readers to reflect on the ways in which their relationships with children underpin all learning and behaviour. It will identify approaches to supporting positive behaviour based on self-direction and mutual respect, such as narrative approaches and peer mediation.

THEORETICAL UNDERPINNINGS OF A HUMANIST APPROACH TO SUPPORTING POSITIVE BEHAVIOUR

Carl Rogers was a psychologist who originally worked as a therapist. Unlike Freud, whose work you explored in Chapter 4, and other therapists who analysed people and told them what they should do, Rogers relied on the capacity of the client to shed light on the issues and decide for themselves what was best to do. In other words, he focused on the ability of the person to direct the course of his own life (Gatongi, 2007; Hayes et al., 2017[1]). Rogers believed that people, including children, were fundamentally good, and would figure out the right course of action and behave well so long as they were given a supportive relationship within which to do so. Humanists consciously reject 'deficit models' of children's behaviour, models that emphasise what a child cannot do rather than recognise and celebrate what he can do. Like the authors explored in Chapter 4, Rogers believed that children develop through the relationships they experience.

Rogers' techniques in therapy very simply involved listening to the person and reflecting back to him what he said, in an accepting and understanding way. For Rogers, this respect for self-direction applies even when the person seems to choose goals that do not make sense to the therapist, and the function of therapy is to provide a supportive relationship within which the person can make decisions for himself. Unlike Freudian and other therapeutic approaches which demand objectivity and separateness from the therapist, a person-centred therapist is an important and significant part of the human equation – 'what he does, the attitude he holds, his basic concept of his role, all influence therapy to a marked degree' (Rogers, 1995, p. 19). Rogers requires therapists to exhibit three central characteristics: empathy (understanding from the client's viewpoint – or 'internal frame of reference'), congruence (genuineness) and unconditional positive regard (acceptance, trust). According to Gatongi (2007), while all three of these conditions are important, empathy is crucial and should be the highest priority of an educator taking a humanist approach to promoting positive behaviour in an educational setting.

Considering the humanist approach in educational settings rather than a therapeutic one, the role of the educator is characterised as a person who creates a supportive, trusting relationship through the Rogerian concepts of 'empathy', 'congruence' and 'unconditional positive regard'. In other words this approach means that the adult must respect each child as an individual capable of positive growth. Of course this can be difficult to achieve at the best of times but can be particularly difficult with the more challenging (often the most vulnerable) children. However, according to Rogers, the greatest tool a therapist or an educator has in supporting the client or the child is acceptance. Acceptance of the child as he presents is an active process on the part of the adult and does not mean passivity or indifference. Indeed such a lack of involvement would be experienced by children as rejection, and for learning to happen, support needs to be provided alongside significant challenge for children (Hayes et al., 2017).

A humanist approach is, as the name suggests, concerned with the human beings in any interaction, and Rogers' approach is often referred to as 'person-centred'. Person-centred approaches, in both clinical and educational contexts, require very active engagement; in person-centred therapy, the counsellor must attempt to take on the client's 'internal frame of reference', striving to see the world as the client sees it (Rogers, 1995). An early childhood educator or teacher applying this approach with a child must therefore try to see the world through the child's eyes and make it very clear that this is what he is trying to do. The educator should never assume that he understands the child's perspective, or that he fully understands why a child is behaving as he is. Rather the educator should ask about the behaviour and try to find a way of understanding the behaviour and the context of the behaviour from the child's viewpoint.

Rogers' concept of person-centredness has been transferred to the educational arena through the ideas of self-direction and the importance of the relationship, in an approach known as 'student-centred teaching' (Rogers, 1995). Its principles have been applied in settings ranging from tertiary to secondary, primary and early years settings (Boyer, 2016; Freiberg and Lamb, 2009; Gatongi, 2007; O'Toole, 2015). The educator's style is non-directive; he becomes more of a 'facilitator', helping children to discover learning for themselves, rather than giving direct instruction. For example, the educator using this approach should work with topics of relevance, interest and concern to children rather than planning from the adult perspective only, and he provides interesting materials for children to make sense of themselves. This is a challenging idea in a world where there is such emphasis on future-oriented education and the achievement of specified child outcomes. However, it resonates with the concept of 'emergent' approaches to curriculum widely used in early years settings internationally, through for example the Te Whāriki curriculum framework in New Zealand (New Zealand, 1996) or the Aistear curriculum framework in Ireland (NCCA, 2009). Recognition of the powerful value of an emergent approach provides a frame within which to identify and make visible early educational curriculum content as emerging from the child mediated through the informed relational and nurturing pedagogy of the educator. This provides a new role for the educator, which is enhanced through the creation of learning environments providing rich and relevant opportunities for learning and making children's learning visible through careful pedagogical documentation.

It may on the surface seem more challenging to be guided by the child's interests, particularly as children progress through educational systems and the curricula generally become more rigid; however, O'Toole (2015) has noted how student-centred methodologies can be adapted even for the most standardised neoliberal systems at tertiary level. Such practice is inclusive and welcoming to children from diverse backgrounds and of diverse ability, and can support the development of children's agency and self-direction. Rogers argues that when children are allowed to direct the course of their own behaviour and learning, they are more likely to make prosocial choices, choices that are positive, helpful, and likely to promote social acceptance and friendship (Rogers, 1995). In simple terms, when educators allow children to make choices for themselves, they tend to behave better in educational settings.

Of course, in practice educators often plan and guide learning towards short- and long-term learning goals that they are aware of although the child is not, and these may be goals of limited interest, meaning or relevance to the child (Hayes et al., 2017). Nevertheless, even in learning situations structured around plans developed externally to the child, if the educators actively focus on the development of relationships and on accessing the internal frame of reference of learners, student-centred approaches can be very powerful (O'Toole, 2015). In considering the educational potential of the person-centred approach Rogers (1974) presents a list of 'questions I would ask myself if I were a teacher', calling on educators to reflect on the relationship between themselves and the children they teach from

> **REFLECTION**
>
> Are there opportunities for children to practise self-direction in your educational setting?
>
> - What decisions can children make for themselves?
> - What decisions do adults make for children?
> - When do children have freedom of movement, expression, choice?
> - When are these freedoms curtailed? Why? Is it legitimate?
> - What specifically could you do to foster an agentic approach in your educational setting?
> - What practices should you change?
> - What practices should you maintain?

a humanist perspective, as a meeting of two human beings with individual strengths and needs. Such challenging questions might include:

> Do I dare to let myself deal with this boy or girl as a person, as someone I respect? Do I dare reveal myself to him and let him reveal himself to me? Do I dare to recognize that he/she may know more than I do in certain areas – or may in general be more gifted than I?
>
> (p. 2)

In asking such questions, Rogers is making serious demands on the educator who, historically, has held a position of power and authority over children in the educational setting. He is emphasising the importance and implications of educator respect for children, and recognises that there may be risk involved in the development of true and genuine human relationships. This highlights the fact that the behaviour of both educator and child develops and is maintained within the context of their relationship. This approach is known as 'humanism' because it recognises the basic humanity of children, and in doing so, their rights as agentic individuals to direct their own behaviour within respectful, reasonable boundaries.

CHILDREN'S VOICE AND A RIGHTS-BASED APPROACH TO CHILDREN'S BEHAVIOUR

The almost universal ratification of the UN Convention on the Rights of the Child (UNCRC) (United Nations, 1989) imposes a responsibility on educators to respond to the idea that children have explicit rights. The Convention supports the view of the active child, and holds participation as a central tenet. Through a rights-based lens, children are seen as competent, strong, active, participatory meaning-makers and young citizens, and educators must make strong efforts to really *hear* the child, being attuned to the many diverse forms of communication that children may use. This perspective moves us as educators from an instructional directive to a democratic, nurturing pedagogy (Hayes, 2013), consistent with a humanist approach. Rogers' concept of entering the internal frame of reference of the child resonates with Article 12 of UNCRC, which grants children and young people the legal right to have their views heard and acted upon as appropriate. This has led to increased interest in recent years in many disciplines, including education, in the concept of children's 'voice'.

In considering the voice of children and their rights to participation in education, Lundy developed a model of participation (2007) which is widely used to explore the concept of voice (Kennan, Brady and Forkan, 2019). According to Lundy (2007), there are four central elements in *really* hearing what children have to say:

- *Space* – it must be safe for children to communicate their opinions, with no fear of reprisals or discrimination
- *Voice* – children must have the right and opportunity to express views, with adult guidance
- *Audience* – children's views must be given due weight, listened to and heard
- *Influence* – what happens to children's views is important; feedback must be respectful and adults must be seen to act on children's views where appropriate and possible

However, this can be difficult to implement in practice (Kennan et al., 2019), and if an educator is to achieve positive behaviour through a humanist approach, he must ensure that he truly understands the viewpoint of the children in his educational setting. Educators must be sensitive to the different power dynamics at play when considering the 'voice of the child' and must respect the multiplicity of voices that children have rather than idealise the idea of a single 'child voice'. This resonates with the idea of the 'hundred languages of children' identified by Malaguzzi as the basis for the pedagogy of Reggio Emilia (Edwards, Gandini and Forman, 1998). This image helps educators focus attention away from difficult or undesirable behaviour towards the child behind the behaviour and the message that the behaviour might be communicating to us.

REFLECTION

How well do you listen to children? Do you try to see the world through their eyes? How can you make time in your busy day to enter the 'internal frame of reference' of children, and what specifically can you do to achieve insight into how they think and feel? How might you access understanding of the internal frame of reference of preverbal or nonverbal children?

HUMANIST PERSPECTIVES ON BEHAVIOUR IN EDUCATIONAL SETTINGS

Educational settings following a humanist approach to supporting positive behaviour are characterised by choice and autonomy for children. The central elements of a person/child-centred approach to supporting positive behaviour within the humanist frame in an educational setting are to value the personal dignity and integrity of children (Doyle, 2009), hold children responsible for their own behaviour, and support them to make good choices in the context of a warm, empathetic relational environment (Gatongi, 2007). According to Doyle (2009), person-centred approaches to behaviour in educational settings can be easily justified on ethical, moral, humanitarian and educational grounds. In an educational setting taking this approach to supporting positive behaviour, children's self-direction is considered very important, with the rationale, as in person-centred therapy, that all humans have the capacity for positive growth, and self-directed action is more likely to be effective than action directed by an outside source, for instance the educator. Cooperative learning and collaboration are valued in this approach and build on the interests of the child rather than the direction of the educator. This may become even more important as pedagogical philosophies aspire to more child-directed methods where curricula that require problem solving and critical thinking from children would be undermined by behaviour 'management' systems that require compliance and obedience (Garrett, 2008).

A humanist educator explains to children why certain standards are important to him, seeks the children's opinions on what rules and standards would be important to them, and negotiates rules and flexible, responsive consequences (Garrett, 2008; Gatongi, 2007). Boyer (2016) recommends a group or class mission statement, renegotiated regularly. In a humanist educational setting, children often have responsibility for various tasks like taking attendance, updating the calendar or caring for a class pet, and they should have autonomy over simple things like when to use the bathroom (Garrett, 2008). The focus is on a cooperative, student-centred, respectful learning environment where children have 'freedom to learn' and behave to their best potential through the development of responsibility and agency within a democratic environment (Freiberg and Lamb, 2009). Peter Moss (2007, 2011) argues that democracy and education are inseparable, and proposes that democratic practice in early childhood settings operates at several different levels, nationally through national framework and curriculum and institutionally through day-to-day practices. Democratic practice in early childhood is sustained through enabling curriculum frameworks and environments and activities where both children and adults are engaged. Whether in early childhood or at later educational levels, approaches such as this, which encourage and support self-discipline, have been found to be more effective on a long-term basis than points systems or punishments based on the behaviourist methods (Freiberg and Lamb, 2009; Laursen, 2003) described in Chapter 3.

Just as the relationship between the therapist and the client is considered crucial to person-centred therapy, the relationship between the educator and the child is considered core to a person-centred approach to supporting positive behaviour. Therefore the strategies for relationship building in educational settings identified in Chapter 4 are relevant here also. Positive relationships between educators and children are seen to lessen the need for control of children (Garrett, 2008). The educator using a humanist approach also achieves such relationship building through the application of the three key elements of empathy, congruence and unconditional positive regard.

Empathy

In an educational context, empathy means that educators wish to see the world the way children do (Gatongi, 2007). Being attuned to the social and emotional realities of children can support them to behave well and develop to their best potential from the earliest years in education (Boyer, 2016). Educators interested in accessing the internal frame of reference of the children in their educational settings, particularly when seeking to understand negative or disruptive behaviour, could draw on the creative methods used by educational researchers to research the viewpoints of children. For example, Kiely et al. (2019) analysed children's drawings of themselves doing homework to access children's perceptions of the links between home and school. If there is a specific topic or issue you would like to find out about from children's perspective, you could ask them to draw it. Alternatively, Greene and Hill (2005) recommend the use of scenarios, vignettes and sentence completion tasks or methods which use computing technology. Christensen and James (2000) highlight the potential of role-play and drama in this regard. Respecting the many different voices of children, Spyrou (2011) explores the use of visual approaches to accessing children's voice, giving a range of examples including visual diaries with pictures and drawings of children's worlds, photo-voice and participatory photography, where children document their lives or explore issues of interest to them by taking pictures of what matters to them. Further methods include photoelicitation where children are invited by the researcher to talk about pictures they took or ones presented to them by the researcher (Nic Gabhainn and Sixsmith, 2006), scrapbooks or media diaries completed by children, maps completed by children of their environments, and videos produced by young people to explore their perspectives of schooling.

TASK

Consider how these research methods could be adapted for early years or primary school setting to access the viewpoints of children. How might accessing children's perspectives impact on their behaviour? Are there any current points of contention between you and the children you work with? Are there any behavioural issues that you find you need to keep revisiting? Begin by identifying a method to access the children's perspective on those issues, and later in the chapter you can discover a humanist approach on how to respond.

Congruence

One crucial element of a student-centred teacher's behaviour is the responsibility of the teacher to bring his own personality into his educational space and be genuine in his engagement with children. To be effective the educator must be prepared to present his personhood, particularly if he is to gain the trust of a child in difficult situations. Such exposure may not come naturally, and O'Brien (2018) notes the traditional, but he argues inappropriate, exhortation to novice teachers of 'Don't smile until Christmas' for fear of losing control. A humanist educator accepts uncertainty and recognises the positive potential for collaborative and cooperative learning, and teaching and shows genuineness by not playing roles or putting up unnecessary barriers between himself and children (Gatongi, 2007). As Boyer (2016, p. 343) puts it, 'It pays to be human in the classroom'. The humanist educator must also practise his values, obey and model the golden rule: treat others as you would have them treat you (Boyer, 2016). In this way a learning environment can be mutually created between the children and the adult, one that builds on the strengths of both the children and adults, encourages dialogue and celebrates diversity and multiple perspectives.

REFLECTION

How might you break down barriers and build relationships between you and the children you work with? What aspects of your personality do you bring with you into the educational space? Are there any aspects of your personality you have been holding back? What skills or talents do you have that the children might enjoy? What interests do you have that you could share? Have you been 'genuine' in your engagement with children to date?

Unconditional positive regard

Acceptance and unconditional regard for the child in an educational setting does not mean that all behaviours must be accepted – it is possible to identify behaviour as inappropriate or damaging while still retaining respect and regard for the child as a fellow human being with needs and feelings, strengths and challenges, just like the adult has. As expressed by Gatongi (2007, p. 208):

> There should be respect and no judgment, however bad the behaviour, thus separating the person from the bad behaviour. But the respect is not a condition for an acceptable behaviour and neither is it an approval of bad behaviour. Therefore drawing a line between what a person does and who they are, it becomes possible to show warmth at the same time as setting boundaries, and expressing different opinions and wishes.

A criticism levelled at the humanist approach is that it creates no boundaries for children and gives unrealistic freedoms to them. Freiberg and Lamb (2009) argue that it is a myth that such approaches mean that children are offered no discipline at all, and Boyer (2016) maintains that limit setting is an important element of creating a safe, person-centred educational setting: 'We accept all students unconditionally, but not all behaviour is safe, kind, forgiving, or loving. The early childhood educator must consider the mental health and physical safety of all students and set appropriate limits' (p. 344). She offers simple language for educators to help young children understand such limits in early childhood settings: 'I am not for hurting, you are not for hurting, and the things around us are not for breaking' (p. 344). It is as a result of such shared limit setting, those in favour of this approach argue, that person-centred classrooms facilitate higher achievement, and have more positive learning environments with stronger teacher–student relationships than teacher-centred or traditional classrooms (Freiberg and Lamb, 2009). By sharing control within educational settings, children become self-disciplined, and so rather than a lack of discipline, Freiberg and Lamb (2009) argue that this approach engenders *more* discipline than in a traditionally structured educational setting.

PRACTICAL APPROACHES TO SUPPORTING POSITIVE BEHAVIOUR THROUGH A HUMANIST LENS

Approaches to supporting positive behaviour are summarised by Freiberg and Lamb (2009, p. 100) into four elements of a person-centred classroom:

- social-emotional emphasis – teachers demonstrate caring for students' social and emotional needs, and for who they are as people;
- school connectedness – teachers ensure that students feel a strong sense of belonging to the school, their classroom, and their peers;
- positive school and classroom climate – students feel safe in school, developing trust for their peers and their teacher;
- student self-discipline – students learn through responsible consequences and a shared respect and responsibility

They can be operationalised within the early childhood setting and classroom through a variety of approaches including narrative practice and peer mediation.

Narrative practice

Narrative practice allows for the practical application of theoretical concepts emphasising respect for the child as an individual, entering the child's internal frame of reference, and understanding negative behaviour as the child's way of adapting to the situation as they see it. Reflecting Rogers' therapeutic approach, narrative approaches to working with children in an educational setting have as their guiding principle the idea that the child is not the problem, the problem is the problem. Narrative approaches maintain that we are natural storytellers and we make sense of our lives through stories, but our lives are made up of many stories (Hegarty, 2007). For example, a child may be a loving son, a challenging student, an excellent midfielder on the football pitch, an aggressive presence in the school yard … all of these stories may be true, but none of them alone is the whole truth. We are all an amalgam of our various stories, but when a child is seen as exhibiting 'challenging' behaviour, that story can often dominate people's perception of him. In such a case, a substantial proportion of the child's 'lived experience' contradicts this 'dominant narrative' (White, 2004). In other words, if we enter the child's 'internal frame of reference', as Rogers advocates, and see the world through his eyes, we understand that in his daily life the child does not see himself as troublesome. He sees himself as bored or as unfairly scolded or as happy a lot of the time. If the child's reputation in school does not sufficiently represent his lived experience, he may 'act out', or withdraw completely (Hegarty, 2007).

This can lead to a 'vicious cycle' where a problem-saturated story dominates the conversations adults have about the child, the child withdraws or acts out further as a result, which causes adults to view him in a more negative light, and so on. Hegarty (2007) tells us that deficit descriptions of a child are often taken on board in a totalising way, as if they touched on the very essence of the person, as if the child is by his very nature troublesome and challenging for all time and in all contexts – as Winslade and Monk (1999) point out, such perceptions can lead to negative behaviours being more engrained. They describe the process as like developing a photograph – 'Like photographic fixing chemicals [deficit descriptions] make images of personhood permanent' (p. 60). Approaches like suspension and expulsion work against change, because they reinforce this image of the child as 'trouble' and the child lives up (or down) to his reputation.

Narrative approaches attempt to break this cycle and present an alternative 'story' for the child based on 'externalising the behaviour'. In other words, this approach takes the problem out of the child – the child is not the problem, the problem is the problem. There is much evidence that this approach decreases unproductive conflict, undermines the sense of failure, and opens up possibilities for people to retrieve their lives and their relationships from the problem (White, White, Wijaya and Epston, 1990). It resonates with Rogers' idea of 'unconditional positive regard' in that it allows the educator to address inappropriate behaviour while still maintaining a positive image of the child. Like Rogers, narrative approaches view the child as the expert on his own life. These approaches invite children to view alternative stories that apply to them, other than dominant negative ones, stories that they might not have even noticed themselves because they are blinded by other people's opinions of them. With this approach, we do not try to change behaviour, we try to understand experience. Consider the narrative approach taken by Hegarty (2007) in understanding a feud between children in two different classes in a primary school:

CASE STUDY

On being asked to conduct an anger management programme with fifth-class children (aged approximately eleven years) Hegarty wrote that she felt that such a programme would only serve to reinforce this narrative of the children as angry and difficult. When she discussed what was going on with the teachers in the school, a picture emerged of a feud between two classes, with the playground turned into a battlefield. This gave her an idea of how to use narrative approaches of externalising the problem – the feud was the problem, not the children, and that is what needed to be addressed. Using narrative approaches, Hegarty:

1 Met each class separately and through Circle Time explored what sort of actions helped the classes get on with each other, and what sort of things got in the way of good relations. She asked the children to assess how well they got on together, and when they said that the classes got on well internally but not well with each other, asked whether they wanted that to continue – all said no.
2 Wrote a letter to each class describing the outcomes of each other's sessions and asking if they were willing to work together with her against their common enemy: 'the feud'.
3 Enlisted the help of one of the more socially 'powerful' children:

   - She had noticed that in the group, a lot of the children made eye contact with one girl before answering, almost as if they were asking her permission.
   - Hegarty told this girl that she could not solve the problem without her, and the child was shocked – she said 'Me! You want to ask me! Nobody here listens to me. I'm only known for fighting' – this shows that the child had an awareness of what the dominant narrative about her was.
   - Hegarty supported the child to develop an alternative narrative where she was a leader in the 'peace process' and the child was then able to identify and draw in the 'leaders' from the other class

4 Hegarty then worked with the two classes together to identify all the things they had in common, and explore ways of being nicer to each other in future
5 The children wrote the story of the feud and the subsequent peace process – a new story or narrative
6 Using language taken from the children's own writings, Hegarty composed a certificate for the children, called an 'Escape from fighting' certificate, which was presented to each child at a ceremony attended by teachers and parents – extending the new narrative to the wider school community.

Source: Hegarty (2007)

Hegarty's narrative approach is consistent with a humanist perspective on behaviour because it allows the adult to enter the children's internal frames of reference, maintains unconditional positive regard for children, separating the negative behaviour from the children as human beings, offers them an opportunity to actively engage in identifying solutions, and locates their behaviours within the context of their relationships with the adults in the school and with each other. Other approaches within a narrative approach through a humanist lens include exploring dreams, hopes and visions for the future with children through some of the methods identified above; the use of a 'quiet room' where experiences can be shared and visualisations enjoyed; the creation of a 'mean-free zone' where children define behaviours that are mean or upsetting and agree to make sure they do not happen in their educational setting; playing games about cooperation; drama and role-play; creating stories with toy animals or puppets on topics like 'the animal school with a serious bullying problem' – any approach that allows children to identify their own narrative, to tell their own story, and not to be 'stuck' in a narrative defined by teachers, parents or other children.

TASK

Individually or with a colleague, come up with a narrative approach to deal with a situation where:

- a child is being disruptive and distracting other children from their learning
- a child is violent towards you
- a child is struggling to make friends

PEER MEDIATION

Another possible approach within a humanist framework for promoting positive behaviour and dealing with negative behaviour if it does occur is the idea of conflict resolution and peer mediation (Cremin, 2007; Garrett, 2008). The central concept behind peer mediation is to return power to children; in educational settings, adults are often in a position of power over children, and peer mediation aims to return a sense of responsibility to children. Peer mediation attempts to encourage children to understand and manage conflict in their own lives and in their own school. It aims to build children's communication skills and problem-solving skills and develop in them a deep-rooted respect for others. It focuses on development of students' social skills through various strategies such as I-messages, classroom meetings, and community-building activities (Garrett, 2008).

Peer mediation involves a third party intervening in a dispute between two children, and the third party is another child. According to Farrell (2005), this approach has the potential to develop children's sense of their own worth and that of others, their capacity to manage their emotions, their ability to learn, and their social and personal skills, because it is based on a fundamental respect for all. This approach may be more appropriate for older children, as it requires a level of self-regulation and objectivity that may be difficult for a younger child to achieve. Peer mediation allows children to develop their communication and problem solving skills (Dummer, 2010), and may allow them to solve conflicts more constructively in their future lives (Gunduz, Uzunboylu and Ozcan, 2017).

A peer mediation system can be set up in a school by first running training for all children on conflict resolution and the mediation process where the rules are explored (Gunduz et al., 2017); for example, 'no interrupting', 'no name-calling'. Situations of conflict can be explored through role-play, group work, discussion and reflection. The whole class can do this training initially, and then children can apply to become peer mediators. This process is taken very seriously – children apply formally and are interviewed before being selected. Those chosen are then always on duty – they may be asked to formally mediate between two of their peers or they may offer their services when they happen to see a disagreement developing. It is important to note, however, that mediation must be entirely voluntary – no child should be forced to take part against his will or the whole point of it is lost. Whole-school approaches to peer mediation are generally seen as valuable (Cremin, 2007). Peer mediation is consistent with a person-centred approach to supporting positive behaviour, because it emphasises respect for children as human beings capable of directing the course of their own behaviour, leading to more responsible outcomes.

CONCLUSION

Humanist early childhood educators and primary teachers believe that children are more likely to behave well when they are given choice and opportunities for self-direction, and encouraged to cooperate and collaborate with the children and adults in their educational environment. Children's behaviour develops and is maintained within the context of the relationships they experience with those around them. Positive, mutually respectful relationships between children and educators are vital for positive behaviour.

Key concepts within this chapter for educational practice

1   Like the psychodynamic and relational approaches, the humanist perspective emphasises meeting basic needs for love, security and belonging to support the development of positive behaviour. In order to support positive behaviour, educators need to create spaces of trust to allow children's voices to be heard, recognising the many different 'voices' children may use. This involves

listening to children in whatever way they communicate, and not only responding but being seen to respond.

2 What is different about this approach is the emphasis on self-direction and autonomy, leading to understanding by children of why they should behave well, and so make positive choices in their behaviour.

NOTE

1 The first section of this chapter draws on the exploration of humanist psychology and student-centred education published by the authors in Hayes et al. (2017).

CHAPTER 6

The biological bases of behaviour

INTRODUCTION

This chapter will help readers to understand how simple biological considerations such as hunger and tiredness can impact on children's behaviour, and to identify simple interventions based on this knowledge that can prevent episodes of negative behaviour from occurring. Readers will also be introduced to the role of temperament, the concept of 'executive function' and how children's brain development over time can have implications for their behaviour through the development of skills such as impulse control and self-regulation. Children's biological needs for movement and play will also be emphasised, along with a caution for educators to avoid mistaking an inability to sit still for misbehaviour. Some additional sensory needs will be considered. However, the hypothesis of a biological basis to behaviour will not be presented uncritically, and the chapter will introduce the 'biopsychosocial' model (Engel, 1977) as one means of understanding the complex and integrated way in which biology interacts with psychological and social factors to influence behaviour.

BIOLOGY AND BEHAVIOUR

When a child presents with difficult or unwanted behaviour it is valuable to take the time to look beyond the immediate presenting behaviour and consider different possible explanations that might explain it and allow for differentiated action from the educator. This is particularly useful when trying to get to know a child or, with children you already know, when seeking to understand an unexplained or unexpected behaviour. There are many different factors that can lead to children exhibiting unwanted behaviour and, in some cases we can identify multiple different potential causes leading to the development of the presenting difficulty – causes such as poor regulation of emotions, environmental stress or genetically based problems. Frequently when a child behaves in an unexpected or unwanted way there is a combination of factors at play and, increasingly, educators are recognising the value of exploring what these factors may be. Such exploration allows an educator to consider a given behaviour from a variety of different perspectives, which can increase the likelihood that the behaviour can be reduced in frequency or altered in form.

Biological theories of behaviour argue that development is a biological process, and so behaviour is seen as primarily determined by genetic potential (Krishnan, 2010). One way to think about genetic influences is as building blocks; while most people tend to have the same basic building blocks, these components can be put together in many different ways to come up with many different outcomes (Cherry, 2018). When we think about our own behaviour, we sometimes recognise similarities between ourselves and family members such as siblings or parents, but is this because we have inherited genetic tendencies towards such behaviour or because in growing and developing under the close influence of these family members, we have learned to behave in similar ways to them? This is known as the nature–nurture debate, and while it has been researched for many decades, few present-day writers now present it as a strict dichotomy. It is generally recognised that both nature and nurture interact in complex and unpredictable ways to influence behaviour. While this chapter aims to explore biological influences, readers should keep in mind that these do not operate in isolation from their psychological and social contexts.

MEETING BASIC BIOLOGICAL NEEDS

One consideration that may not come to mind in educators is that simple biological considerations like hunger, tiredness or physical discomfort can play an important role in behavioural outcomes for children. This is particularly true for small children or children with additional needs who may not have the language to express physical discomfort. According to Eurostat (2019) statistics, children are the group at highest risk of poverty and social exclusion in Europe and in 2017, 69.2% of the 'very low work intensity households' with dependent children and 48.4% of the 'low work intensity households' with dependent children in the EU were at risk of poverty. Kelly, Gavin, Molcho and Nic Gabhainn (2012) found that 21% of Irish schoolchildren reported going to bed or school hungry as there was not enough food at home. In research in Dublin schools, Downes and Maunsell (2007) found that between 6% and 33% of children were either often, very often or every day too hungry to do their work. Their research also found that 15% were not able to concentrate from lack of sleep, often due to anxiety. Considering the fact that Bub et al. (2011) found links between sleep difficulties and cognitive ability, it is important for educators to consider such physical needs when thinking about children's needs and evaluating their behaviour. If a child is hungry, it is very difficult for her to behave well in an educational setting. Very often when children misbehave they are letting you know that they have an unmet need (O'Brien, 2018). If children are hungry they may misbehave and they certainly cannot participate in education to the best of their ability (Flaherty, 2012). Some children may come into your educational setting tired for lack of sleep or lack of opportunity for deep and replenishing sleep. Tired children, as many educators will know, can exhibit difficult behaviour, and often the best approach is to provide them with space to rest, and if necessary sleep. Napping may not be beneficial for all children but the opportunity to nap should, if possible, be available, and is a must for the youngest children and babies. Sleep routines should be tailored to the unique needs of individual children rather than designed to cater to the needs of a setting's timetable or staffing requirements. Physical discomfort resulting from inadequate or ill-fitting clothes or shoes will impact on a child's ability to settle at ease, attend to activities or focus in a consistent manner. In order to ensure that children start the day well fed, rested and comfortable and, as a result, more likely to behave well and learn to the best of their ability, many educational settings provide various resources such as, in relation to hunger, snacks for children in the morning, and some develop a breakfast club and may have kitchen services to provide other meals. The organisation Healthy Food for All (Flaherty, 2012) has published a *Good Practice Guide* for educators who would like to set up a breakfast club. The Guide can be accessed here: www.welfare.ie/en/downloads/Good-practice-guide-for-breakfast-clubs.pdf. Such approaches to meeting physical needs are important in the present lives of children but are also important from a long-term perspective.

While the current chapter presents some biological, developmental, genetic and brain-based impacts on present behaviour, it does so with the full understanding that development over time involves a complex interaction of both nature and nurture. In fact, the most-up-to date understandings of 'epigenetics', or how genes are 'switched on' by environmental experiences, would seem to indicate that not only have we moved on from nature *versus* nurture to nature *and* nurture, but in fact we now understand that nature *is* nurture. According to Cherry (2018):

> While the genetic instructions a child inherits from his parents may set out a road map for development, the environment can impact how these directions are expressed, shaped or even silenced. The complex interaction of nature and nurture does not just occur at certain moments or at certain periods of time; it is persistent and lifelong.

Nurturing children's physical, emotional and psychological development is crucial for behavioural and other outcomes across the lifespan through the impact on the child's developing brain structures.

BIOLOGY, BRAIN DEVELOPMENT AND THEIR INFLUENCE ON BEHAVIOUR

As introduced in Chapter 4, from the beginning the infant brain is affected by the environmental factors in the world around the child. The National Scientific Council on the Developing Child, in their report on the science of early childhood development (CDC, 2007), argue that research into early brain development confirms the importance of early life experiences and their impact on the basic architecture of the brain. They present evidence that brains are built up over time beginning before birth and continuing into adulthood, and highlight the significant value of early interactions and relationships:

Young children naturally reach out for interaction through babbling, facial expressions, and gestures, and adults respond with the same kind of vocalizing and gesturing back at them. In the absence of such responses – or if the responses are unreliable or inappropriate – the brain's architecture does not form as expected, which can lead to disparities in learning and behaviour.

(pp. 1–2)

There is evidence indicating that the stress associated with poverty, neglect, abuse or poor parenting can compromise the positive brain development essential to later achievement, success and behaviour. The kinds of behaviour that are expected of children in schools and early childhood settings in order to be successful include creativity, flexibility, self-control and discipline, and central to all of these are brain-based systems known as 'executive functions' (Hayes et al., 2017). The executive functions are those functions we use to manage our behaviour, our emotions and our attention, and to organise and order our actions and thoughts (Diamond, 2013). These skills, necessary to control and coordinate information, are critical to success in life in general and school success in children in particular, and begin to develop in early childhood, providing the foundation for later learning and development. The actual term executive function has come to be used increasingly to refer to a wider variety of skills than originally intended, including attention, self-control, emotion regulation, creativity and problem solving, among others. This poses a challenge for early childhood educators and others who wish to seek out relevant research findings that are tied to specific skills. For clarity it is more helpful to refer to executive function (EF) and self-regulation together (CDC, 2017; Miyake and Friedman, 2012; Jones, Bailey, Barnes. and Partee, 2016).

Executive function and self-regulation involve both concrete behaviours and abstract concepts, and research indicates that children who have good executive functioning and self-regulation do better in both the academic areas such as literacy and numeracy and in general social adjustment (Jones et al., 2016). The development of executive function and self-regulatory skills depends on the biological maturity of the child, and the process is heavily influenced by environmental experiences. It appears that through the quality of their early learning experiences children access the opportunities to develop these functions, and the adults in their lives are of critical importance in facilitating this. For the purposes of considering the role of early childhood educators in the support and development of executive functions and self-regulatory behaviours, it is useful to view them in terms of three interrelated types of brain function: working memory, mental flexibility and self-control:

- Working memory governs our ability to retain and manipulate distinct pieces of information over short periods of time
- Mental flexibility helps us to sustain or shift attention in response to different demands or to apply different rules in different settings
- Self-control enables us to set priorities and resist impulsive actions or responses (CDC, 2017)

Children are not born with these skills but have the potential to develop them. Their development depends on the quality and intensity of the interactions and relationships available to children, and educators have an important role in 'scaffolding' children in this development until they can perform them alone. If they do not receive the necessary supports from their environments and those around them, children's development of executive function and self-regulation skills may be delayed. According to Diamond (2016) executive functions and self-regulation skills include the ability to mentally play with ideas, give a considered response rather than an impulsive one, change perspectives as needed, resist temptations and stay focused. Research studies indicate that executive functioning and self-regulation may be developmental in nature; that is, they begin to emerge in early childhood but develop over time because the frontal lobes of the brain are growing and are not fully mature until adulthood. As a result, our expectations for self-regulation, inhibitory control or cognitive flexibility in young children should not be the same as for those of older children or adults (Cepeda, Kramer and Gonzalez de Sather, 2001; Davidson, Amso, Anderson and Diamond, 2006; Garon, Bryson and Smith, 2008). Skills like reasoning, problem solving and planning require children to use a number of executive functions simultaneously including working memory, inhibitory control and mental flexibility (Diamond, 2016), so educators should not mistake young children struggling with these skills as misbehaving.

There is evidence that executive functions, comprising skills of self-regulation alongside attentional and motivational dimensions of development, can impact on children's behaviour in educational settings, and thus can be critical for success from the early years, all the way up through primary, secondary and even into university and workplace settings (Diamond, 2016). Diamond provides some thought-provoking guidance for early educators in this regard:

> The prefrontal cortex is not fully mature until early adulthood (one's mid-20s). Some people have asked, therefore, 'Isn't it nonsense to try to improve EFs in pre-schoolers? There isn't enough of a biological substrate to work with; wait until prefrontal cortex is more mature.' In response, I think it is helpful to consider an analogy. Certainly toddlers' legs are not at their full adult extent, and they probably will not be for another 15 years or so, but with those immature legs toddlers can walk and even run.
>
> (p. 20)

While it is true that such development tends to unfold naturally over time with the development of the frontal cortex of the brain, executive function and self-regulation in children is also sensitive and responsive to experience, and some environments have been found more supportive to the development of strong executive function and self-regulation in children than others (Hayes et al., 2017). These environments include calm, predictable, loving environments with secure, consistent boundaries and attuned responses to expressions of physical and emotional need. Children who experience such environments are likely to develop strong executive functions, good self-regulation, and generally exhibit positive behaviour, appropriate for their age group in educational settings. On the other hand, chaotic environments that are unpredictable, abusive or even overindulgent with few or inconsistent boundaries tend to lead to limitations in the development of children's executive function and self-regulation skills, leading to negative behaviours in educational settings – behaviours such as aggressive outbursts, inability to cope with frustration, poor inhibitory control so that children tend to blurt out the answer, jump out of their seats, take things from other children, and have difficulty paying attention and completing tasks. Poverty has particularly been identified as a significant stressor for the delayed development of children's executive functioning (Raizada and Kishiyama, 2010; Sektnan, McClelland, Acock and Morrison, 2010), and its effects can be cumulative, so that children marginalised by poverty can fall progressively farther behind each school year (O'Shaughnessy, Lane, Gresham and Beebe-Frankenberger, 2003). A small difference in executive functioning and self-regulation in the early years can lead to a gap in achievement and mental health that grows ever wider each passing year so that quality early education, intervention and support has an important contribution to make in reducing inequality (Diamond, 2016).

Through observing play, adults can gain insight into children's executive function and self-regulation at work when, for instance, they talk themselves through an activity as they move objects around or place things in a particular order. The example below is an illustration of a young child at play. If you follow closely you will see different skills in action and the early educator's role in supporting and extending the opportunities presented towards strengthening positive adaptive behaviours (Hayes et al., 2017, pp. 139–140).

At planning time, Gabrielle says, 'I'm going to play with the doggies and Magnatiles in the toy area. I'm making a tall elevator.' At work time, Gabrielle builds with the magnetic tiles while playing with the small toy dogs, as she planned. She stacks the tiles on top of one another in a tower-like form – her 'elevator' – then places some dogs in it. The elevator then falls over. She repeats this several times but the elevator continues to fall over. Gabrielle then arranges the magnetic tiles into squares, connecting them to form a row. Gabrielle says to Shannon, her teacher, 'I'm making doghouses because the elevator keeps falling down.' Shannon says, 'I was wondering what you were building, because you planned to make a tall elevator going up vertically, and now you are using them to make doghouses in a long horizontal row. You solved the problem by changing the way you were building.' Gabrielle uses pretend talk while moving the dogs around. At one point she says, 'Mommy, Mommy, we are hungry' and opens one of the doghouses and moves the dog inside where a bigger dog is placed. Gabrielle says, 'Mommy says the food's not ready, so go play.'

While moving the dogs around, Gabrielle says to herself out loud, 'We have to find something to do until the food is ready.' Gabrielle says to Shannon, 'Let's pretend we are going to the park.' Shannon agrees and says, 'I'm going to slide down the slide three times and then jump off the climber.' As Shannon pretends to do this with one of the dogs, Gabrielle watches then copies her and says, 'My dog jumped higher than yours.' She then says, 'Mommy says we have to go home now. We need to move our dogs over there so they can eat.' The pretend play continues.

At recall time, Gabrielle is using a scarf to hide some objects she played with. When it is her turn to recall, she gives clues about what is under the scarf. She shows the group a couple of magnetic tiles and dogs. Shannon asks her what she did with these materials during work time. Gabrielle talks about the problem with the falling 'elevator' and then recounts the story about the doggies.

Source: Drawn from research data (Lockhart, 2010, pp. 1–2)

You will notice how, with the careful intervention of Shannon, the early years educator, Gabrielle was made aware of the fact that she had solved a problem. Later in her play she was given the opportunity to see planning in action when Shannon talked through her plans for sliding on the slide. Finally we see Gabrielle given the opportunity to recall and share her activity with others. Where playful everyday experiences are available in well-designed and interactive early childhood settings children have the time, encouragement and context within which to develop the dispositions and skills necessary to function competently and effectively at their own level. The presence of observant, well-informed, attuned and engaged educators enriches children's experiences, expanding and strengthening their learning and development. For all children, but particularly for those who may struggle with executive function, the importance of a sensitive and knowledgeable adult to support them to co-regulate in the early years cannot be overestimated. This allows them to gradually develop the skills required to move towards self-regulation so that as their brains develop the capacity to inhibit impulses, pay attention and behave in ways that are more generally acknowledged as positive, they can begin to do so independently.

TEMPERAMENT AND INDIVIDUAL DIFFERENCES IN BEHAVIOURAL TENDENCIES

The mechanisms that influence the development of executive functions and self-regulation are complex and include the child's temperament. The term 'temperament' refers to behavioural tendencies that appear early after birth, are stable, and have a constitutional, biological basis. Examples given by Saudino (2005) are that some children cry easily and intensely whereas others are more easy-going; some are highly active and always on the go where others are more sedentary; some attend and persist in tasks for long periods of time where others' attention wanders quickly, and Saudino indicates that it is these individual differences and the variations in between that are of interest to behavioural geneticists. Saudino (2005) notes a dramatic increase in studies that elucidate temperamental and environmental interactions, documenting the importance of environmental factors on temperament dimensions, tracking the developmental course of genetic and environmental contributions to temperament, addressing the issue of genetic and environmental overlap between temperament and problem behaviours, and relating specific genetic markers to temperament dimensions. These studies illustrate how temperament can mediate environmental conditions. A number of studies illustrate how parental hostility and child negative reactivity relate to child maladjustment, including one study where children who were high in negative reactivity were likely to demonstrate externalising behaviour problems if their mothers were high in hostility (Morris et al., 2002).

In their seminal study, Temperament and Development (the New York Longitudinal Study [NYLS]), Thomas and Chess (1977) collected data on the behavioural development of a group of 133 children from early infancy into adult life, gathering data on each child at different stages in their development. From their data they identified three distinct types of temperament in the infants. They called the different types of temperament the 'easy baby', the 'difficult baby' and the 'slow-to-warm-up baby' and found the following distribution in the population studied:

- The easy child (40%) was quick to establish regular routines in infancy, generally cheerful and adapted easily.
- The difficult child (10%) was irregular in daily routine, slow to accept new experiences, tended to react negatively and cry a lot and showed a greater risk of adjustment problems in later life.
- The slow-to-warm-up child (15%) was inactive, a bit negative, and showed low key reaction to her environment.
- Other babies (35%) who did not fit the above categories neatly were deemed to exhibit 'no pattern'.

'Easy' babies are far less demanding than those deemed 'difficult'. They are smiley, cheerful, adaptable, friendly and rewarding. Difficult babies, on the other hand, are irritable, reject new foods, new situations, new people, and fuss strenuously about their frequent complaints. They are finicky, fussy and trying. All babies (and of course children and even adults!) have their fussy moments or occasional periods of irritability but they are not necessarily difficult. A difficult baby is consistently irritable and over-reactive. These differences can cause problems in the interaction between the mother and her child in the very early stages of the relationship. For the mother who can accept a difficult child the problems will be less than for the mother who considers that the child's difficulties reflect on her own capacity as a mother. That brings us to an important concept in the study of child development, not only in respect of infant development but development in general, and that is the concept of 'goodness of fit'.

Thomas and Chess (1977) found that the development of children's behavioural problems in later life could not be predicted from a knowledge of the child alone or, for that matter, of the parent alone, but rather from the goodness of fit – or lack of fit – of the characteristics of both parties. They also established that the nature of the child's temperament right from the moment of birth was a factor. This is a hugely important concept for educators wishing to understand the dynamics of children in educational settings (Hayes, 2013). Thomas and Chess stress how mistaken it is to assume that a child's behaviour problem must inevitably be due to unhealthy parental influences. Such a view results in a mistaken emphasis on the supposed pathogenic, or damaging, influence of the mother. The reality is that a wide variety of factors, including the temperamental nature of the child, can influence development. McClowry (2012) observes that when goodness of fit is examined through the lens of self-regulation the focus of attention shifts from the parent–child dyad to situations where a child's temperamental tendencies have to accommodate to environmental demands. This is illustrated in the example below.

Goodness of fit becomes more difficult to achieve as children get older and enter environments where parents have less direct control. Parents who have adequate personal, financial and community resources may be better able to access child care and educational environments that match their child's temperament. For example, a small nurturing preschool with a teacher who exudes warmth is likely to be a good choice for a child whose temperament is high in withdrawal. In contrast, a stimulating, fast-paced day care center may be more suitable for an active child.

Source: McClowry, (2012)

Attachment theory and the work of Tony Ryle noted in Chapter 4 highlighted how our own temperaments as adults can also enter the equation. Therefore it is equally important in an educational setting not to blame the child or blame yourself if things have gone awry in the past. Sometimes a temperamental fit can be explosive or unhelpful, but since it is unlikely that a child will be in a position to figure out how to develop 'goodness of fit', it is up to the educator as the adult to work that out as best as possible.

REFLECTION

Are there any children with whom you work whose temperament does not match well with your own temperament? Could any past incidences that you previously attributed to 'challenging behaviour' perhaps have been explained by an absence of 'goodness of fit'? How might you approach this situation differently if faced with something similar in the future?

CHILDREN'S BIOLOGICAL NEED FOR MOVEMENT AND PLAY

Throughout the theoretical and research literature in early childhood education there is the repeated acknowledgement that children learn through movement and play. For example, Maria Montessori (1870–1952) emphasised how thought and movement were closely linked, and how learning required independence and autonomy. Friedrich Froebel (1782–1852) developed a child-centred approach to education based on movement, creativity, activity and play. Jean Piaget (1896–1980) showed how children learn through their exploration of the world, and coined the phrase that the child was a 'little scientist'. Lev Vygotsky (1896–1934) influenced decades of researchers to explore the link between learning and play, and told us that 'in play it is as though he were a head taller than himself' (Vygotsky, 1978, p. 102). Margaret McMillan (1860–1931) emphasised learning and exploring in the outdoors, an approach underpinning the modern day 'forest schools'.

These theoretical perspectives have been confirmed by more up-to-date research on developmental neuroscience. According to Kiser (2015), babies' brains make 700 new neural connections, or synapses, a second, and by the age of three, a child has 1,000 trillion synapses. These are created, she writes, by the infant and toddler exploring the world holistically, with hands, feet and body, as well as eyes, ears, nose and mouth. 'Sensorimotor, materials-based learning was the bedrock of our evolution, and it shapes the brain: in his book *The Ascent of Man* (1973) mathematician and biologist Jacob Bronowski wrote: "The hand is the cutting edge of the mind"' (Kiser, 2015, p. 286). Instead of harnessing this wondrous, inbuilt capacity to learn through movement, very often we develop behavioural strategies to figure out how to get small children to sit still! This is particularly inappropriate for children under six years of age. Research is clear that physical inactivity can increase the risk for several chronic diseases across the lifespan. However, the impact of physical activity on childhood behaviour and cognitive and brain health has only recently gained attention. A recent Institute of Medicine (2013) report reviewing physical activity in schools outlined the benefits of physical activity for health outcomes, noting also that achieving 60 minutes of moderate to vigorous physical activity during a school day emerged as necessary for optimum classroom-based learning. Khan and Hillman (2014) have noted that emerging research suggests that regular physical activity and higher levels of aerobic fitness have weak but positive effects on academic achievement, although the size of the effect is a matter of debate. They conclude that while more research is necessary, 'the current evidence points to the benefits of physical activity and aerobic fitness for cognitive and brain health in childhood' (2014, p. 143).

The transition from preschool to primary school has repeatedly been identified in the literature as challenging for small children (Graham, 2012; O'Toole, Hayes and Mhic Mhathúna, 2014), in no small measure due to the increased expectation in many primary schools for more extended periods of physical inactivity and adult-directed sedentary learning. Although not always the case, in general early childhood settings tend to have a clearer sense of the need for learning through play and movement for small children than primary schools do, and the move to primary school is often characterised by increasing expectations for children to sit still (Ring et al., 2015). It is little wonder therefore that many children struggle with behavioural expectations in this transition, and in recent years researchers are beginning to understand that rather than focusing on getting children ready for school, the problem may rest with the fact that schools are not ready for children (Graham, 2012; Ring et al., 2015).

Vygotsky's[1] work illustrated how children develop rules and self-regulation through play; in order to engage in an episode of sociodramatic play, for example, children must agree certain roles, and they must stick to those roles or else the play breaks down. If we are playing at schools, and one child is the teacher and the other is the student, the game no longer works if both children insist on being the teacher. Therefore, play allows for negotiation and sharing and requires self-control, and this is something that can be leveraged. Consider how early childhood educator Ingrid uses a play episode to support an orderly transition from outdoor to indoor play:

The children in Ingrid's preschool are playing outside, drawing on the ground with chalk. It is time to move indoors, and many of the children are reluctant to do so as they are enjoying the activity, but it is almost time to go home, so Ingrid is aware that unfortunately she cannot allow it to continue for much longer. One of the children, Tom, is drawing circles with the chalk and telling the other children that they are puddles. The other children are jumping up and down in the circles, pretending to splash in the puddles. Taking a piece of chalk, Ingrid says, 'Wait until you see my big puddles!' She draws a series of large circles leading towards the preschool door. The children happily 'splash in the puddles' all the way into the preschool.

Source: Author observation in practice

In this example, Ingrid could have scolded the children for not coming inside when she wanted them to, or used star charts to reward children for formally lining up and coming inside. Instead, she tapped in to their natural wish to move and play. Turning a desired behaviour into a game is a key tool in an educator's arsenal, and very pleasant way for both educators and children to achieve their mutual goals.

ADDITIONAL PHYSICAL OR SENSORY NEEDS

Adult–child interaction is a two-way affair; what the adult does is affected by what the child does and what the child does is affected by what the adult does. O'Brien (2018) makes the point that this dynamic may be complicated even further if a child has an additional physical or sensory need that is not being met in an educational setting. According to O'Brien (2018), educators often make the mistake of thinking that 'special educational needs' and 'challenging behaviour' mean the same thing. He maintains that children with additional physical or sensory needs are not predisposed to misbehave, but at the same time schools and classrooms can be difficult places for them if their needs are not being met, and this can have a significant influence on their behaviour. This can get worse as children get older – for example, while early childhood educators may be attuned to difficulties for young children in communicating, and skilled in supporting communication to prevent behavioural outbursts, educators at later educational stages experience language and communication difficulties less often and as a result may not recognise them, presuming instead that communication difficulties are in fact behavioural difficulties. This is 'because the behaviour is overt and the unmet need may be covert. The behaviour is in your face, sometimes literally, and that dominates your attention with the cause potentially remaining hidden' (O'Brien, 2018, p. 137). Equally, O'Brien states that the labels that come with special educational needs can be misleading because children with the same diagnosis can behave in very different ways. By its nature early childhood education and care is inclusive and embedded within a child's rights framework which offers educators a way forward from the limiting conceptualisation of 'special educational need' towards the more inclusive consideration of 'educational rights' for all children (Hayes, 2018). Such an approach will be less constrained by labels and more responsive to each individual child, her unique abilities and interests and the contributions all children can make to the group in the early childhood setting.

Therefore, this section does not attempt to outline the features of specific neurological, physical or developmental disorders such as autism, attention deficit hyperactivity disorder (ADHD) and so forth. Rather, it makes the point that educators have the responsibility to get to know the strengths and challenges of individual children in their educational setting, because otherwise there is the significant risk of misinterpreting responses to unmet need as inappropriate behaviour, and punishing when we should be supporting. Consider the perspective of Mairéad, a seven-year old girl who agreed to be interviewed in order to help educators understand how the world feels through the eyes of a child who is defined by adults as exhibiting behavioural difficulties. At time of interview, Mairéad was undergoing a process of assessment for a sensory processing disorder and other potential neurological and psychological difficulties. She had experienced some episodes of extreme explosiveness, emotional and behavioural outbursts and exceptional sensitivity, while at other times being extremely affectionate, funny and kind. Here she gives her perspective on her behaviour and her advice for adults on what helps and what makes the situation worse:

> I'm very good at giving hugs and I'm very artistic. That means I'm very good at art. I have a lot of emotions – I have shyness, I have sadness, happiness, and sometimes when someone annoys me I get a bit angry. I sometimes have no words. My head feels funny when it's too noisy and I have a blow-up, my head hurts. Everybody gets hurt, everybody starts

to cry and feels sad and I feel really really angry and really sad. It feels all upsetting and my head feels sore in my brain. [Grown-ups] help me stay calm by helping me breathe, telling me to put my hand on my tummy and letting me feel it go up and down. I do chair lifts, or I jump up and down. [Grown-ups make it worse when they] shout. I get even angrier and my head gets even sorer when they shout. It's because I'm only seven that I can't manage. Maybe if I was eight, nine or ten it'd be okay, but [my advice to teachers would be] help kids stay calm.

Author interview

Here Mairéad describes techniques that work for her to support her to reconnect with her body through breathing or releasing excess energy, allowing her to disconnect from other overloaded senses. On the other hand, she describes how it feels when she is already overwhelmed and an adult adds to that sense of overwhelm by shouting. The techniques that work for Mairéad may not work for all children, and you will need to work with individual children and their parents or other professionals to figure out how best to support their unique physical needs. This example highlights the fact that biology does not work in isolation. While Mairéad may be dealing with a biologically or neurologically based challenge, an attuned adult supporting her to manage this challenge, or exacerbating it, can make all the difference to her behaviour. Therefore, it is crucial to understand the interaction between biology, psychology and social context.

THE BIOPSYCHOSOCIAL APPROACH

Rather than focusing on biology alone, many educational psychologists now use an approach known as the biopsychosocial approach for understanding behaviour and developing interventions in educational settings. As the name implies, this approach examines biological, psychological and social factors affecting an individual child, and how they might combine and interact to influence behaviour. For example, the National Educational Psychological Service (NEPS) in Ireland recommend this framework as it:

recognises that the causes of difficulties may be multiple and complex and even a single causative factor may lead to different behaviours in different pupils and in different situations. It is also important to remember that behaviour may often be described according to the particular perspective adopted by the teacher, parent or others

(NEPS, 2007, p. 8)

The 'bio-psycho-social' (BPS) model stems from an original theoretical approach developed by Engel (1977) which sought to contextualise the study of medicine and health. The BPS model was adopted by psychologists, who saw its relevance to linking the many factors leading to the development of psychological disorders such as genetics, difficulty regulating emotions, or environmental stress (Saudino, 2005). Engel's holistic approach in proposing the BPS model (within the clinical context) could be seen as a significant shift from reducing phenomena to their smaller, molecular parts in order to address singular problems, thus limiting recognition of the complexities of the human. It could be seen as a response to the reductionist approach proposed by behaviourists and a move towards a more humanistic and relational model of clinical practice. Cooper, Bilton and Kakos, (2012) have observed that 'the distinctive feature of the biopsychosocial approach is to focus on the ways in which the psycho-social systems and internal and external biological systems interact with and influence one another' (p.2). The strength of the BPS model lies in the combination of different perspectives to be considered when a child presents with a social, emotional or behavioural difficulty. Cooper et al. (2012) point out that the first step in any intervention is to consider what is expected of the child and make judgements as to the appropriateness of these expectations. They go on to identify a variety of early interventions that can be applied to address a range of social and psychological difficulties in educational settings, including behavioural training such as rewards, cognitive strategies such as anger management, and various therapeutic strategies.

The BPS model is applied in many different fields including education. The 'bio' component of the theory examines aspects of biology that influence behaviour. For example, a child might have a neurological condition, such as a sensory processing disorder that makes it difficult for her to tune out all of the overwhelming sensory input that she experiences within an educational setting to allow her concentrate on the educational activities. This can in turn impact on the 'psycho' component of the model in that this biological aspect of the child's make-up might influence how she feels about herself and about school, which could lead to anxiety in certain situations. The 'psycho' component of the theory examines psychological components, things like thoughts, emotions or behaviours (Saudino, 2005). The 'social' component of the model considers social factors that might be influential, for example our interactions with others, our culture or our economic status. The role of the educator is crucial here, and again the concept of 'goodness of fit' comes into play. We see for example how Mairéad advises an adult to be calm in order to support the child to be calm as well. The research on the impact of poverty on the development of executive functioning is also relevant. Biological functions do not develop in a vacuum and it is important to note that the elements of the BPS model are all connected. Biology can affect psychology, which can affect social well-being, which can further affect biology, and so on (Saudino, 2005). As a result, responding to a child's behavioural needs must always be considered in context.

CONCLUSION: STRATEGIES TO SUPPORT POSITIVE BEHAVIOUR FROM A BIOLOGICAL PERSPECTIVE

One particularly important element to note from a biological perspective is that if a child's behaviour stems from an unmet need, then punishment or sanctions are likely to be at best ineffective or at worst may actually exacerbate the problem. A child acting out through hunger is not likely to behave more appropriately by being placed in time out; rather a slice of toast is more likely to do the trick. Equally, if a child with a sensory processing disorder is overwhelmed by noise and acting explosively as a result, then shouting at her will only make the situation infinitely worse.

The following strategies summarise the key messages of this chapter and have been synthesised from a number of published sources including O'Brien (2018) and the website www.synapse.org.

- Provide as much structure and routine as possible within your settings while ensuring that children's physical needs are met in safe and risk-rich environments [indoors and outdoors] that incorporate movement and play.
- Communication should be clear, direct and frequent; where possible, use plain and concise language. Do not be vague in explaining which behaviours you like and do not like and have unambiguous, explicit limits and rules about what is expected and what is desirable.
- Developing setting rules with the children where possible gives them a sense of ownership and belonging and the rules are more likely to be respected. It can be helpful to assist their understanding if you respectfully allow them repeat back your instructions and expectations. Give children feedback and information about their behaviour.
- Use strategies that defuse behaviour and help a child calm down – talk it through, change the topic, change the task. Work on attuning your own behaviour to children's needs and maintain awareness of sensory overwhelm. Use redirection, distraction and diversion to shift behaviour and use visual support to break up complex tasks.
- Children's natural instinct for movement and play can be leveraged to support positive behaviour. If there is a specific behaviour you would like to encourage, think about how you could turn it into a fun activity or game.

Not every difficulty that children present with in early childhood settings needs to be examined exhaustively for its cause, and in many cases it can easily be explained. Cooper (2006) recommends that educators take what he calls 'progressive focusing' approach, arguing that the most effective and efficient approach to understanding behaviour is to know your children well and be systematic in seeking explanations. Adults who are well trained and knowledgeable are more likely to recognise the source of difficulties and intervene constructively and sensitively to ameliorate problems. Questions that should be considered when seeking to understand a particular behaviour or change in behaviour include what factors in the environment might be contributing, how the environment can be altered to diminish or prevent a recurrence of the behaviour or how we, as educators, can change our demands or our responses. In educational settings, when it comes to ideas of impulse control, self-regulation or behavioural problems, it may be that the source of difficult or challenging behaviour lies not, in fact, within a particular child, but rather with a combination of factors which may include adult expectations, the behaviour of other children and adults, and the strictures of the educational settings and the wider community.

Key concepts within this chapter for educational practice

1   Simple biological considerations like hunger or tiredness can impact on behaviour so educators should consider eliminating them to eliminate negative behaviour.
2   Executive functions have a biological component that develops over time as the frontal lobe of the brain grows, but they are also responsive to the environment, and educators play a crucial role in their development, especially for at-risk children.
3   Both children and adults have their own temperaments, and it is important to understand and work towards 'goodness of fit'.
4   Children have a biological need for movement and play. Having difficulty sitting still is not misbehaviour. Educators can leverage this by turning desired behaviours into games or fun activities.
5   When children have additional physical or sensory needs, this may impact on their behaviour, and educators should be attuned for negative behaviour as a communication of unmet need.
6   The BPS model describes the integrated nature of biological, psychological and social influences on children's behaviour.

NOTE

1   *The Collected Works of L. S. Vygotsky* Volumes 1–6 have been published by Springer Publications. You may wish to explore his original writings on topics including child psychology, play and the development of higher mental functions.

CHAPTER 7

Behaviour in context
Bioecological theory and the web of development[1]

INTRODUCTION

According to the psychologist Urie Bronfenbrenner (1917–2005) it is impossible to understand a child's behaviour unless we consider the *context* in which it occurs. Rather than focusing on the individual as the site for development and change, Bronfenbrenner believed that it was the interactions between the individual and the social and material worlds that drove individual development, resulting in further changes to these environments. In its most recent iteration (Bronfenbrenner and Morris, 2006) the bioecological model of human development identifies *process* factors (such as relationships between children and adults), *person* factors (such as temperament), *context* factors (such as classroom climate) and *time* factors (such as the child's age) that must be understood in interaction with each other in order to understand, explain and respond to behaviour. The bioecological model of human development allows us to explore the interactive, dynamic and entangled relationships across and within systems that impact directly and indirectly on children's development to explore and perhaps explain how we can foreground and support children through pedagogy to enhance the development of culturally sensitive, positive behaviour and learning.

In this chapter readers will be supported to use Bronfenbrenner's Process–Person–Context–Time (PPCT) framework to draw together the learning from previous chapters, deconstruct the root causes of specific examples of children's behaviour and identify potential responses. In addition, the creation of 'linkages' in the 'mesosystem' will be emphasised – in more simple terms, this means recognising that the 'taken for granted' in one setting may not match that in another (Reay, 2010), and when links between important settings for children (such as home and school) are strong, behaviour tends to improve. The key role of relationships between parents and educators will be explored, both conceptually and with practical ideas to support relationship building.

While the biopsychosocial model of development outlined in the previous chapter does recognise the complex interplay between the biological, psychological and social in individuals, and has progressed from an earlier focus on the individual child in isolation to exhibiting a greater appreciation of the importance of reflective and caring engagements with children (Borrell-Carrió, Suchman and Epstein, 2012), it fails to take account of the child in context and how this perspective can provide an enhanced understanding of behaviour. The bioecological model broadens out the understanding of development to explicitly attend to context and consider the interactions and relationships between individual children, people and things within multiple influencing environments, and consider how these interactions and relationships impact on behaviour and are, in turn impacted on themselves. An awareness of and sensitivity to children's own backgrounds and experiences can help inform pedagogy and provide deeper insights into factors that contribute to an individual child's behaviour in an educational setting. Evidence suggests that positive behaviour is more likely to occur when there is an atmosphere of mutual respectful understanding, and this applies to even the very youngest children.

General Comment 7 from the UN Committee on the Rights of the Child notes that:

> The Convention requires that children, including the very youngest children, be respected as persons in their own right. Young children should be recognised as active members of families, communities and societies, with their own concerns, interests and points of view.
>
> (United Nations, 2005, p. 3)

This does not mean that children always get to decide what they will or will not do, but as explored in Chapter 5 it does require adults to attend to the voice of children, actively listen to and consider their views, and seek to understand things from their perspective as much as possible. In practice this means that the educator must try to see the world through the child's eyes. This can be achieved in many ways. For instance, rather than saying 'That's a lovely picture of a house' ask the child to 'Tell me about your picture' – it may turn out to be a story rather than a static image! We should never assume to understand the child's perspective without carefully attempting to understand it in all its complexity. In this way we are less likely to make unreasonable or thoughtless demands on children.

We have discussed in earlier chapters ways in which to create positive learning environments and develop positive tactics to encourage desired behaviour, rather than resorting to more negative controlling techniques. We also established that it is important to find a balance so that the praise for good and appropriate behaviour to any one child at least equals the negative attention he gets. Observational studies of adult–child interactions, particularly in school settings, have found that often the only attention some children receive is negative attention! Children are individuals with different interests, temperaments and coping skills. In your daily contact with groups of children you are likely to come across a wide variety of difficult or problem behaviours that will vary from the simple to the more complex. It is important to remember that children behave in response to their experiences and are not always able to tell us how they feel or express why they are behaving in a particular way. For this reason it is necessary to try to understand a child's behaviour, what is causing him to behave in a particular way at a particular time, and to take account of that when meeting his needs, while at the same time working towards more positive behaviour. This can be done, for instance, by equipping a child with new skills, for example encouraging him to use words rather than hit out at other children when frustrated.

Bronfenbrenner's model of development was a response to an increased understanding of the non-linear nature of learning and development, and the value of considering multiple theoretical positions from within which to consider both psychological theories of learning and development alongside theories of educational practice, as we have done in this book. It is a framework, which can accommodate the multiplicity of factors, proximal (close to) and distal (distant from), influencing learning and development. What distinguishes Bronfenbrenner's model from much of psychology is its basic assumption that one cannot improve the developmental trajectory of individuals by focusing primarily on the individual in isolation (Wertsch, 2005). Many of the views articulated by Bronfenbrenner in his early policy presentations and articles are echoed in our current theorising and understanding of child development and education (Siraj and Mayo, 2014) and his work looked beyond individual development to take account of wider influencing factors and the context, or ecology, of development. The model has been influential in both early education practice and curriculum development, most explicitly by New Zealand where it informed the development and implementation of their early years curriculum Te Whāriki (Ministry of Education, New Zealand, 1996).

FROM AN ECOLOGICAL TO A BIOECOLOGICAL MODEL OF DEVELOPMENT

Bronfenbrenner's original model introduced the idea that humans develop within a nested and interconnected environment or ecology of four systems – the *microsystem*, the *mesosystem*, the *exosystem* and the *macrosystem* (Bronfenbrenner, 1979). These interconnected systems, or levels, are organised from those closest, or proximal, to the child (microsystems) to those whose influence is indirect or distal (exosystem and macrosystem) (Greene and Moane, 2000). Reflecting his Russian background, Bronfenbrenner, who was born in Moscow, referred to these systems as 'nested' each within the next like a set of Russian dolls (the Matryoshka dolls). Later, recognising the important role of time and history in development, he included a fifth system which he called the *chronosystem*. In its final iteration the model extended the focus to a *bioecological model* (Bronfenbrenner and Morris, 2006) foregrounding the importance of the developing individual and the relational nature of development in context – an emphasis Bronfenbrenner felt had been lost with too much focus on systems in the earlier iteration of his model. This new model stressed that context was not only something that impacts *on* the child but is more dynamic, reflecting the view that the context or environment impacts *with* and *through* the child's participation. Giving children a central role in their own development acknowledges children as agents who can express desires and wishes but also negotiate and interact within their environments, ultimately changing these environments.

Given the increased understanding of the integrated and dynamic nature of learning and development, and the value of considering many theoretical positions when studying behaviour, Bronfenbrenner saw the need for a developmental framework within which to consider psychological theories of learning and theories of educational practice. This required a level of complexity to accommodate the variety of factors influencing children's behaviour, whilst at the same time providing a framework within which the factors can be considered, reconciled and responded to in psychological and pedagogical practice, policy and planning. The bioecological model of human development presents such a framework. From his earliest work Bronfenbrenner recognised that good practice in understanding child development, including educational practice, required a deep understanding of the developing child in context and this, he argued, required a complex ecological theory of development. He used the word 'ecological' to capture the socially and materially embedded and holistic nature of human development. His most influential book *The Ecology of Human Development: Experiments by Nature and Design* (1979), described such a model. The ecological approach to understanding development recognises that individuals are embedded in and affected by different levels of context at both a macro (the large-scale, at a distance) and micro (small/local, close by) level. In considering research into human development, Bronfenbrenner was critical that researchers studied development out of context. For him, development was a function of the interplay between the individual and his environment. Therefore, he insisted on locating development within environmental systems. He defined the 'ecology of human development' as involving:

> the progressive, mutual accommodation between the active, growing human being and the changing properties of the immediate settings in which the developing person lives, as this process is affected by relations between settings, and by the larger contexts within which the settings are embedded.
>
> (1979, p. 21)

From the very beginning and through its various iterations, this model has addressed both the structural or biological aspects of development alongside the process or sociocultural dimensions (Bronfenbrenner, 1979, 1989; Bronfenbrenner and Ceci, 1994; Bronfenbrenner and Morris, 2006). An additional feature of the model is the emphasis on the dynamic, bidirectional relationships of people and context. Studying individual development through the lens of this model allows early years practitioners to contextualise child development and to take account of the overlapping and interacting nature of each system.

The child's closest and most familiar *microsystem* is the family but there are other microsystems, including settings close to the child such as day care, preschool and school. The *mesosystem* refers to the communication and interactions between the various elements of the microsystems of the individual. In education this would include the relationship between family members and educators. The third level in the ecological system model is the *exosystem*, which refers to more distant influences, factors external to the children and adults but impacting on them nonetheless such as educational policy or curriculum design. The *macrosystem* represents the influence of even more distant factors such as societal values and the cultural view of the child. Finally, the *chronosystem* refers to the influence of time on development. It takes account of time from the individual perspective but also in terms of historical time; it is of relevance to educators when, for instance, considering issues of transitions either in to, within or across settings.

REFLECTION

As a teacher in the junior class of an established school in the centre of Dublin, consider the differential experiences of six-year-old Sean and six-year-old Jamal. Sean has been brought up in a middle-income home in the middle-class suburbs of the city. Jamal is a recently arrived refugee from Syria living in temporary hostel accommodation in inner city. What factors might you take account of when responding to the attention-seeking behaviour of both boys? How would you ensure that your responses were fair and just?

The ecological model of human development was appealing and very quickly was accepted as a useful framework within which to study development; it was taken up by psychologists, sociologists and teachers. It began to feature in textbooks and the idea of the nested systems seems to have provided a very useful visual guide accounting for the myriad factors that affect development. In fact, Bronfenbrenner himself considered his original model 'an instance of what might be called "the failure of success"' (2005, p. 288) pointing out that having argued over the years that research in developmental psychology had failed to take sufficient account of context he now found 'a surfeit of studies on "context without development"' (p. 288), which were in danger of losing sight of the developing child (and the kinds of considerations explored in Chapter 6) altogether.

To address this concern Bronfenbrenner developed his model further and in its final form he extended the focus to a *bioecological model* (Bronfenbrenner and Morris, 2006) foregrounding the importance of the developing individual and the relational nature of development in context. The focus on making the child more visible at the centre of his development sits well with the notion of 'agency', involving children's capacity to understand and act upon their world and foregrounding children's competence (James, Jenks and Prout, 1998; Mayall, 2002). Such an approach seeks to understand development in context, taking into account the definitions and meanings children give to their own lives. This revised perspective also sits well with an approach that sees the child as actively participating in his own childhood in accordance with Malaguzzi's (1993) concept of the 'rich child' – the child who is 'rich in potential, strong, powerful and competent' (1993, p. 10). Giving the child a central role in how his development plays out acknowledges that children as agents can express not only their desires and wishes but can also negotiate and interact within their environment and these interactions may ultimately result in them changing their environment.

THE CENTRAL ROLE OF PROCESS

Within the bioecological model Bronfenbrenner highlighted the development of the individual within context and also drew a critical distinction between 'environment' and 'process' (relationships and interactions), with *process* occupying a central, driving position in development and having a meaning that is quite specific to the model. In fact, process is at the core of the bioecological model. The construct of process (P) encompasses particular forms of interaction between individual and environments, often termed nature (genetic) and nurture (environmental). Bronfenbrenner called these processes the *proximal processes* to emphasise the fact that they are located within the microsystems of development and operate over time; they are posited as the primary mechanisms producing human development. It is through *proximal processes* that an individual's genetic potential is made visible in his behaviours and actions. The emphasis is on the reciprocal nature of interaction and understanding that relationships with people and environments are bidirectional. Proximal processes are not unidirectional and the presence of other people in the immediate environment alone does not necessarily lead to the occurrence of a proximal process (Griffore and Phenice, 2016). Neither are proximal processes only about social interactions; they include interactions with the objects and symbols that make up the context. Specifically, Bronfenbrenner and Morris (2006, p. 797) highlighted the importance of proximal processes in children's development as follows:

> Especially in its early phases, but also throughout the life course, human development takes place through processes of progressively more complex reciprocal interaction between an active, evolving biopsychological human organism and the persons, objects, and symbols in its immediate external environment. To be effective, the interaction must occur on a fairly regular basis over extended periods of time. Such enduring forms of interaction in the immediate environment are referred to as proximal processes.

The concept of proximal processes has important implications for education, highlighting the power of interactions and the important role of the adult. Through reflective observation of the child, adults can come to understand the characteristics of the child and the environments which facilitate positive development and learning. Drawing on many different studies of child development with children of different ages, Bronfenbrenner and Morris (2006) describe the positive, generative dispositions valued by western culture. An example of generative disposition given is the extent to which the child tends to engage and persist in progressively more complex activities. For example, given a facilitating environment, children will elaborate, restructure and create new features in an environment, not only physical and social but also symbolic. Another class of developmentally generative disposition they describe reflects the increased capacity and active propensity of children, as they grow older, to conceptualise their experiences. This, Bronfenbrenner and Morris argue, contributes to the development of 'directive belief systems' about oneself as an active agent both in relation to the self and the environment. This is particularly important and relevant in education as these personal belief systems, emerging in early childhood, are the foundations for self-directed learning, attention and problem solving. The manner in which adults respond to, guide and support children's development can profoundly impact on behaviour and even on the adult the child becomes.

When we use the concept of 'proximal processes' to make sense of children's behaviour it becomes obvious that relationships are vital for children's development emotionally, socially, cognitively, and of course behaviourally. Building good relationships should be a central area of concern for education. The bioecological model emphasises that such vital relationships are informed and shaped by the person characteristics of both the children and adults involved, the context in which they take place, and the time (both of the person's life, and historically) in which those relationships are embedded. Bronfenbrenner says that we must understand process, person, context and time if we are to understand the child. The power of these processes [P] to influence development varies based on characteristics of the person (P), of immediate and remote environmental contexts (C) and the time periods (T) in which they take place. To capture the integrated nature of the various elements of the model Bronfenbrenner characterised it as the Process–Person–Context–Time, or PPCT framework. Consider the vignette below and reflect on how you, as an educator, might respond to the situations in light of what you understand about the impact of process, person, context and time on individual behaviour.

> Luka is usually an independent boy who likes to engage in self-directed play in his early childhood setting. However, today he has a cold and is not feeling well. He has spent the morning following his early educator around the room, and cries when she leaves to go to the bathroom.
>
> Source: Author observation in an early years setting

PERSONAL CHARACTERISTICS

As we have seen, Bronfenbrenner's bioecological theory went beyond simply high-lighting or stating the active role which the child or individual plays in his own development. It emphasised the fluid and relational nature of development through a focus on the question of how personal characteristics influence present and future development. Three kinds of characteristics were emphasised as fol-lows: active behavioural characteristics (also known as dispositions), resource characteristics and demand characteristics. Below we elaborate on these types of characteristics and illustrate them in vignettes framed within the context of early childhood and primary learning.

Active behavioural dispositions as shapers of development

Active behavioural dispositions are related to variations in motivation, persistence and temperament. Bronfenbrenner notes that even when children have equivalent access to resources, their developmental courses may differ as a function of char-acteristics such as the drive to succeed or the persistence in the face of hardship.

> Lauren is eighteen months old, and sitting on the floor in her crèche sur-rounded by toys and colourful objects. However, she is only interested in reaching for the soft teddy, which is sitting beyond her reach on the sofa. She crawls near the sofa and tries for some time to pull herself up, hang-ing on to the sofa in order to try to reach the teddy. After several attempts she falls back into a sitting position on the floor. Having looked around the room to see if anyone can come to her aid, she finally begins to tug slowly and cautiously on a rug hanging down from the sofa. As she pulls the rug, slowly Teddy, who is sitting on the rug, begins to move forward. Lauren stops and looks around again, not sure about what she should do next. Eventually she pulls on the rug again and this time Teddy comes tumbling down into her arms.
>
> Source: Author observation in an early years setting

Lauren is demonstrating evidence of positive active behavioural dispositions such as the motivation to gain access to the teddy and the perseverance to patiently experiment in different ways until she finally succeeds in achieving this. While her success in reaching the teddy may not be a significant achievement regarding her developmental pathway, at the same time the positive dispositions she has shown are likely to be reinforced by the success of her attempts. By leav-ing her to find a way to retrieve the teddy the educator has recognised her power of perseverance and has not intervened too soon in the process. Too early an intervention in children's activities can limit the development and strengthening of the dispositions, which can in turn lead to frustration. Once Lauren has achieved her ambition the educator could take time to praise her perseverance, thus rewarding the positive disposition displayed, one valued within early childhood settings.

Active behavioural dispositions may be positive or negative in impact. *Generative* dispositions are characteristics that are likely to enhance interactions and elicit responses from and reactions to the environment. Generative dispositions are associated with the ability to initiate or maintain reciprocal interactions with parents or other care-givers (Bronfenbrenner, 1989). Such characteristics include curiosity, attentiveness and ability to defer gratification. *Disruptive* dispositions, on the other hand, are those characteristics that prevent or disrupt responses from and reactions to the environment. Such characteristics include distractibility, aggressive tendencies, inability to defer gratification and tendency to withdraw from activity.

Apply your understanding of the role of active behavioural dispositions to this vignette and consider how you would respond to minimise the disruption while at the same time respecting both the group and Lena's positions.

At free play time, Lena wants to play at the sandbox in her primary school. Julie, the teacher, has explained that at the moment there are too many children playing at the sandbox, and encourages Lena to wait a short while until there is more space for her to play safely there. Julie invites Lena to join another activity and Lena ponders this for a moment, but then turns and insists on joining the other children at the sandbox. As there is not enough space for all children to play at once, some of the other children who were already playing with the sand become annoyed and refuse to allow Lena to play with them.

Source: Author observation

Bronfenbrenner highlights the potential for personal characteristics to change environments. The interaction between humans and their environments is, therefore, one of reciprocity – the environment or context in which a child is developing is likely to impact on his development and, in turn, the child may shape or change his environment through these interactions. The particular characteristics of children, their ability to focus, to show interest in things, to become engaged in and excited about events, contributes to shaping our responses to these children. In turn, we are affected by and through our interactions and responses to the different children in our educational settings.

Resource characteristics of the child as shapers of development

Resource characteristics are not as immediately visible or recognisable as dispositions; they include mental and emotional resources such as past experiences, intelligence and skills, as well as material resources such as access to housing, education and responsive care-givers. According to Bronfenbrenner and Morris

(2006, p. 812), these characteristics involve no selective disposition to action but rather are described as 'biopsychological liabilities and assets' influencing the capacity of the child or individual to initiate and sustain interactions. Developmental assets can take the form of ability, knowledge, skill and experience, which, as they develop and evolve, expand the range and diversity of options and sources of growth available to the child.

Resource characteristics may operate to limit or disrupt the extent to which a child can thrive or even become involved in the interactions and activities available within an educational setting. These characteristics include genetic inheritances like low birthweight, physical disability and severe or persistent illness. However, Bronfenbrenner shows how the impact of these characteristics depends on a variety of factors. As Brewster (2004) points out in the context of a 'social model' of disability, the physical and attitudinal environment can disable a child far more than any impairment. Consider how a supportive early childhood setting limits the impact of a potentially disruptive resource characteristic in the following example.

Elena is a bright, outgoing three-year-old, and today is her first day in preschool. Elena's mother has been quite anxious about her starting preschool, largely because she has cerebral palsy and uses a wheelchair, so her mother is worried about the ability of preschool staff to meet Elena's needs. However, since the family and the preschool have spent time planning together, this morning Elena is met at the door by the preschool teacher Sarah, who wheels her chair up the ramp, through the doors and into the school, where she introduces Elena to another three-year-old, Hanna. 'Hanna is feeling a bit shy this morning, Elena. I know that you really like chatting and playing, so can I ask you to spend a bit of time with Hanna and help her feel less worried?' As the girls get to know each other, Sarah shows Elena's mother the accessible bathrooms and the raised flowerbeds in the garden, where Elena will be able to take part in the planned gardening with the other children.

Source: Composite of author experiences working with children with disabilities

---

Resource characteristics: disruptive characteristics

In Elena's case, her cerebral palsy could potentially have represented a disruptive resource characteristic limiting her ability to benefit from early education. In some early childhood settings, she may not even have been able to enter the building due to a lack of ramps for her wheelchair, and staff fears may have prevented them from being willing to engage with Elena as a child with strengths as well as challenges. In this case, the accessible environment and Sarah's recognition of Elena's social skills frames her experiences and the perception of her resources very differently, to the benefit of Elena, her mother, and Hanna, the little girl who may now have a supportive friend to help her through the transition from home to preschool.

Demand characteristics of the child as developmental influencers

Demand characteristics are those easily noted qualities of the developing person that can invite or discourage reactions from the social environment, influencing the way in which proximal processes are established. Bronfenbrenner and Morris (2006) provide examples of demand characteristics such as an agitated or calm temperament, attractive versus unattractive appearance, hyperactivity and passivity (both of which can be considered problematic in early education). Other characteristics which are more externally accessible, such as age and gender, can also affect the establishment of effective interactions. Bronfenbrenner shows how a child's characteristics prompt certain reactions from others, and those reactions then impact on the future development of the child's characteristics, which in turn prompt further reactions, and so on. This dynamic process is illustrated in the following vignette:

Tania is four years old and attends Alison's reception class. Tania is bright and full of energy, and loves to take control of her own activities. She very much dislikes being told what to do by adults, and when she feels that her autonomy is being challenged, she tends to react badly, sometimes shouting and becoming quite stubborn. Alison knows Tania well, and the two have developed a warm way of working together that meets both of their needs. When it is time to end activities and get ready for lunch, Alison gives Tania the job of setting out the plates for everyone to use because she responds well to the sense of responsibility. As a result, she usually agrees to end her activities at the appropriate time, even when she is engrossed and enjoying herself.

On Monday, Alison is out sick, and a teacher, Christine, is in Tania's class. When the time comes for activities to end, Christine asks Tania to put everything away. Tania is enjoying herself so she refuses. Christine tells Tania that she must do what she is told, as it is time for lunch. Tania sits on the floor holding tightly to her work and refuses to move. Christine raises her voice slightly, and warns Tania to comply. Tania throws her puzzle on the floor and marches over to where the plates are kept. Christine, unaware of Tania's usual job, tells her to come immediately to the lunch corner and sit down. Tania picks up the plates and in temper throws them on the ground, shouting that it's not fair. Christine removes Tania to a corner to calm down.

Source: Author experience of practice

In this example we see how an active child with a 'disruptive' tendency towards stubbornness and temper provokes two different reactions from two different early childhood teachers, leading to two very different outcomes. Bronfenbrenner shows how such interactions over time can influence the dispositions developed by children. The bioecological model predicts that if Tania regularly experiences calm, supportive interactions, like those with Alison, she will over time learn to manage her emotions more appropriately. In sociocultural terms, she will learn self-regulation. Alternatively, if Tania regularly experiences interactions based on conflict such as those with Christine, she is likely to become even more prone to temper and stubborn responses. This is a good example of the concept of 'internalisation'. Here we see again how personal characteristics both shape and are shaped by experiences in context.

The bioecological model of human development draws attention to the importance of the interaction between 'person' and 'context', in that the personal characteristics and dispositions of the child elicit certain responses from the environment in which the child is developing. These responses influence the personal characteristics of the child and elicit further responses from the child. So, demand characteristics, and indeed active behavioural dispositions and resource characteristics, first appear as one of the components of the bioecological model and, therefore, as an influence on development and, at the same time, as a developmental outcome, or a result of development (Bronfenbrenner, 1995a, 1995b; Bronfenbrenner and Morris, 2006). This process of interaction and influence can be understood as a spiral dynamic where the personal characteristics of the child interact with and influence the people and the environment around them in an ongoing cycle of transformation. In understanding these influences, educators may gain insights into children's behaviour, recognising the variety of factors that may influence behaviour. This allows educators to respond more sensitively and so effectively to individual children.

The bioecological model envisions the child as an active agent in his world, both influenced by and influencing the environment, or 'context,' in which he is living. As we have seen, a child's dispositions may be 'generative', inviting positive interactions with other people, or 'disruptive', potentially leading to negative interactions with others. These positive or negative interactions then impact on the child's behaviour and the direction that his development will take, through the power of proximal processes. This is significant, since most developmental research treats personal characteristics as developmental outcomes rather than recognising that they are both outcomes and producers of development (Bronfenbrenner and Morris, 2006).

ACTIVATING THE MESOSYSTEM

As an educator you occupy a significant place within the educational microsystem on a number of levels. At the interactive level we have seen that you are a key participant in engaging in and providing for the proximal processes, which drive development. You are also central, at a communication level, to activating and maintaining the mesosystems through which contacts with parents in the home and educators within the school system occur. In this second level of contextual influence on development, the mesosystem, Bronfenbrenner drew attention to interactions and interdependencies between the elements within the child's different microsystem, and the important role they play within a healthy bioecological education system. Planning to maximise opportunities for bridging communication between children's home and educational settings takes time and thought. A number of studies have identified the profound influence of children's home environment on their well-being in education settings and more broadly (O'Toole, Kiely, McGillacuddy, O'Brien and O'Keeffe, 2019). The Effective Provision of Pre-School Education [EPPE] study (Melhuish, Phan, Syvla, Sammons and Siraj-Blatchford, 2008; Sylva, Melhuish, Sammons, Siraj and Taggart, 2004), found that the quality of the learning environment of the home (where parents are actively engaged in activities with children) promoted intellectual and social development in all children. Although parents' social class and levels of education were related to child outcomes, the quality of the home learning environment appears to be more important. The importance of enhancing continuity and alignment between learning environments offered by the home and educational settings is emphasised in these research findings. Drawing attention to the notion of the malleability or fluidity between home and educational settings, Kernan (2015, p.6) talks of 'softening the boundaries' between these environments and reinforcing the connections between children's families and communities and the learning environments they inhabit. Such 'softening' is critical in laying the foundations for trusting and respectful engagement across the two key microsystems in the lives of young children, and becomes even more important where a child may be exhibiting difficult or undesirable behaviour. By working together and sharing information, parents and educators can help to facilitate access to and sharing of valuable information which can enhance understanding in adults and contribute to more meaningful experiences for children in both home and educational settings. As explained by the bioecological model, outcomes such as 'behaviour' or 'motivation' are not solely a function of individual child factors, but result from complex interactions with contexts and relationships experienced. Parents can act as the interpretive bridge between home and educational setting for children.

REFLECTION

How can educators gather and exchange information with children's parents and families to improve the learning environment? How can educators help parents to support their children's learning and development?

While encouraging close engagement with families is valuable and can, in certain instances, lead to improvements in both learning environments, this is an issue that must be handled with great cultural sensitivity and in real partnership with parents, who are the experts of experience regarding their own children (Gaylor and Spiker, 2012). The onus is on educators to be proactive on these issues, because previous experiences of education can leave some children and adults vulnerable to marginalisation and intimidation. In developing strategies for parental involvement, Kiely et al. (2019) found that it was not specific strategies that worked per se, but rather the support for relationship building underlying them that was effective. For instance, it is important that educators realise that expecting all parents and families to behave in the same way or hold the same values, beliefs and capacities regardless of background or personal circumstances may be futile. The concept of 'family' is open to a diversity of interpretations, and different parenting arrangements bring different challenges and benefits for the social and emotional development of children. Increasing pluralisation and diversity in family contexts is likely to exert influences on parenting styles and practices, which, in turn, impact on children's psychological well-being (Halpenny, Nixon and Watson, 2010). While an extensive body of research has shown the benefits of traditional family structures involving two parents (Bronfenbrenner and Morris, 2006), it is the relationships or 'process' within family contexts that actually matter rather than who is a part of the family per se. The presence of another adult who gives support and love to the primary care-giver is key to positive functioning within families (Bronfenbrenner and Morris, 2006), and that 'other adult' could be a same-sex partner, a grandparent or some other close individual, rather than explicitly the other biological parent of the child. As Bronfenbrenner and Morris put it, 'it would seem that, in the family dance, it takes three to tango' (2006, p. 824). This prediction of the bioecological model has been supported by research showing that children of same-sex couples are in many cases happier and healthier than population samples (Crouch, Waters, McNair, Power and Davis, 2014).

Previously, much of what we knew about the effects of family transition (such as divorce, for example) on children focused solely on child outcomes. However, present-day research has focused upon the profound importance of the quality of family processes or interactions prior to, during and following family transitions (Halpenny et al., 2008). Consistent with bioecological thought, this approach draws our attention to the importance of family interactions and how these interactions may evolve and progress over time, impacting on children's behaviours. Proximal processes and positivity of relationships within families may be more influential on outcomes for children than whether families are structured in traditional ways. This is important to remember when responding to the influential culture of testing for 'school readiness' using checklists that impose a 'cultural arbitrary' on what constitutes 'good' parents and 'home learning environments', disregarding diversity in families (Brooker, 2015). Educators must be cognisant of and sensitive to the needs of different types of families and different family contexts.

REFLECTION: CONSIDER THIS QUOTE FROM ADRIENNE RICH (1986, P. 199)

When those who have the power to name and socially construct reality choose not to see or hear you, whether you are dark-skinned, old, disabled, female, or speak with a different accent or dialect than theirs, when someone with the authority of a teacher, say, describes the world and you are not in it, there is a moment of disequilibrium, as if you looked into a mirror and saw nothing.

Would the children in your educational setting see themselves in the 'mirror' that you provide? What about their parents? What assumptions do you bring to your interactions with them that are based on your own cultural, linguistic, social, class-based and gendered 'normality'? Could these assumptions create challenges for children and parents in the early years setting? What practical measures could you take to minimise such challenges, and instead create 'linkages' between the contexts of home and school[2]?

Differences based on factors such as socioeconomic status, language, culture and religion can contribute to disjuncture in the mesosystem, and can be implicated in difficulties for children, parents and educators alike. However, contextual factors can exacerbate or ameliorate these potential difficulties, and thus it is important that educators contemplate these considerations through a bioecological lens. This understanding highlights the fact that 'children' and 'parents' are not homogeneous groupings, and 'processes' in educational settings may be extensively impacted by both 'person'-based and 'context'-based factors.

One mechanism that has proved very powerful in establishing good communication between families and educational settings is that of documentation. Observing, listening to and creatively documenting children's activities in their daily routines provides unique insights into children's collective interests and pursuits and also into their individual curiosities and learning dispositions. Significantly, documenting children's ideas and activities generates new information, which can inform pedagogical planning and identify additional props and resources that can be used to extend their learning. In addition to providing opportunities for close engagement with children and informing pedagogical planning, documentation makes visible children's learning and can act as an important tool in communication across the mesosystems into the child's home and future educational settings.

CONTEXT: THE LEARNING ENVIRONMENT

One of the key components of children's microsystems is the learning environment, which plays a central role in supporting and facilitating children's development and learning (Sylva et al., 2010). Educators have a significant role to play here as they, in effect create and maintain the learning environment. The learning environment (indoors and outdoors) is the context within which children interact with other people, materials and symbols, and where they are given the time and encouragement to learn about the world and their place in it. This role is crucial as the environment can amplify, suppress or ameliorate behavioural difficulties in children. Context is one of the key concepts elaborated in the bioecological model of development and is identified as central to understanding development and to informing quality practice. The importance of the environment as the 'third educator' has been highlighted by, among others, those who follow the Reggio Emilia model of early education (Smidt, 2012, p. 100). It is here that the educator has the power to be a creative architect of learning and development, where careful environmental planning can create points of interest, of exploration, of quiet creativity, safe risk and aesthetic pleasure for the child. Perhaps the most important feature of any learning environment is that it is welcoming – a space where children feel not only a sense of security and belonging, but also a dynamic and stimulating space which offers them an invitation to explore and discover new experiences and concepts. Curtis (2001, p. 42) highlights the importance of creating responsive environments that encompass the values of 'co-operative play, large muscle activities, high drama, messy play, the sounds of childhood, working through conflict and the importance of family engagement'. Spaces carefully designed and drawing on children's perspectives are welcoming, and encourage children's natural responses of curiosity, exploration and communication (Hayes and Kernan, 2008). Inviting surroundings also enhance children's positive disposition towards learning. Children love to create their own worlds at their own pace and to their own scale in any environment they can manipulate or modify (Strong-Wilson and Ellis, 2007). Spaces allowing for opportunities to experiment with and transform the environment are also likely to be rich in learning experiences. Young children thrive in calm and predictable learning environments, which give them opportunities, encouragement and the time to develop and learn, where the pedagogical process is relational, responsive and reciprocal (Hayes, 2013).

One concept that helps to bring together Bronfenbrenner's proximal processes with the notion of a rich learning environment is that of *affordances* – those features of the environment that contribute to the positive interactions that occur within these environments. Kernan (2007) draws attention to the fact that the concept of affordances is being used increasingly within research on pedagogy to describe and gain insight into the relationship between children and their environment. Guerrettaz and Johnston (2013) further conceptualise affordances as the potential starting point of the meaning-making process, which involves active engagement between children and the environment in which they spend time.

A key feature of designing and shaping a rich learning environment for children is the ability to tune in and attempt to perceive the environment from the perspective of the children inhabiting their space. Educators and parents can play a significant role perceiving affordances of environments from children's points of view and thereby generating shared moments of discovery (Kernan, 2015). Significantly, drawing deeply on how children perceive and use space to create meaning, in keeping with a bioecological approach, positions the child at the centre of his learning environment.

REFLECTION

Discuss with a colleague your understanding of the concept of affordances in learning environments. To what extent are you aware of the affordances that may enhance the learning opportunities for children in their educational setting? How can we learn to better perceive affordances from children's perspectives?

Finding the balance between indoor activities and outdoor explorations is also part of a purposeful planning process and can provide particularly valuable developmental opportunities for excitable and more distractible children. Children benefit from rich and stimulating play choices both outdoors and indoors. Outdoor space and adult support have been identified as important factors particularly in respect of promoting physical activity and providing risk-rich spaces to encourage risky play. Affordances for risky play in the learning environment create invitations for children to challenge themselves and to extend and push out the boundaries within a setting where the safety and well-being of the child are paramount. The emphasis on outdoor play in Nordic countries has prompted educators in different cultural contexts to revisit and review ideas on establishing greater fluidity between indoor and outdoor learning environments. Research into the relationship between environmental affordances and children's play and development, with particular reference to outdoor experiences, suggests that environmental complexity and diversity in nature are highly associated with increased play opportunities and are rich in opportunities for developmentally demanding activities.

Access to outdoor play opportunities can be influenced by views held on the benefits and challenges of outdoor play experiences. Research exploring understandings of outdoor play in early childhood (Kernan and Devine, 2010) generated a construction of the outdoors as simultaneously a space of freedom, discovery and risk for children in the early years. The former was spoken of in terms of spontaneity and freedom to explore, the latter reflected concerns around traffic, 'stranger danger' and fear of litigation in the event of personal injury. The authors conclude that in the context of an increasingly risk-averse society, especially with respect to children, this construction and experience of the outdoors has given rise to the marginalisation of the outdoors from the experiences of many children in early childhood services and the consequent invisibility of children in outdoor spaces.

Rich learning environments, indoors and outdoors, for younger and older children, provide affordances for children's learning, which invite and support complex reciprocal interactions, capture children's interest and curiosity, and challenge them to explore and share their adventures and discoveries with others. Such environments can stimulate children's thinking, imagination and creativity, thereby enriching communication. As children's interests change, possibilities for changing and transforming their surroundings contribute significantly to expanding on and extending learning experiences. By capturing children's interest and curiosity and reflecting these interests, educators play an important role in fostering and promoting positive learning dispositions and so positive behaviour in children. Through their interactions with other children, with adults, with materials and with concepts, children learn about the world around them and their place within that world.

A rich learning environment is one that invites and accommodates individual differences in abilities, skills and competencies of children who inhabit these spaces, reflecting diversity in family types and configurations as well as diversity across capabilities, socioeconomic class and culture. There are multiple influences, at the micro and meso levels, that can affect the impact of learning environments, and recognising them is important to planning and providing for calm, extended and enriching periods for play and learning. Influences may also be at the macro level where changing values, new technology and societal expectations can impact on educator and learner roles and modes of learning and discovery.

CONCLUSION

Bronfenbrenner's model of human development provides an impetus for responding to contemporary understandings of child development and behaviour. Changing educational practice to incorporate this new knowledge, based on scientific understandings of development, is not an easy task. Such transformation rests with all those concerned with quality educational practice and requires ongoing reflection and a commitment to learning and change. As Bronfenbrenner (2005, p. XXVII) puts it:

> Human beings create the environments that shape the course of human development. Their actions influence the multiple physical and cultural tiers of the ecology that shapes them, and this agency makes humans – for better or for worse – active producers of their own development.

Educators play a central role in building and developing an environment that motivates children to interact with each other, with the participating adults and with the objects within their space. These experiences support children in becoming confident and competent communicators who behave positively in their educational settings. An important aspect of the design of learning environments is that they can help to promote positive learning and behavioural dispositions in children. As adults we have a powerful role in facilitating this development through providing quality learning environments that encourage children to develop positive, generative dispositions of curiosity, persistence, responsiveness, the tendency to initiate and engage in activity (alone or with others), and inhibit the more disruptive dispositions of impulsiveness, explosiveness, distractibility or at the opposite pole, apathy, inattentiveness, unresponsiveness, lack of interest in one's surroundings, feelings of insecurity or shyness.

Key concepts within this chapter for educational practice

1   Children's behaviour develops from a complex mix of influences at proximal (close) and distal (far away) levels. It is impossible to understand a child's behaviour out of the context in which it develops.
2   Relationships are crucial for the development of positive behaviour. Bronfenbrenner thought that relationships were so important that he called them 'the engines of development'. He named them 'proximal processes'.
3   Children's behavioural dispositions develop through the power of proximal processes and are influenced by the 'affordances' provided in the learning environment by the educator.
4   Strong links with a child's family are considered crucial within a bioecological perspective.

NOTES

1   Much of this chapter draws its material directly from Hayes, N., O'Toole, L. and Halpenny, A. M. (2017) *Introducing Bronfenbrenner: A Guide for Practitioners and Students in Early Years Education*. London: Routledge.
2   These issues will be explored in greater depth in Chapter 8.

An intercultural perspective on behaviour

INTRODUCTION

Developing the ideas introduced in Chapter 7, this chapter will further interrogate the influence of culture on behaviour, and on perceptions of that behaviour. Through the lens of sociocultural theory, we see that many beliefs and practices relevant to children's behaviour vary across cultures – norms of behaviour, images of children, and their competence and responsibilities, beliefs regarding the appropriateness of various forms of discipline, and ideas on how relationships between adults and children should be conducted. When there are differences between home and school in terms of such beliefs and practices, there can be potential for a child to be seen as misbehaving when her behaviour would be acceptable in a different context. Children's responses to disciplinary approaches can vary and approaches can be unsuccessful as a result of cultural differences. The French sociologist Pierre Bourdieu shows that this applies to contrasting socioeconomic cultures as well as those based on language, ethnicity and religion.

Since culture is in many ways invisible when we are immersed within it, educators' attempts to support children to behave positively are often guided by biases and assumptions of which the educator is unconscious. This chapter will support readers to deconstruct their own class-based, cultural and linguistic 'taken for granted' assumptions, with a view to analysing how these could, if unchallenged, potentially contribute to or trigger children's so-called 'challenging' behaviour within educational settings. Sometimes it may in fact be that it is the behaviour of adults that is 'challenging' for children! A number of approaches will be identified to facilitate the development of warm, inclusive, intercultural educational settings, where all children are welcome and are supported to behave appropriately.

SOCIOCULTURAL THEORY

Sociocultural theory largely draws from the work of the Russian psychologist Lev Vygotsky. He showed that children's learning and behaviour rely on social interaction rather than simply developing within the mind of a child in isolation.[1] Sociocultural theorists believe that 'mediated minds are developed out of the social activity that is embedded in the cultural values of particular communities' (Ellis, 2012, p. 524). To put it more simply, this means that, as human beings, we learn how to behave by living within a culture, and from the viewpoint of an educator trying to make sense of the behaviour of a child in a primary classroom or early childhood setting, the key message of sociocultural theory is that the individual cannot be studied or understood in isolation but only as part of a history, a culture and a society (Dunphy, 2012; Swain, Kinnear and Steinman, 2015). Rogoff (2003) writes that culture is embodied within children in terms of their beliefs, influencing the very way in which they approach making sense of the world. Vygotsky (1978) is often quoted explaining this:

> Any function in the child's cultural development appears twice, or on two planes. First it appears on the social plane, then on the psychological plane. First it appears between people as an interpsychological category, and then within the child as an intrapsychological category... It goes without saying that internalization transforms the process itself and changes its structures and functions. Social relations or relations among people genetically underlie all higher functions and their relationships.
>
> (p. 163)

The language of this may seem complicated, but what Vygotsky is proposing is that a child experiences culture first outside herself, through interaction with family members, important adults and other children, but, little by little, culture becomes 'internalised' into the mind and behaviour of the child. In sociocultural theory, psychological tools 'mediate' children's psychological processes. Such tools include language, play and interactions with adults, and so they are drawn from the culture in which the child lives (Vygotsky, 1978). Each child's behaviour depends on these mediated processes, so in a very real way, every child's behaviour depends on the culture in which she has developed her psychological functioning. Experience becomes incorporated into the characteristics of the child, and thus, in a process of mutual influence and reciprocity, influences the direction of future development. For Vygotsky, the starting point for the development of behaviour is the culture, whose characteristics determine the formation of the mind of the child (Hayes, O'Toole and Halpenny, 2017).

For sociocultural theorists, language is key to such internalisation, as social speech becomes inner speech with children's development, thus shifting the direction of activity from external control by adults to internal control and self-regulation by children themselves. For example, in the 1980s a well-known sociocultural theorist Wertsch (1985) showed how children developed self-mediation through private speech as they moved from reliance on verbal instruction from parents to complete a puzzle, to verbally instructing themselves. This is known as 'private speech' and its development is one way in which sociocultural theorists recommend that educators support children to self-regulate their behaviour. Vygotsky's work on the link between language and thought inspired generations of researchers (Bartlett and Burton, 2012), and there is even some evidence from studies of bilingualism that switching the language we speak can significantly alter our perception of events and the way we experience the world (Boroditsky, 2018).

All of this means that for human beings our understanding of what is appropriate behaviour is entirely rooted within the culture we come from and the language we speak. Culture, by its nature, is invisible when we are immersed in it – when surrounded by our own culture we do not see it, it is 'normal'. It is only when we step outside that culture that we notice its existence. Vygotsky's (1978) ideas of the social formation of the mind and modes of thought through the mechanism of culture mean that while children are active learners, their individual behavioural choices are not easily reduced to their being either 'naughty' or 'well behaved'. Rather, cultural norms are so deeply embedded that little choice is involved in automatic responses to certain situations; from this perspective, 'adult and child learners are seen as situated in particular social, cultural and historical contexts. Learning is constrained (i. e. limited) by the beliefs, artefacts and practices of the particular context in which learning is taking place' (Dunphy, 2012, p. 204). If a child finds herself in an educational setting that mirrors the cultural norms of home, behavioural expectations may be easy to meet. If, on the other hand, cultural norms of home and school are at odds, some confusion can be caused for children. Consider the experience of Shamifa in negotiating the different demands of the adults in her life.

Shamifa is six years old and attends her local primary school. Her teacher Janet has asked her to stay after class because she would like to talk to her about her handwriting. Janet feels Shamifa is capable of better work and has not been putting enough effort into her handwriting. 'You know that this is not acceptable Shamifa', Janet tells her. Shamifa looks at the floor. 'Have manners and look at me while I'm speaking to you', says Janet.

When Shamifa comes out of class her mother is angry with her. 'Where were you? I was worried!', she says. Shamifa looks at her and says, 'I'm sorry, the teacher wanted to talk to me about something'. 'Do not look me in the eye like that, you impertinent girl', says her mother.

Source: Author observation in practice

In this case, conflicting cultural norms about whether a child should look an adult in the eye have led to trouble for Shamifa. Different cultures may hold differing beliefs on appropriate relationships between adults and children, how authority should be expressed, and how children should behave towards their elders. However, her behaviour in neither case was inherently negative, it was merely interpreted as so by the adults involved based on their own cultural norms, which according to sociocultural theory, have been internalised by them through living within their own cultures. The problem arose for Shamifa in trying to negotiate the journey between the two. Derrington (2007, p. 357) calls this 'cultural dissonance', referring to culturally determined differences regarding the adult–child relationship, accepted communication styles and responsibility for discipline.

REFLECTION

In ethnography (the study of culture) researchers discuss the 'insider/outsider dilemma' (Gregory and Ruby, 2011). Consider a time when you felt like an 'outsider'. Why did you feel like an 'outsider'? Would 'insiders' have been aware of your discomfort? What was 'taken for granted' that you did not understand? What might have helped you in that situation? Structural supports? Personal responses by particular individuals? Anything else?

Now consider a child who is at risk of being an 'outsider' in your educational setting. Who, based on her internalised linguistic, cultural, socioeconomic, norms might not automatically understand your 'taken for granted' expectations? Who, like Shamifa, might be trying to negotiate a journey across differing cultural norms between home and school? What expectations do you need to explain to her? Are there any inappropriate expectations in your setting educational setting that you might need to alter? What supports might you need to offer?

To further develop the idea of cultural norms, and the potential challenge of negotiating cultural clashes for children and children's behaviour, it is useful to move beyond the disciplinary boundaries of psychology to consider the contributions of sociology. In this regard, the work of the French sociologist Pierre Bourdieu may be particularly relevant.

BOURDIEU'S THEORIES OF CULTURAL CAPITAL AND SOCIAL AND CULTURAL REPRODUCTION

For Bourdieu, the goal of research is to uncover the most deeply buried structures of different social worlds, as well as the mechanisms that tend to ensure either their reproduction or transformation over time (Bourdieu, 1996; Reay, 2010). According to Alanen, Brooker and Mayall (2015), his work allows 'better understanding of why and how childhoods "on-the-ground" are as they are, through interrelating private troubles with public issues' (p. 1). Bourdieu shows how, as with sociocultural theory, our social and cultural experiences become internalised when we are children. As Reay (2010) explains, in Bourdieu's theories people's relationships to dominant culture are conveyed in a range of activities, including eating, speaking and gesturing

(Bourdieu, 1984). As such, the social becomes 'embodied' and is inscribed in the body of the biological individual (Bourdieu, 1985). This embodied 'way of being' is known in Bourdieu's theories as 'habitus', or 'a set of dispositions, reflexes and forms of behaviour that people acquire through acting in society' (Bourdieu, 2000, p. 19). An example of this is accent, and Glock (2016) has noted how children's accents can impact on educators' treatment of them, and interpretation of their behaviours.

A central aspect of Bourdieu's theories is that our individual habitus leads us to '"reproduce" the social conditions of our own production' (Bourdieu, 1990, p. 87). This idea of social reproduction has been used to explain intergenerational cycles of poverty and disadvantage. Reay (2010) indicates that habitus is primarily a method for analysing the dominance of dominant groups in society and the domination of subordinate groups, and it can easily be applied to the analysis of gender or racial (as well as socioeconomic) disadvantage. One of Bourdieu's best known and most widely cited concepts in this context is that of 'cultural capital', or the idea that the habitus (or taken-for-granted behaviours and ways of being) of certain groups and individuals are valued by the dominant culture whereas the habitus of other groups and individuals are devalued – in other words, some groups and individuals possess better 'cultural capital' than others. This is particularly important to consider in educational settings when thinking about behaviour – one culture's norms of behaviour can be valued more than another's but that does not mean that a child behaving according to those norms is necessarily a better-behaved child.

In this regard it is important to note that the basis of cultural capital is in fact a 'cultural arbitrary' (Bourdieu and Passeron, 1977). As Brooker (2015) explains, 'Culture is itself arbitrary: there is no objectively right or wrong way to bring up children. Instead every culture, and every type of cultural capital, derives from the field of practice in which it develops' (p. 43). The operation of habitus regularly excludes certain practices that are unfamiliar to the cultural groupings to which the individual belongs (Reay, 2010), so that, for example, the cultural capital possessed by children and parents from working-class backgrounds may not be appropriately valued in school settings that are based on middle-class culture (Mulkerrins, 2007).

Thus, Bourdieu's theories can be used to focus on the ways in which the socially advantaged and disadvantaged play out the attitudes of cultural superiority and inferiority that are ingrained in their habitus in their daily interactions (Reay, 2010). Habitus, capitals and fields, or social spaces, interact, to the advantage of some and the disadvantage of others. Bourdieu specifically explores the impact of cultural capital on educational achievement, describing 'the domestic transmission of cultural capital' as 'the best hidden and most socially determinant educational investment' (Bourdieu, 1986, p. 243. The habitus, or the 'taken-for-granted' (Reay, 1995, p. 365) in one field or culture may not be valued in another. This means that there may be a sense of 'disjuncture' when moving between fields because an individual child's habitus may not fit well with the expectations of the new field. Consider again the experience of Shamifa in negotiating the move between home and school. Reflect also on the types of 'cultural capital' needed to succeed in education:

REFLECTION

- What cultural capital do you need to succeed in education systems? Knowledge? Behaviour? Dispositions? Understandings? Skills? Prior experiences?
- Can early education 'give' this capital in a way that may enable children to negotiate later educational stages more successfully? How?
- How can we recognise and value existing cultural capital (funds of knowledge)?
- Consider identity – 'I have long experienced myself being read through the grid of elitist values – a powerful complex of ideologies and cultural practices which splits cleverness ... from working-classness' (Hey, 1997, p. 142) – how can we enhance children's 'cultural capital' while ensuring not to enforce the culture of the dominant group and subjugate the culture of minority groups?

Crucial to the success of children like Shamifa and many others in traversing the journey from one culture to another is the behaviour of educators, and the creation of educational settings where diversity is valued and respected and where multiple identities can be celebrated – where children do not have to make a choice between who they are at home and who they are at school. However, teacher expectations of pupils whose backgrounds differ from their own have been found to be consistently low (Robinson and Harris, 2014), and there is extensive research to show that teacher expectations can often become 'self-fulfilling prophecies'.

TEACHER EXPECTATIONS, BIAS AND CHILDREN'S BEHAVIOUR

In many countries, educators come predominantly from the dominant culture, and minority cultures are under-represented on teaching staff. This is important to consider because children from minority cultures are often disadvantaged in such circumstances by negative stereotypes held by educators, even when educators express egalitarian and multicultural beliefs (Glock, 2016; Hachfeld, Schroeder, Anders, Hahn and Kunter, 2012). With regards to behaviour, there is evidence that often educators are subconsciously inclined to be more lenient with children from the same cultural background as themselves (Gregory et al., 2010; Gregory and Mosley, 2004). This could be explained by prejudice but also by the internalisation of cultural norms of behaviour explored earlier in this chapter – a child of a similar cultural background is likely to have internalised similar behavioural norms and so to behave in a way an educator is likely to recognise and approve of. This does not mean of course that the child is objectively better behaved. For example,

Downey and Pribesh (2004) showed that the implicit bias of White teachers led them to develop more negative interpretations of the behaviour of Black children, and Glock (2016) also highlights negative teacher expectations and stereotyping of ethnic minority children. Lindsay and Hart (2017) note how these processes can mean that children of colour experience harsher discipline in educational settings – up to and including expulsion – but that when children have access to teachers of colour these effects can be mitigated.

Educators' (often unconscious) bias can lead them to expect misbehaviour from children from different cultural backgrounds from their own, and this can cause them to treat children differently. This in turn may cause children to disengage, or misbehave, creating a self-fulfilling prophecy. There is a longstanding body of research dating back to the 1960s documenting such processes. Rosenthal and Jacobson's (1968) classic work 'Pygmalion in the Classroom' showed that when teachers had high expectations for children, the interactions they had with them were of higher quality, impacting positively on the children's learning and behaviour. When the teachers had low expectations for children, the quality of their educational and personal interactions was lower, impacting negatively on the children's learning and behaviour.

Rubie-Davies (2010) tracks the history of teacher expectation research from the early 'Pygmalion' studies, showing repeated evidence of how race, culture and unconscious bias can shape teachers' interpretations of children's behaviour. An example of this is Alison St George's work in the 1980s that showed how teachers perceived Maori children more negatively than New Zealand European children (St George, 1983). Later, Brophy and Good (1986) and Good (1987, 1993) found that once teachers were given a child's IQ score (not always accurately), they adjusted their expectations and their teaching. With those of lower IQ, teachers waited a shorter time for them to answer questions, gave them the answers more frequently rather than giving them clues or chances to respond, praised them less frequently, smiled at them less often and demanded less work from them. These researchers also found that such teacher behaviours had a negative effect on the educational outcomes of such children. Teachers with low expectations of children tend to manage behaviour negatively, relying on punishment and control, whereas teachers with high expectations of children tend to work towards supporting positive behaviour through relationship building (Rubie-Davies, 2010). This is particularly true of groups such as those from those from minority cultural backgrounds or those from lower social class backgrounds that, for various reasons like cultural bias in testing and poorer educational and social opportunities, tend to score lower on IQ tests (MacRuairc, 2009).

According to Derrington (2007), children's behavioural responses to such experiences with educators may fall into three categories: fight, flight or playing white. The 'fight' response involves aggressive reactions to cultural dissonance that are often interpreted by educators as bad behaviour. The 'flight' response enables the child to escape, avoid and distance herself from the source of any perceived or actual threat, driven by neurophysiological reflexes. It is not rational or logical and examples include nonattendance, withdrawal or pretending to be sick; a form of what Derrington calls 'avoidant coping' (p. 363). 'Playing white' requires the child to conceal or adapt her cultural or linguistic heritage in an effort to fit into the dominant culture. This can have a devastating impact on a child and family's cultural identity (Kraftsoff and Quinn, 2009; O'Toole et al., 2019). Read the three vignettes below to see how children and their families might adopt some of these strategies in engaging with early educational settings, and the various impacts they might have:

Vignette 1: Fight

'We've been teached [sic] that if somebody hits us then we hit them back. If somebody says something to us, we say something back' and teachers observed that Traveller students, in particular, preferred to deal with bullying in their 'own way'. In some cases, students had developed or earned a reputation for being 'hard'. Whether or not this was con-sciously achieved, it was a successful strategy in that it offered protection from future abuse. Kieran, Joe, Becky, Crystal and Kimberley all felt that their reputations made others more wary about provoking them, 'They know I'll stick up for myself. They don't pick on me as much now because they think I'm hard so they stopped picking on me.' (Becky)

> In the minority of schools where several Gypsy Traveller students were enrolled, there was a distinctive sense of group loyalty and cohesiveness, which could generate group retaliation. 'If anyone calls us "Stinking Gyppo" we stick together.'
>
> Source: Derrington (2007, p. 362)

Vignette 2: Flight

> Tim came to a new early childhood setting mid-year. He was a shy child, small for his age and wearing glasses. Although the educators wel-comed him in and introduced to him to the other children, he did not settle. They noticed that he was often playing alone and did not enjoy going outdoors. Over time his attendance slipped. In discussion with his parents it became clear that he was resisting coming to preschool, com-plaining of stomach ache and getting very upset. His parents found it easier to keep him home than to put him through further distress. When explored it appeared that he felt lonely, isolated and hurt by the name-calling of some of the older children. The early educators and parents together agreed on a set of strategies to address the issue of name-calling and isolating within the setting while at the same time equipping and supporting Tim with skills necessary to stand up to others.
>
> Source: Author observation in practice

Vignette 3: Playing white

Lejla moved to London in the early 1990s when her family fled Bosnia during the war. As a refugee with no English, going to school each day was challenging, but little by little she began to understand more and more of what people were saying to her. She acted as translator for her parents, and filled in forms for them when they needed her to. As she got older, she developed an English accent and often people told her they thought she was English. When Lejla grew up she married a fellow Bosnian, and they had a little girl together called Asja.

When the time comes for Asja to go to preschool, Lejla meets with her teacher Lorna and tells her, 'Don't worry, we have only been speaking English to Asja, not Bosnian, so she will be ready for school.' Lorna says 'No, no, you mustn't feel that you can't speak your own language! Bosnian is a great gift to Asja. We would love to include some Bosnian in the preschool, and we can help her with her English too.' Lejla bursts into tears and shares her story with Lorna of feeling scared, alone and unable to understand or be understood. She is very determined that her daughter will 'fit in' and never experience that sense of isolation.

Source: Author observation in practice

While 'fight' responses to cultural dissonance may be more challenging to educators, the 'flight' and 'playing white' responses may be much more damaging to children themselves. In the case of Tim, the shared approach by educators and parents to addressing his isolation and shyness will go some way to improving his day-to-day experiences while raising awareness among other children of the rights of all children to belong, and feel they belong, in the early childhood setting. With Lejla and Asja, in an effort to protect her daughter from the isolation and fear she herself experienced in childhood as a refugee, Asja was alienated from the richness of her mother's Bosnian culture, and Lejla was left with a painful schism in her identity.

According to Glock (2016), teachers with high multicultural beliefs do not neglect cultural differences but emphasise them as enriching daily classroom interactions. A reflective approach is crucial in combating the effects of teacher expectation and cultural bias because as Glock (2016) points out, stereotyping operates on an automatic level, and may draw on evolutionary processes – early in its evolution, the human brain needed to be able to make rapid judgements and respond quickly to situations in order to be able to avoid potential threat. In the modern world of education, this means that we often make judgements too quickly, based on inappropriate stereotypes involving unawareness, unconsciousness and unintentional processes. Stereotypes free up brain power, because they provide predictions about behaviour that we do not have to think about, but the obvious problem with this is that stereotypes can provide erroneous predictions that can cause us to mistreat children, or to think that they are misbehaving when in fact they are not (Murray and Urban, 2012). Since stereotyping may be the default position of our brains (Glock, 2016), it is important to make a conscious, reflective effort to view the behaviour of each child for what it is, rather than through the lens of a stereotypical response. We need as educators to try much harder and much more mindfully to genuinely see what is in front of us rather than to just allow our brains to categorise automatically based on a stereotype. Drawing on socio-cultural theory, an alternative approach for educators, which may help to avoid stereotyping and respond to such 'fight', 'flight' and 'playing white' responses, is to ensure respect for and development of the 'funds of knowledge' children bring with them to the educational settings.

FUNDS OF KNOWLEDGE, DIVERSITY, AND CREATING SPACE FOR DIFFERENCE AS SUPPORT FOR POSITIVE BEHAVIOUR

From a sociocultural perspective, interactions within educational settings are seen as key to underpinning the learning that happens (Dunphy, 2012). Relationships between children and educators are highlighted as mediating tools that help children to develop appropriate understanding of the kinds of behaviours that are expected of them – behavioural norms, like other learning, can be co-constructed between children, adults and the context in which learning is taking place (Anning, Cullene and Fleer, 2009). This underlines the importance of understanding the rich 'funds of knowledge' (Hedges, 2010, 2011; Wood, 2013) that children bring with them from the various contexts in which they are developing.[2] Increasingly, the number and range of contexts that young children need to traverse on a day-to-day basis is expanding, and educators need to be aware of the potential for children to experience a type of 'culture shock' when those contexts are very different from each other. For example, when the culture of the home and that of the educational setting are significantly different, it can be difficult for children to adjust (Brooker, 2015). Support structures for families are sometimes based on 'socialisation' (Hornby and Lafaele, 2011; O'Toole et al., 2019). This means that schools and preschools attempt to shape parental attitudes and practices so that they facilitate and meet the needs of the educational setting or of the broader society. However, educators who attempt to shape education to ensure the creation of a context where everyone 'fits in' tend to be more successful in supporting children and accommodating wider variations in behaviour than those advocating a 'one-size fits all' approach.

This is central to the work of sociolinguists such as Cummins, 2005; Cummins et al. 2005; Ntelioglou, Fannin, Montanera and Cummins, 2014) who emphasise the need to draw on children's home culture and language as both a learning resource and an important repository for children's pre-existing knowledge. Some educators make explicit their interest in learning and sharing information about all the different cultures represented in their setting and may host annual events such as an Intercultural Day. However, if these are merely once-off events and are not reflected in the fabric of the educational setting or the pedagogy of the staff they can be seen as tokenism and a sort of 'tourist' interculturalism (Murray and

O'Doherty, 2001). Equally, children sometimes do not want attention drawn to their cultural and linguistic backgrounds in this way, as it increases their sense of difference and 'otherness' (Eriksson, 2013). For example, asking parents to speak the language of the dominant culture in the home should be avoided, since maintenance of the primary language in their children may be essential to cultural identity and ethnic pride (Edwards, 2009; Kraftsoff and Quinn, 2009; Siraj-Blatchford and Clarke, 2000), and the potential for language loss is great when the parent chooses to, or is required to, predominantly speak the dominant language (Burck, 2005), as in the example of Asja and Lejla above.

Fleer (2003) challenges us to question the assumptions underpinning how we consider communication and conversation with children, and many of these assumptions have relevance to, and implications for, children's behaviour in educational settings. Children are embedded in the social world and are active in their communication with it through various verbal and non-verbal processes. When reflecting on our practice do we, Fleer asks, see both child and adult as partners in learning together or separate from each other with the adult in the powerful position? While there is of course an inequity between the child and the far more experienced adult, this should not negate the value of considering children as partners and working to manifest this. The process of distancing children, of treating them as a separate 'other', is well bedded in, in our society. Such 'othering' may be exacerbated when the cultural backgrounds of children and educators do not match.

Carefully planned child-friendly environments facilitate social and collaborative learning. Therefore, there is a need for explicit consideration and for creating occasions, spaces and time for meaningful communication, or what Fleer calls 'conversational opportunities'. Real communication, in a meaningful way, between adults and children (and children and children) is not simple; it takes understanding and thoughtful planning, and goes beyond reading stories or asking questions. In fact limiting conversation and dialogue to a question-and-answer style of communication or to organisational and management activities is insufficient and also disrespectful to children. It runs contrary to the inclusive and respectful pedagogy that underlies a democratic approach to practice, which research suggests equips children with important developmental proficiency (Mitchell, 2011; Moss, 2008), and may support self-regulation and pro-social behaviour in educational settings (Freiberg and Lamb, 2009).

Just as children come to educational settings with 'funds of knowledge' (Hedges, 2014) we need to recognise what educators bring to their practice with regards to the 'taken-for-granted', and to actively reflect on our own norms, in order to ensure that we do not hold inappropriate ethnocentric expectations that 'other' some children, and set them up for failure. An important aim for an educator who wishes to support positive behaviour in a mutually respectful, intercultural classroom is to eliminate the sense of cultural dissonance identified by Derrington (2007). Machowska-Kosciak's (2019) innovative and interesting study tracing the experiences of children of Polish heritage growing up in Ireland from early childhood through to later stages of education describes the importance of supporting children to be proud of multiple identities so that they do not feel they have to choose between them. She maintains that allowing for a 'comfortable bi-cultural identity' (p. 172) is one of the main factors in children's educational, social and emotional outcomes. Equally, in Derrington's (2007) research, the minority of Traveller students who completed their education to the end of secondary level had stronger affiliations with both Traveller and non-Traveller cultures than those who left school early, and this was coupled with a firm sense of cultural identity of which the students were proud. Derrington notes similar findings regarding a sense of belonging to and being able to switch between two cultures, without compromising one's own sense of cultural and familial identity correlated with psychological adjustment and well-being in research with Hispanic students (Szapocznik, Kurtines, & Fernandez, 1980) and American Indian students in mainstream schools (Whitbeck, Hoyt, Stubbon, and LaFromboise, 2001).

In increasingly diverse societies it is insufficient to simply focus on the similarities between children – 'Well, we're all the same really' – particularly where there are manifest differences. Far better to acknowledge and celebrate diversity and recognise that all of us are part of that diversity. Louise Derman-Sparks (1989), originator of the anti-bias curriculum, was clear that children are well aware that language, gender, colour and physical abilities are connected with privilege and power. In her writings she defined 'anti-bias' as an active approach to challenging prejudices, stereotypes and bias of all kinds. Bias can occur for many reasons and can give rise to difficulties in educational settings if not explicitly recognised and addressed. In early childhood children are beginning to understand fairness and unfairness, and need guidance in expressing their feelings to adults and to other children if they are feeling hurt or if someone else has been hurt. In summarising some key points to consider when thinking about creating a learning environment that respects and promotes equality and diversity, Murray and O'Doherty (2001) drew on the anti-bias curriculum and identified four goals to strengthen the sensitivity to a fair and just early childhood environment for all children. These goals were to nurture each child's construction of a confident self-concept; promote in children skills for empathetic interactions; foster the development of critical thinking about bias, even in very young children; and cultivate children's own strength to stand up to others in the face of bias.

For many children, joining an early childhood setting is their first exposure to wider society. Vandenbroeck (2018, p. 2) points out that this:

> presents them with a mirror reflecting how society looks at them and thus how they should look at themselves, since it is only in a context of sameness and difference that identity can be constructed. In this public mirror, every child is confronted with a critical existential question: Who am I? And is it OK to be who I am? A positive self-image is closely linked to well-being and the capacity to succeed in school.

For this reason he stresses the importance of the family connection, suggesting the early childhood curriculum should also be a 'family-centered curriculum'.

CONCLUSION

In primary schools and early childhood education settings adults can limit the jarring challenges that new environments can present to children, and assist and strengthen the development of children's sense of identity by working to really get to know each individual child, her likes and dislikes, her fears and her dreams. This can be done through a willingness in the setting to work together to overcome any unconscious biases that may exist, exchange experiences with families and other children, discover similarities and difference, and explore more thoroughly these contrasts to use them as instruments and contexts for creating an inclusive and caring educational environment for all. Such consciously intercultural pedagogical approaches can mitigate unnecessary tensions and misunderstandings that may arise from cultural differences in beliefs and values. In addition they can contribute to limiting the dissonance between children's educational settings and the socioeconomic, linguistic, ethnic and religious cultural environments in which children grow and develop.

Key concepts within this chapter for educational practice

1 Norms of behaviour are developed within cultures and there are no universal 'right' ways of behaving. If the norms of behaviour in a child's family culture are different from those of an educational setting, a child can experience confusion regarding how she is supposed to behave.
2 Educators who are mindful of this reality will create environments that welcome diversity and encourage sharing of different cultural customs and rituals. However, educators also bring their own deeply held cultural norms of behaviour to educational settings, and in the absence of reflective practice, bias and negative expectations of children from different cultural or socioeconomic backgrounds can lead to self-fulfilling prophecies and negative behaviour.
3 Creation of supportive educational settings in which diversity is welcomed and multiple identities are celebrated creates nurturing environments in which children thrive and positive behaviour is supported.

NOTES

1 Here we give a brief overview of some key ideas within sociocultural theory as they apply to understanding children's behaviour in early education settings, but if you would like to develop your learning on this theory further, you may like to consult Schmidt, S. (2009). *Introducing Vygotsky: A Guide for Practitioners and Students in Early Years Education.* London: Routledge.
2 This section draws on previous work by the authors published in Hayes, O'Toole and Halpenny (2017).

CHAPTER 9

Combining theoretical approaches

The example of bullying

INTRODUCTION

While the various approaches to supporting positive behaviour outlined in this book were necessarily presented in a linear format for ease of comprehension, Chapters 6 and 7 showed how, in reality, children's behaviour is not straightforward, but rather is messy and complicated, with many factors combining and interacting to influence outcomes (Hayes et al., 2017). Therefore, in real-life situations, educators need to draw on a variety of theoretical perspectives simultaneously, incorporating a wide range of practical solutions in supporting children's positive behaviour. Approaches that may work very well with one child or group of children, or in a particular situation or culture, may be ineffective or may even exacerbate a problem with another child, a different group of children or in an alternative situation or culture. This chapter will begin the process of allowing the reader to develop his or her individualised, personal theories on behaviour that can then be translated into a dynamic repository of practical responses and proactive ideas upon which to draw in educational settings. It will do so by assisting the reader to synthesise the theoretical ideas presented in previous chapters by applying them to the practical example of countering bullying in educational settings.

Bullying is aggression that is unprovoked, intentional, involves an imbalance of power and is repeated over time. It can have devastating, long-term implications for the victim's self-esteem and physical and mental health, with effects including anxiety, depression and reduced academic performance. Various issues related to bullying among children will be presented in this chapter, such as definitions and categories of bullying, warning signs that bullying may be taking place and gender differences in bullying behaviour. The chapter will then proceed to analyse how the approaches and understandings outlined in previous chapters might be adapted to counter bullying in the educational setting.

DEFINITIONS AND TYPES OF BULLYING

Some children use aggressive and destructive behaviour to manage their relationships in educational settings, to achieve and maintain popularity, and to meet psychological needs to control, dominate or gain attention (Caravita and Cillessen, 2012; O'Moore, 2010). Sims-Schouten (2015) notes research linking bullying behaviour to parenting styles, or to egoistic aims regarding popularity or self-worth. The long-term implications of bullying have been established by decades of research, with both perpetrators and victims of childhood bullying more likely to experience mental health and disciplinary difficulties right into adulthood, and even those who are uninvolved but witness bullying suffering adverse effects (Foody, Murphy, Downes and O'Higgins Norman, 2018).

Much of our understanding of what bullying is and how its dynamics work in schools can be attributed to the early studies of the Swedish researcher Dan Olweus (e. g. Olweus, 1978, 1993, 2000). Among many honours for his important research, Olweus won the 2003 Award for Distinguished Contributions to Public Policy for Children by the Society for Research in Child Development, the 2011 Award for Distinguished Contributions to the International Advancement of Psychology by the American Psychological Association and the Award for Distinguished Contributions to Research in Public Policy from The American Psychologist in 2012 (American Psychologist, 2012). The definitions of bullying and its types and forms provided here are drawn from an amalgamation of the work of Olweus with that of other prominent researchers on bullying such as Mona O'Moore, founder of the Anti-bullying Centre in Dublin, Ireland (https://antibullyingcentre.ie/) and a variety of published research sources (see citations below[1]). There is no universal definition of bullying but there are some common aspects that are mentioned often in the literature. Following Olweus, it is generally agreed that bullying involves aggression that is:

- Unprovoked – contrary to myth, victims do not bring the bullying on themselves through their own behaviour.
- Intentional – bullying entails wilful and conscious acts of aggression. It is intended to cause as much upset and hurt as possible to the victim.
- Involves an imbalance of power, either physical (when one child is bigger or stronger than another) or psychological (when one child is afraid of the other or when one is more popular than the other).
- Repeated over time – a once-off incident does not generally constitute bullying.
- Can be perpetrated by an individual or by a group.

The idea of bullying as intentional becomes somewhat unclear when referring to very young children, however (Helgeland and Lund, 2017), and it may be that definitions of bullying need adaptation for early years settings (Saracho, 2017). Until recently, almost all research on bullying was located in primary and secondary schools rather than in earlier educational settings, with new studies in preschools and other early educational settings now beginning to emerge. What research does exist on bullying among younger children provides an inconsistent picture, ranging from some identifying similar rates of bullying in preschools and in later educational stages to others stating that the behaviour of children under five can easily be misconstrued (Sims-Schouten, 2015). For example, incidents that might be considered physical assault in older children could be reasonably interpreted as younger children using their bodies to solve their differences, claim items or assert themselves in the absence of more developed language and social skills. Additionally, in self-report studies, pre-schoolers can sometimes include behaviours in their definitions of bullying that adults would not necessarily consider to be so, since they may not include repetition, imbalance of power or intention (Psalti, 2017). Sims-Schouten (2015) highlights the agentic image of children as learners in most up-to-date thought in early childhood education, for example in studies such as the Mosaic approach by Clark and Moss (2011). In contrast, she notes the sense of discomfort many writers have when discussing young children as agentic in their behaviour, perhaps even as aggressors, reverting instead to images of young children as 'incapable, vulnerable and premoral' (p. 235) when discussing issues like bullying:

> It is these views of the vulnerable young child who is in need of total care and protection that may also, paradoxically lay the foundation for a view of young children as passive, inexpert and lacking valuable knowledge, whilst at the same time placing agency and knowledge in the sphere of the adults (Hogan, 2009). This in and of itself can feed into the viewpoint that bullying … does not apply to young children as they are simply not capable when it comes to making judgements about 'right' and 'wrong' behaviour towards others … However, it could be argued that … there is a need for an awareness of children's agency and choice.
>
> (pp. 235–236)

Helgeland and Lund's (2017) exploration of preschool children's perspectives on bullying showed that children did feel a guilty conscience when excluding another. Saracho (2017) found that peer aggression is more frequent at preschool (age three to five years) than in any other age group, and there is emerging research evidence that bullying is indeed a common, perhaps even extensive, occurrence at preschool level (Helgeland and Lund, 2017; Humphrey, 2013). Sims-Schouten's (2015) research findings were that behaviours fitting the definition of aggression that was intentional and repeated over time were observed in preschool but were explained away by parents and early educators by saying that the children did not understand or were not capable of making judgements about right or wrong. This is confirmed by Lund (2015) who found that adults tended to overlook children's bullying at preschool level, and to trivialise young children's aggressive behaviour. Perhaps, therefore, even educators of the youngest children should ask themselves whether bullying might be a concern in their educational settings after all. It is also interesting to note that there is evidence, contrary perhaps to intuitive understandings, that incidences of bullying are higher at primary level than at secondary level (Foody et al., 2018).

Some researchers question whether preschoolers' behaviour can in fact be classified as 'bullying' due to the instability of the victim role and the lack of repetition of the victimisation over a long period. However, even when referring to bullying at primary level O'Moore (2010) questions the idea that aggression must occur on multiple occasions to constitute bullying. She argues that we need to take into account the fact that there are often once-off, isolated incidents that can cause children to feel harassed on a daily basis. For example, if a child is threatened with violence, he may then live in daily fear of the threat being carried out. She describes bullying that is masterminded by a 'ringleader' but actually carried out by a group of children, known in the literature as 'henchmen' or 'hangers-on'. She describes an incident from her research at primary level whereby a 'ringleader' gave notes each morning to different children, giving instructions on different ways to torment a specific victim. To the adult eyes, this would have appeared like multiple unrelated individual incidents, when in fact it was an orchestrated bullying campaign. Therefore, O'Moore (2010) recommends that we adapt the traditional definition to include repeated attacks of aggression on any one child even if they are not carried out by the same 'bully'.

Research generally also identifies a number of different *types* of bullying. *Verbal bullying* involves name-calling, teasing and all forms of verbal aggression, with malicious, demeaning or humiliating intent. *Psychological bullying* involves attempts to upset, confuse, dominate or otherwise damage another child emotionally and psychologically. *Physical bullying* is the traditional image of aggression, and the extent of physical aggression reported in the literature as experienced by some children is extreme. O'Moore's (2010) research with primary level children describes pushing, shoving, kicking, biting, headbutting, punching, scratching and even urinating on a child's head. Children gave examples like, 'People walked on my head and spat on me.' In research by O'Moore, Kirkham and Smith (1997) and Minton (2010) on the experiences of Irish schoolchildren, it was noted that both boys and girls regard physical bullying as the worst sort. However, Psalti (2017) points out that teachers may be more likely to respond and offer support to victims of physical bullying, while ignoring more social types and forms of bullying. This suggests that the outcomes of social bullying, which can be as extensive in the long term as those of physical bullying, may be under-reported.

Sexual bullying can include abusive, sexualised name-calling and insults, spreading rumours of a sexual nature online or in person, and inappropriate or unwelcome touches without consent. Sexual bullying may be homophobic in nature. Minton, Dahl, O'Moore and Tuck (2008) investigated the experience of Irish gay, lesbian and transgendered young people, and half of those who took part in the study admitted to being bullied, with 71% indicating they had at some point been called nasty names and teased about their sexuality. The most common difficulties reported in international studies are homophobic name-calling, and sexual comments, jokes and gestures. *Gesture-based bullying* may involve non-verbal aggressive and threatening gestures that can be very frightening for children, for example mimed throat-slitting or 'dirty looks'. *Extortion* includes demands for money or possessions, often accompanied by threats, which are sometimes carried out, if the victim does not comply.

There are a number of different *forms* that these types of bullying can take. Bullying can happen *directly* – direct verbal attacks, physical aggression, assaults, gestures or extortion. However, bullying may also be *indirect*. This is bullying that tends to be more covert and anonymous so that the aggressor is not readily identifiable by the victim; perhaps circulating nasty notes, putting derogatory graffiti on toilet doors, or damaging personal property. *Relational bullying* causes or threatens to cause damage to a child's relationships with others. It manipulates social connections by ignoring, excluding, isolating, spreading rumours, and turning other children against the victim. Such exclusion from peer relationships has been found to be one of the most common forms of bullying in early educational settings (Kirves and Sajaniemi, 2012), and the form most feared by small children (Helgeland and Lund, 2017). The aim of this bullying is to damage the victim's reputation and ultimately create peer rejection. The kinds of behaviours involved in relational bullying are withdrawing one's friendship out of jealousy or anger, isolating a member from a peer group, spreading malicious rumours and lies, cold-shouldering and isolating, and embarrassing the child. This form of bullying can be devastating, and the perceived slight that triggers relational bullying can often be so obscure that the child has no idea why this is happening to him (O'Moore, 2010). O'Moore also points out that children who assist in this type of exclusion bullying often have a sense of social insecurity and a strong dependency on group membership. They try to solidify their own position within the group by excluding the victim. In spite of the intense distress caused by relational bullying, educators often consider it to be less serious than other forms of bullying, have less sympathy for victims, and are less likely to intervene (Bauman and Del Rio, 2006; Psalti, 2017).

A relatively new and increasingly noted form of bullying is *cyberbullying*. This involves using electronic devices such as mobile phones and computers to abuse the victim through text messaging, camera or video-clips (often circulating nasty pictures that have been altered to make it look as if the victim is engaged in something compromising or sexual), internet postings using social networking sites to post messages or create false profiles or even to orchestrate bullying campaigns, mobile phone calls, etc. Worryingly, for children experiencing cyberbullying there is essentially no escape. With traditional forms of bullying at least when the child leaves school he is free of the bullying until the next day, but with cyberbullying, even if the child turns off the phone and the computer, there is a sense of worry about what is still happening online, and of course the reach and audience for potential humiliation is much wider. While the methods of achieving aggressive acts are different in instances of cyberbullying and traditional bullying, the two are often interlinked, and sometimes an incident of bullying online is a result of actions offline or vice versa (Foody et al., 2018).

Across the types and forms of bullying, the roles of bullies, victims, bully-victims (children who experience both roles) and bystanders have been repeatedly identified across the decades of research since Olweus's pioneering studies in 1970s.

THE ROLE OF THE ADULT IN COUNTERING BULLYING IN EDUCATIONAL SETTINGS

By its nature, bullying involves a power imbalance, and so a child experiencing bullying is very unlikely to be in a position to deal with this alone and unsupported (Saracho, 2017). Adults in educational settings play a key role in ensuring that bullying is prevented, and when it does occur, addressed, as they can contribute to the creation of a positive school climate by the way they respond to bullying (Psalti, 2017). According to Dawes, Chen, Farmer and Hamm (2017) the norms of children's aggressive or non-aggressive behaviour within classrooms are established and nurtured by how schools and teachers address and respond to these behaviours, and this has critical implications for how and whether victimisation occurs. The role of school principals and educational leaders has particularly been highlighted, both in terms of creation of positive school climates, and due to the support principals can give in building teachers' self-efficacy beliefs for addressing problems of bullying (Foody et al., 2018). Principals and other educational leaders set the tone for how teachers conceptualise and respond to bullying of all types and forms (Foody et al., 2018).

However, research has consistently shown that teachers and principals underestimate the extent of bullying in their classes and in their schools (Foody et al., 2018; Fröjd, Saaristo, & Ståhl 2013; O'Moore, 2010). When children were asked about bullying in Irish schools not one single school was reported by children as free of bullying, and it was more common in schools where teachers were not aware of what was going on or when adults did not make concerted efforts to prevent bullying (Minton, 2010). It is interesting to note that even when adults are aware of incidences of bullying, adults and children tend not to agree on who is at fault, and there is some evidence that teachers tend not to be aware of the true dynamics at play between children during bullying behaviour (Dawes et al., 2017). If an educator does not have a clear picture of what is going on with children, there is a risk that a victim of bullying who strikes back may end up at the receiving end of punitive discipline (O'Moore, 2010). Hamm, Farmer, Dadisman, Gravelle and Murray (2011) found that greater teacher–student attunement was positively related to students' sense of belonging at school, students' willingness to protect peers being bullied and students' sense that peers would stand up for them if they were bullied.

REFLECTION

Most educators tend to believe that they would be aware if there were bullying happening in their early years setting or school classroom. However, research indicates that in fact adults are very often unaware of bullying dynamics between children. Therefore, if you believe that there is no bullying happening in your educational setting, it is likely that this is a naïve assumption. How might you identify, prevent or address potential situations of bullying in your educational setting? Are there particular children in your setting who might be at risk of bullying?

While educators often believe that children would talk to them about experiences of bullying, research indicates that for most victims of bullying, telling a teacher or other adult is not an option, and the reluctance to tell is one of the greatest challenges that educators face in dealing with bullying. The reasons given for why children do not tell adults what they are experiencing include fear of reprisals, shame, humiliation, degradation, inability to figure out how to change the situation because of low self-esteem and feelings of helplessness, the notion that seeking help confirms taunts of being weak and incompetent, and fear of losing respect of parents and teachers (O'Moore, 2010).

However, there are some warning signs of bullying identified by research (Arseneault et al., 2006; O'Moore, 2010; Saracho, 2017) that may help educators to identify a potential situation of bullying without having to rely on a child's report. These include unexplained bruising, cuts or damaged clothing, visible signs of anxiety or distress, often with refusal to say what is wrong, unexplained changes in mood or behaviour, for example becoming withdrawn, clingy or attention-seeking, out-of-character behaviour like fighting (remember that when victims strike back it is often misinterpreted by educators and the victim ends up being punished), deterioration in academic achievement, erratic attendance (perhaps due to fear of going to school), lingering behind in school after class (the child may be hoping to avoid the bully), artwork expressing inner turmoil, psychosomatic symptoms like sleep disturbances, bad dreams, tummy aches and headaches, and even suicide ideation or enactment.

Once identified, it is crucial that educators address all instances of bullying, as it is when children seek help and do not receive it from adults that they are particularly vulnerable, with many serious instances documented, sometimes to the point of suicide ideation and enactment, even in young children (O'Moore, 2010). Saracho (2017) argues that bullying prevention programmes need to be introduced with young children as early as possible in their educational career, preferably in early years settings, but certainly by the junior years of primary school. Each of the theoretical perspectives explored in the previous chapters offers a lens on how to understand the dynamics of bullying, and how best to prevent it and address it when it does occur. You will now have the opportunity to remind yourself of the key elements of each theoretical lens, to read about examples of how they might be applied to counter bullying in practice, and to think about how the various approaches could best be combined in your unique educational setting to best suit the children, educators and families you work with.

BEHAVIOURISM: POSITIVE REINFORCEMENT AND CLEAR SANCTIONS

Reminder

The central tenets of behaviourism include the idea that children learn through association and reinforcement – behaviours that are followed by positive consequences tend to be repeated whereas behaviours that are ignored or that are followed by negative consequences tend to disappear. The role of the educator within a behaviourist approach is to identify a systematic set of reinforcers to shape the behaviour of children towards desired outcomes.

Bullying through a behaviourist lens

Using a behaviourist framework, bullying can be interpreted as a behaviour that has achieved a desired outcome for the perpetrator in the past, and the role of the educator is to either render it more attractive to behave in a kind and supportive manner towards other children through the use of positive reinforcement, or to ensure that bullying behaviour becomes so unattractive through the use of punishment that it ceases to be used. While traditional behaviourism has been criticised on ethical grounds (explored in detail in Chapter 3), the adaptation and use of behaviourist strategies in modern educational settings can be very appropriate and successful when applied in an ethically informed manner. For example, Simon Lewis, principal of a primary school in Carlow, Ireland, describes how he uses positive reinforcement as part of a whole-school anti-bullying approach, based on application of a behaviourist reward system. Could this work in your educational setting?

As one element of a broader relational approach to education, rather than focusing on punishment of bullying, the team aims to create a positive school climate by reinforcing and rewarding children for kindness, empathy and treating each other well. Children are encouraged to report examples of kind behaviour to their teacher, and when this happens both the child who acted kindly and the child who brought that kind act to the attention of the teacher may be invited to visit the principal to have their name added to the 'Golden Book'. Children's own teacher and teachers from other classes as well as other school staff such as Special Needs Assistants, the School Secretary, the Cleaning Staff and everyone in the school community are also on the look-out for opportunities to highlight a child's positive behaviour and send them on their way for entry into the Golden Book. The most important thing is that my office is a place where children love coming to. They always know they will leave with a smile and a high-five and that their hard work has been recognised.

FIGURE 9.1 A wall display on bullying created by the children in Simon's school.

In this case, positive reinforcement is very successfully used to proactively prevent bullying. However, behaviourist approaches can also be used to respond to bullying when they occur. At this point, revisit Chapter 3, and consider how approaches like behaviour contracts, token economies and ABC analysis might be applied to prevent and respond to bullying in your educational setting.

PSYCHODYNAMIC AND RELATIONAL THEORIES: RELATIONSHIP BUILDING AND EMOTIONAL EXPRESSION

Reminder

The central tenets of psychodynamic theories include the idea that emotions and the workings of the unconscious mind may explain much behaviour. The experiences that children have early in life with their primary care-givers create internal working models of relationships and reciprocal roles that influence how new environments and relationships are experienced and responded to. Some children may experience 'fight–flight–freeze' reactions when under challenge or when experiencing something new.

Bullying through a psychodynamic lens

Through this theoretical perspective, bullying behaviours can be interpreted as a defensive mechanism whereby a child has learned that the most effective management of a relational role is to aggressively externalise fear in order to maintain personal safety, and the appropriate response for an adult is to support the child to express emotion more appropriately while teaching to child to feel empathy and mutual respect for his victim. Emotional support for the child experiencing bullying is also seen as crucial. Consider the potential implications of the responses of some participants in Psalti's (2017) study of early educator's perspectives on bullying to the following vignette, from a psychodynamic perspective:

VERBAL AGGRESSION

In your classroom you hear Child A saying to Child B, 'Go away! You stink!' Child B tries to ignore this, but frowns. You saw this same thing happen the other day (pp 398).

In the verbal bullying incident of mockery, more than one out of four respondents indicated that they would advocate a be tough action, encouraging the victim to ignore bullying by not letting it bother him/her. This suggests that teachers believe that directing someone not to feel emotions can be quite comforting.

(Psalti, 2017, p. 395)

From the viewpoint of this theoretical perspective, encouraging children not to feel or express painful emotion acts as an agent of repression, and creates the likelihood that this painful emotion will be either externalised into aggressive behaviour by the victim of bullying, or internalised into withdrawn or self-destructive behaviour by him. Supporting children to express emotion appropriately, to develop their social and emotional skills, and to build resilience within a relational educational environment is central to a psychodynamic, relational approach to countering bullying. Creating an emotionally supportive environment where children feel able to talk about their difficulties can prevent the kinds of externalising behaviour that, this perspective argues, may lead to aggression manifested as bullying. Saracho (2017) maintains that when bullying situations are identified in educational settings, social and emotional skill building can help children avoid bullying behaviours and instead cultivate solid social relationships. O'Moore (2010) indicates that as an educator, it is crucial not to dismiss a child's efforts to tell his experiences of bullying. When an account of what has happened to him is not taken seriously, a child may come away feeling even more humiliated and helpless. If a child is disbelieved or made to feel foolish for reporting bullying, educators create an atmosphere that feeds into the wall of silence that supports the development of bullying. Instead, educators should proactively make it very clear to children that seeking help for themselves or others experiencing bullying is in fact a sign of strength and a responsible thing to do (O'Moore, 2010). The best anti-bullying strategy of all is prevention, and if it cannot be eliminated altogether, the next best option is early intervention. A psychodynamic perspective argues that educators can do this by creating the kind of atmosphere where emotional expression is normalised and supported, and children can come forward if there is a problem. Now revisit Chapter 4, and consider which of the approaches for supporting emotional expression and communication between adults and children might best be adopted for preventing and responding to bullying in your educational setting.

HUMANISM: SELF-DIRECTION AND SPACE FOR EXPLORATION OF THE ISSUE OF BULLYING WITH CHILDREN TO UNDERSTAND THEIR 'INTERNAL FRAME OF REFERENCE'

Reminder

The central tenets of a humanist or student-centred approach are that all humans, including children, have the capacity for positive, self-directed action, and the role of an educator is to create a positive climate in which a supportive relationship can facilitate positive choices.

Bullying through a humanist lens

From a student-centred perspective, the role of an educator is to discuss issues of bullying openly with children, explore with them the kind of environment they would like their school to be, and negotiate fair and equitable rules by which everyone agrees to live. While it may be easy to underestimate children's capacity to explore these kinds of issues, research like that of Helgeland and Lund (2017) shows the ability of even three- and four-year-olds to discuss bullying in nuanced and detailed ways. A common theme running through the literature is that children in early years and primary settings are very capable of understanding and working through these complex issues – they can often be a lot more insightful than adults! Consider the insights of the children from a kindergarten in Porto, Portugal, taking part in the THRIECE (Teaching for Holistic, Relational and Inclusive Early Childhood Education) project described in Chapter 4, who spent some time with their educators working out how they should treat each other:

'Do not take toys from friends'

'Do not push friends'

'Do not bite friends'

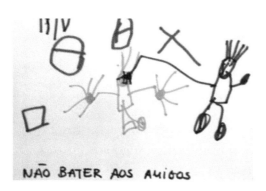

'Do not hit friends'

'Love the friends'

The educators revisited these rules with the children periodically and they decided whether or not the rules were still relevant and needed to be kept in place. Such humanist approaches may be effective in preventing bullying from occurring, but this theoretical approach may also be useful in identifying responses when it does happen. For example, Saracho (2017) maintains that faulty social relationships at school can be repaired through restorative justice techniques that include assembling all children (for example, bullies, victims, bystanders, other children) 'in a participatory process that addresses wrongdoing while offering respect to the parties involved' (Morrison, 2007, p. 198). Restorative approaches based on a humanist theoretical framework can support the aggressor to take responsibility for their hurtful behaviour in a meaningful way, gain insight into the effects of that behaviour on others and change their negative/anti-social behaviour. Now revisit Chapter 5 and consider how student-centred methodologies like narrative approaches and peer mediation might be useful in preventing and responding to bullying in your educational setting.

BIOLOGICAL BASES OF BEHAVIOUR: VULNERABILITIES TO BULLYING

Reminder

Biological understandings of behaviour emphasise the impact of genetic and physical influences. Chapter 6 identified how physical concerns like hunger, tiredness and discomfort can affect behaviour, and also introduced concepts like executive function and temperament, highlighting the fact that while these may have biological roots, they are highly sensitive to environmental influence. Another consideration within a biological perspective is the impact of additional physical and sensory needs.

Bullying through a biopsychosocial lens

The biopsychosocial model put forward in Chapter 6 would posit that bullying happens due to a complex interaction of biological, psychological and social factors. Educators should ensure children's physical needs are met, so that aggression is not triggered by physical discomfort. They should also work with children to work on impulse control and the development of executive function, through approaches that develop 'goodness of fit', especially for children who show signs of aggressive temperament. It is also important to be aware of evidence that children with disabilities and additional physical or sensory needs may be vulnerable to becoming targets of bullying, rendering them at a double disadvantage (Chatzitheochari et al., 2016). Now revisit Chapter 6, and consider how you could counter bullying in your educational setting by ensuring to meet physical needs, leveraging children's instincts for engagement with play, and helping children to maintain calmness and avoid overstimulation.

BIOECOLOGICAL THEORY: STRONG LINKS WITH PARENTS AND COMMUNITIES

Reminder

The central tenet of a bioecological perspective is that behaviour results from a complex, dynamic interaction of genetic factors with social and environmental experiences at immediate and societal level, through the power of interactions and relationships.

Bullying through a bioecological lens

With regards to bullying, bioecological theory would recommend understanding the behaviour in context, and forming strong links across the contexts in which the child is developing in order to facilitate the development of positive behavioural dispositions. Consider this example of home–school communication in different contexts, and how it could impact on a child's behaviour and treatment of other children, drawn from research by O'Toole (2016) which is theorised through a bioecological framework. Interviewed after her child had transitioned from preschool to primary school, this parent described how things changed in terms of her communication with each setting, and how that impacted on her son's behaviour with other children.

Two parents in particular identified their children's behaviour, in the wake of family crises, as challenging in this transition (from preschool to primary school). Providing a good example of the interactive nature of relevant factors, and in particular how 'process' may be more influential than 'person', one of these parents noted how strong and positive communication with the preschool had alleviated these difficulties:

> Myself and the kids' dad are separated, so at one point S. found it very difficult because there was no contact with his dad … He was having a really bad time in [pre]school. I was able to go in and explain … They asked, which was nice, they weren't just saying 'Oh he's biting and he's kicking', they asked [was there something going on for him] … I was able to explain to them and felt OK about explaining to them.
>
> Source: Parent of junior infant

However, she was still in the process of building such a relationship with the primary school, and that exacerbated the problem:

> Yesterday I was asking S. how did school go and he said 'Let's get out of here mammy' and I was thinking 'Oh right, what's gone on here now?' Whereas at the [preschool] I would have known because they would have been at the door asking could they talk to you for a second and they would let me know. I had to go back to the teacher yesterday … and ask if something had happened … now in her head they had dealt with it at school but I just wanted to know.
>
> Source: Parent of junior infant

The role of schools and particularly school principals in forming strong links with parents and communities in the context of prevention of bullying has been identified by Foody et al. (2018). Parents know their child far better than educators ever can, and are in a better position to notice changes in behaviour that may be indicative of a problem that has gone unnoticed at school. Teachers should provide information on bullying to parents and should take them seriously if they come to them with concerns (O'Moore, 2010). Now revisit Chapter 7, and consider whether a process–person–context–time (PPCT) analysis could cast any light on the bullying behaviour of any children in your educational setting, or provide any insight to you on how you might prevent or respond to such behaviour.

INTERCULTURAL PERSPECTIVE: EARLY EDUCATION FOR SOCIAL JUSTICE

Reminder

The central tenet of an intercultural perspective on behaviour is that there is no objectively right or wrong way for children to behave, but rather expectations for behaviour are rooted in deeply held encultured beliefs and norms.

Bullying through an intercultural lens

The idea that behaviour is culture-bound applies to aggression and bullying as much as to all other behaviours. For example, Psalti (2017) identified cultural differences between early educators from the USA and UK who indicated that physical bullying was the most serious form, and the Greek educators in their replicated study who identified verbal bullying as the most serious. While any child may become a victim of bullying, and a narrative identifying the victim as the source of the problem of bullying is damaging and unfair, studies have shown that in a world sometimes characterised by prejudices such as racism, ableism, misogyny, homophobia and other forms of bias, educational settings are not immune from the injustices of the society outside them, and as a result some children may be more vulnerable to experiences of bullying than others (O'Moore, 2010). Consider the experiences identified in the Norwegian context where a child who is not from a Norwegian family background is at risk of exclusion by children and adults alike.

Sunita speaks Norwegian, but she is not a native Norwegian. She is often alone, walks around the playground or stands watching the others without taking initiative. She usually is not invited to join the game, the other girls ignore her or run away from her. Sometimes she is allowed to join, but is quickly excluded. The other girls may say: "'it's not like that, you don't know the rules, it's no fun.'"

The children who are adamant receive attention from the adults in connection with the conflicts in which they get involved. Sunita and several other children are more "'invisible,'" and are overlooked by the adults as well as the children. They mostly walk around by themselves, observing others playing, rarely being invited in. Occasionally they are allowed to join for a short while, but they are quickly excluded from the game.

Helgeland and Lund, 2017 p. 139

In this case, the authors note that educators not only fail to protect the child from exclusion, but in fact contribute to it themselves. This highlights the importance of reflecting upon and challenging one's own personal prejudices or cultural 'blindspots' as highlighted in Chapter 8, and this applies to prevention of and responses to bullying as much as to other behaviours. For example, in a recent content analysis of anti-bullying policies in schools in Northern Ireland, Purdy and Smith (2016), noted minimal reference to racist, religious, homophobic or sexual bullying, in spite of good awareness of traditional and cyberbullying. Adults who work with children should be aware of this both within themselves and within the group of children with whom they work, with a view to prevention and teaching tolerance and inclusion. Psalti (2017) has noted that teachers play a vital role in the detection of at-risk children. Bullying is often based on so-called gender-atypical behaviour (Felix and Greif Green, 2010), and anything that marks a child out as different leaves them at risk of victimisation. Boys tend to experience stricter rules of gender conformity – boys who have interests beyond the usual male preserves of football and other sports, or who show traits perceived to be effeminate, are twice as likely to be bullied as gender-typical boys (Felix and Greif Green, 2010). Sims-Schouten (2015) argue that early interventions in relation to bullying behaviour in early childhood should include educating children about diversity and social justice, and notes that this is supported by Trevarthen (2004) who argues that there is a need for a stronger focus on infants as innate companions and cooperators. The role of school leadership is noted in the literature as crucial in creating an environment where differences are nurtured and equality is demanded (Foody et al., 2018). Now revisit Chapter 8, and consider how education for social justice can work to prevent bullying in your educational setting.

CONCLUSION: A MULTI-THEORETICAL FRAMEWORK FOR TACKLING BULLYING IN EDUCATIONAL SETTINGS

In preventing and responding to bullying, as in preventing and responding to other negative behaviours, while promoting positive behaviours and children's flourishing, a multi-theoretical framework drawing on many ideas, approaches, concepts and strategies is most likely to be effective. In the decades since Olweus's pioneering research, a strong body of literature has developed, identifying the practical approaches that tend to be effective in countering bullying in educational settings, and they draw on a variety of theoretical frameworks. In order to be successful in tackling bullying, it is generally acknowledged that a whole-school approach is required – in other words, the whole educational community must give high priority to prevention and intervention in bullying, as in the example of the use of the 'Golden Book' in the primary school mentioned earlier. This includes educators, children, parents, traffic wardens, even local shopkeepers. It should be clear to all that bullying of any kind will not be tolerated – for example, an educational setting could develop a charter of rights, detailing that every child has the right to feel safe. Drawing on a humanist perspective, the educational setting could involve the children in developing that charter, and drawing on a bioecological perspective it could also involve families and communities.

An anti-bullying policy can be crucial in tackling bullying. This should be explicitly written down, and may be one of the most important aspects of a whole-school or early childhood setting approach to bullying (DES, 2013). It is a framework for how to deal with bullying, regularly reviewed, nominating a specific member of staff to deal with bullying, and including formal reporting of bullying. In developing the policy, the whole educational community develops clear expectations, commitment and consistency in addressing all forms of bullying. In developing a policy, O'Moore (2010) recommends that we:

- Accept that bullying exists.
- Consider the key issues (what do we mean by bullying, what misconceptions are there, who are the victims, the aggressors and the bystanders, what strategies do we have/want to reduce the risk of bullying and to respond to it when it happens, what is the line of reporting incidents, etc.).
- Determine the current level of bullying.
- Communicate the results.
- Investigate the literature and seek anti-bullying strategies.
- Prepare a draft policy.
- Review the policy.
- Implement the policy.
- Review, revise and renew the policy.

In synthesising the literature and theoretical perspectives explored above, other key practical responses to bullying emerge. Playground supervision is considered essential, as unsupervised playtime is often considered a particularly opportune moment for bullying to occur, so prevention is an important consideration. Taking into account the evidence explored in this chapter on educators' common misconceptions on bullying, training in the issues around bullying and how to prevent it is also crucial to empower educators. Drawing on many of the theoretical perspectives explored here, including psychodynamic theories, humanist theories and intercultural perspectives, an important consideration is the creation and reinforcement of a positive, friendly ethos in the educational setting and the promotion of a culture of respect and dignity. Educators must discourage all bullying behaviour that comes to their attention and challenge all single acts of aggression in order to promote a culture of disclosure. Educators may wish to draw on behaviourist reward systems to empower bystanders to take action and develop a classroom climate that is positive and rewarding to the students. A student-centred approach could promote restorative approaches to dealing with indiscipline and bullying, or use the curriculum and visual materials to highlight the topic of bullying with children and prevention strategies that build empathy, respect and resilience.

Now reflect on how these approaches might fruitfully be applied in your educational setting. The practical implications of this multi-theoretical perspective are well summarised by Helgeland and Lund (2017, p. 140), who indicate that an appropriate response to the challenge of bullying in early educational settings:

calls for attentive and available adults, who see all the children and each individual child. It demands a focus on context and relational processes rather than defining individual children as the cause, as a result of 'how they are,' based on personality variables. Adults must be able to look behind the behavior and be curious about what might trigger a situation of conflict.

FINAL ACTIVITY

Saracho (2017, pp. 456–457) identifies well-established anti-bullying programmes for use with children from preschool to primary level, which you may wish to investigate further. See if you can identify some of the theoretical underpinnings of each:

Olweus Bullying Prevention Program (Ages 8–15)

The Olweus Bullying Prevention Program (OBPP) decreases bullying and assists in improving the peer relationships of elementary, middle, and junior high school students in their school and home environments. It is based on four fundamental principles: (1) the adults' warmth, positive interest, and participation; (2) stringent parameters that explain unacceptable behaviors; (3) persistent concentration to nonphysical restrictions for acceptable behaviors, disturbances, or regulations; and (4) adults are considered authorities and positive role models (Olweus, 2005).

Steps to Respect: a bullying prevention program (Ages 8–10)

Steps to Respect: a bullying prevention program focuses on relational types of aggression such as spiteful gossip and social segregation (Low, Frey and Brockman, 2010) of children who are in the third, fourth, and fifth grades. Its components combine positive norms that create and reinforce policies to eradicate bullying and to encourage appropriate behavior. The Steps to Respect program teaches children skills to deal with bullying, to recognize bullying and aggressive behaviors, to become sensitive toward bullied children, to generate positive social norms, and to respond with socially acceptable behaviors when they observe bullying behaviors (Committee for Children, 2005).

Second Step: a bullying prevention program (Ages 4–14)

Second Step: a bullying prevention program is a social skills program for children who are 4–14 years of age. They learn to diminish impulsive, high-risk, and aggressive behaviors and develop their socioemotional competence. Through modeling, practice, role playing, and developmentally appropriate verbal intervention strategies, young children learn perspective taking (empathy), impulse control, and anger management. The program includes "'A Family Guide to Second Step'" and curricula for children who are in preschool, kindergarten, and elementary school, which includes first through fifth grades (Committee for Children, 2014, 2015).

Bernese Program against Victimization in Kindergarten and Elementary School (Be-Prox)

The Bernese Program against Victimization in Kindergarten and Elementary School (Be-Prox) is an anti-bullying and victimization program for young children. This thorough and practical approach is used to change the teachers' attitudes and abilities to manage bullying and to generate positive principles that are necessary to promote the children's interactions. Teachers learn how to deal with bullying behaviors and prevent victimization in a variety of situations in kindergarten and elementary classrooms (Alsaker, 2004; Alsakser and Valkanover, 2001, 2012). They are provided with a 4-month concentrated program that includes (1) supervision, (2) group discussions, and (3) shared support and collaboration between consultants and teachers and between teachers and parents (Alsaker 2004).

In this chapter, we have taken the example of bullying as an illustration of how you might go about consolidating your theoretical knowledge. We encourage you to take this multi-theoretical approach to supporting positive behaviour in other regards in your educational setting.

NOTE

1 Sources drawn on to identify definitions, types and forms of bullying include (see bibliography for full references): DES (1993, 2013); DfE (2013); Foody et al. (2018); Helgeland and Lund (2017); Jansen et al. (2017); Jimerson, Swearer and Espelage, 2010; Olweus (1978, 1993, 1997, 2000); Olweus and Limber (1999); O'Moore (2010); Psalti (2017); Saracho (2017); Sims-Schouten (2015); Small, Neilsen-Hewett and Sweller, 2013; Vlachou et al. (2011).

CHAPTER 10

Reflecting on positive approaches to engaging with children's behaviour

INTRODUCTION

In this final chapter, key points of learning will be identified with regards to support for children's positive behaviour. Previous chapters have presented a range of theoretical and practical approaches, some of which may even have seemed contradictory. For example, Chapters 3 (behaviourist) and 4 (psycho-dynamic/relational) offered approaches to understanding and responding to displays of emotion that are in direct contradiction to each other. A behaviourist would recommend ignoring a child who is crying, for fear of reinforcing and thereby increasing crying behaviour; an attachment theorist on the other hand would maintain that it is vital for an adult to comfort a crying child to build a secure attachment, and a psychoanalyst would view crying as an important means of releasing emotion (catharsis) which should be encouraged, not feared.

This chapter will support readers to come to terms with these tensions, helping them to identify their own preferred approach to supporting positive behaviour, and also articulating some common threads that weave through all or most of the theories and practices explored in this book. Such common threads include the importance of warm and caring relationships between adults and children in supporting positive behaviour, the need to understand children's experiences, perspectives and agency in developing self-regulation, developing approaches based on reciprocity and respect, and the importance of reflective practice.

THEORETICAL PERSPECTIVES: A REMINDER

In this book, readers were introduced to a number of well-known theories that may offer insight into the behaviour of children in educational settings:

Baumrind's parenting styles

Diana Baumrind's (1971) concept of authoritative parenting has in recent years been translated into the concept of authoritative teaching (Gregory et al., 2010). The central argument of this approach is that, rather than creating a dichotomy between 'structure' (boundaries, clear rules) and 'support' (a sense of belonging, care and self-direction), children need both.

Behaviourism

The key ideas within this approach to understanding children's behaviour relate to learning through association (Watson and Rayner, 1920) and learning through reinforcement (Skinner, 1953). Behaviourists believe that all behaviour is learned and so can be unlearned or reshaped through judicious application of association and consequence. They are not interested in children's inner experiences, emotions or thoughts. Behaviourism has benefits in that it views all children as capable of behaving well with support and it offers clear direction for educators, but it should be treated with caution, as it seeks to control rather than understand children, and it gives little insight into children's inner lives. Those who view children from a human rights perspective based on the United Nations Convention on the Rights of the Child (1989) tend to be uncomfortable with a behaviourist approach.

Psychodynamic and relational approaches to supporting positive behaviour

Chapter 4 drew on psychodynamic theories like those of Freud (1955), attachment theory (Bowlby, 1969) and Cognitive Analytic Therapy (Ryle, 1998) to explore the impact of relationships and emotions on behaviour. Key concepts include 'internalising' behaviour, whereby the emotions related to traumatic experiences are directed inwards, leading to withdrawal and/or self-damaging behaviours; 'externalising' behaviours, whereby such emotions are directed outwards, leading to aggression and violence; 'hypervigilance', whereby a child who has experienced trauma is constantly on the alert for danger, and may see it even when it does not exist, leading to inappropriate 'fight or flight' responses; and 'catharsis', or achievement of emotional release to avoid misdirection of energy into negative behaviour. Early experiences impact on later behaviour through the power of 'internal working models' and 'reciprocal roles'. Relationships are seen as dynamic, two-way, complex and crucial for supporting positive behaviour.

Humanist approaches to supporting positive behaviour

A humanist perspective foregrounds the idea that a child's behaviour is a manifestation of a complex inner world, and that approaching the development of positive behaviour solely from the adult's perspective shows only half the reality. Such approaches emphasise the capacity of all human beings, including children, to develop positively, and frames negative behaviour as a form of communication and a coping strategy in a world perceived by the child as hostile (Rogers, 1995). In supporting children's positive behaviour, humanists emphasise genuineness, empathy, unconditional positive regard and self-direction rather than coercion (Freiberg and Lamb, 2009).

The biological bases of behaviour

This perspective investigated behaviour and development as a biological process. It explored the impact of simple biological imperatives like hunger or tiredness, and the need for movement and play in childhood. It introduced the concept of 'executive function' based on brain development, and how children move from co-regulation to self-regulation over time. The biological perspective also considers the idea of 'temperament', or early appearing and relatively stable traits that may impact on behaviour. Additional physical or sensory needs could also be considered from a biological perspective. However, in this chapter readers were introduced to the biopsychosocial model that draws together biological concerns with psychological and social influences on behaviour.

Bioecological theory

Bronfenbrenner's bioecological model of human development (Bronfenbrenner and Morris, 2006) identifies *process* factors (such as relationships between children and adults), *person* factors (such as temperament), *context* factors (such as classroom climate) and *time* factors (such as the child's age) that must be understood in interaction with each other to explain behaviour. This theory can be used as a framework to draw together many of the other theories explored within this book to help understand children's behaviour.

An intercultural perspective

This chapter drew on sociocultural theory, which showed that many beliefs and practices relevant to children's behaviour vary across cultures – norms of behaviour, images of children and their competence and responsibilities, beliefs regarding the appropriateness of various forms of discipline, and ideas on how relationships between adults and children should be conducted. When there are differences between home and school in terms of such beliefs and practices, there can be potential for a child to be seen as misbehaving when her behaviour would be acceptable in a different context. It also explored Bourdieu's (e.g. 1997) concepts of cultural capital, social and cultural reproduction, cultural arbitrary which explore the impact of society, dominant and subordinate groups, the 'taken-for-granted' and impacts on individual behaviour.

REFLECTION

In reading any of these theoretical perspectives, did you have any 'lightbulb moments'? Were there any theories, or particular elements of theories, that 'rang true' to you? In reading this book, were there any moments that made you think of children you know, or that explained experiences you have had more clearly?

In Chapter 1, we explored how each of us has our own, sometimes naïve or uninformed personal 'theories' of why children behave as they do, and how often unbeknownst to us or at least unacknowledged, these theories guide our responses. Now take the time to redevelop your theories into a more informed perspective.

Alone or with a colleague, identify the key themes that you noted recurring throughout the book, across different theories and different chapters. If you were developing your own personal theory of why children behave as they do, and what are the most important things to consider when developing responses to support positive behaviour, what points would you now include?

The rest of the chapter represents the response that we as authors present to this reflection. These are the common themes that we identify across theoretical perspectives, and the crucial points that we feel educators should consider in developing their understanding of children's behaviour as well as their responses to it. It is not important that you agree with us, but it is important that you think about why you think as you do. As you progress, think about the children you work with, or those you know well. How do your experiences with them fit within the framework we present? By the end of the chapter (which will be the end of the book) we hope you will feel more confident, if not in knowing all the answers, at least in knowing the questions to ask.

COMMON THEMES ACROSS THEORETICAL PERSPECTIVES ON BEHAVIOUR

The crucial nature of relationships

While different theoretical perspectives identify varying approaches and ideas for supporting positive behaviour in educational settings, it may be that it is not the strategies in themselves that work, but rather the relationships and the opportunities for relationship building underlying them that are effective. Some theories, like attachment theory, CAT, humanist/student-centred theories and the bioecological concept of proximal processes, explicitly name the power of relationships to support children's positive behaviour, learning and development. In other strategies, for example the interpersonal negotiation and mutual respect involved in a well-executed behaviour contract, the relational aspect may not be articulated, but it is nonetheless crucial to success.

In reality, the relationships underpinning positive behaviour are complex, messy and multi-faceted. Such relationships do not simply involve the educator and the child alone, but many of the theories in this book (particularly the bioecological model, sociocultural theory and Bourdieu's theories) show how relationships are embedded within the contexts, culture and societies in which they develop, and an educator seeking to draw on the power of relationships to develop positive behaviour should be cognisant of this.

Let's take an illustration of how sensitivity to the complex web of factors influencing relationships might work in practice for an educator working on strategies to support positive behaviour.[1] A child may develop a close and trusting relationship with an early childhood educator or teacher. This relationship evolves over time, supported and fostered by interactions between the characteristics of the child and those of the educator with whom she is working closely. For example, both might have a shared interest in music, and because they play music together their relationship develops well and the child is more likely to behave well with that educator. The relationship is also undoubtedly influenced by more distal influences and less visible influences beyond the immediate setting, but in this case the educator may have little information about that, and those influences may be difficult to determine. On the other hand, with another child a positive, trusting relationship with educator may develop, but the quality of these interactions may be dependent on close communication and a positive relationship between the child's parent and this educator. This can sometimes be the case when a child has an additional physical, sensory or learning need, and so parents and educators need to communicate in more detail in order to be able to meet that need so that positive behaviour can be maintained as explored in Chapter 6. The precise and quite distinct pathways to the quality of the relationship between the educator and these two children, and thereby to the positive behaviour of the two children, is to some extent obscured if we see both relationships as similar and only identify difference in terms of features specific to the child while ignoring other factors of importance from the wider context. By placing more emphasis on the network of influences operating to build close and trusting interactions between children and adults working alongside them, we can identify more clearly the precise points of contact within these interactions, thus facilitating greater insight into the factors influencing children's development and behaviour.

However, building such relationships does not happen of its own accord. Relationships must be valued and time must be taken to build them. Remember the experience of the early educator in Chapter 4 who described the little girl pushing her away before finally trusting her. Taking the time the child needed to feel safe may have interrupted a negative behavioural trajectory for her, so while it is tempting to measure the quality of educational practice in terms of immediately verifiable outputs, it is crucial to note that what is really important in terms of quality is often much less measurable. Supports for positive behaviour should be aimed at facilitating strong connections, rather than tick-box or politically motivated systems with false models of 'quality'. An ethos of respectful consideration and caring for children and families is vital for the protection of potentially vulnerable children and adults, as well as support for agency and capacity, fostering positive social, emotional and thereby behavioural outcomes. Such an ethos can be hard to measure, and requires proactive efforts and on-going reflection to achieve and maintain. A theoretically informed approach to supporting positive behaviour can give educators the language and confidence to defend spending the time and energy required to invest in the kinds of relationships that are likely to lead to positive behaviour in children.

Reciprocity and respect for children as human beings with agency

Another key concept that we identify across most of these theoretical perspectives, with the obvious exception of the behaviourist lens on children, is the importance of viewing children as human beings with agency and rights. Adults who seek to dominate and control children to their own ends rarely achieve genuine self-regulation or true moral understanding in children. Rather, positive behaviour is achieved through reciprocity and respect for children's agency particularly evident in the humanist and sociocultural models. Hayes' (2004, 2013) concept of a 'nurturing pedagogy' is a commitment to democratic principles that recognise the need to respect and engage meaningfully with children. This approach is reflective of an understanding of quality educational settings as sites of democratic practice where children and adults can participate collectively in interpreting experiences and shaping decisions affecting their own behaviour, learning and development and the nature of the context within which they occur.

In order to scaffold the move from co-regulation to self-regulation of behaviour over time, some recommended approaches are to prioritise mastering the skills of looking after self and belongings, sharing, active listening, problem solving and persistence, and this is relevant not only to younger children, but to older children in primary schools also, since such skills have been shown to present problems for children in the transition to secondary school (O'Toole et al., 2014). Sensitive educators, while locating the child at the centre of practice in supporting positive behaviour, balance an awareness of children's vulnerability, children's need for protection and their dependence on adults to develop appropriate boundaries with their need for space for their self-development, greater autonomy and independence.

Educational environments rich in affordances for children to engage in joint activities and tasks and to provide opportunities to work together and negotiate shared meanings with other children and adults in early years settings do not require sophisticated tools or equipment but will be enhanced through innovative and creative inputs from both children and adults working together. The unique constellation of dispositions and characteristics which individual children bring to their educational settings influences and shapes the experiences they will have within these settings, and the behaviour they exhibit within them. As explored in Chapter 6, early childhood educators and primary school teachers play an important role in facilitating and supporting children's emerging agency and participation in their learning and development, and this has a huge impact on their behaviour. Working closely alongside children in educational settings, we soon become familiar with and tune into the particular and distinct characteristics of each individual child, and the extent to which we succeed in doing this is undoubtedly influenced by the characteristics of individual educators and their associated responses to individual children.

Equally important within this conceptualisation is mindfulness of the need of children for movement and play. Through a psychodynamic, relational lens, play arose as an outlet for emotional expression and development of empathy for others. In Chapter 6, we explored play as a biological imperative, and as a result of this, a strategy for supporting positive behaviour. The sociocultural perspective on play described in Chapter 8 showed how play is a mediating tool through which children internalise cultures and rules for self-regulation. Play is quite simply a crucial part of childhood and is a right for all children.

Reflective practice

Chapter 1 introduced the idea that as educators our approaches to children's behaviour are often based on our own experiences of discipline as children, whether these are positive or not. Equally, for many educators, decisions regarding behaviour can be based on fear of losing control rather than active choices. In Chapter 4, concepts of internal working models and reciprocal roles showed how a simple conception of a rational adult taking control of an immature or misbehaving child is a naïve representation of the classroom dynamic. Rather our own 'baggage' as adults can have a huge influence on our responses to children's behaviour which in turn influences their response to us and so on. In Chapter 8 then, we saw how (often unconscious) biases and prejudices as well as unfounded expectations can influence children's behaviour. Understanding that our behaviour as educators has so profound an impact on children, and at such a crucial and deep level, can be daunting and even paralysing! The thing is that even without understanding the influence of our practice, it has an impact on the children we work with – knowledge helps us to consider our practice a little more carefully; it challenges us to consider the implications such knowledge has for our practices and it allows us recognise that feedback and the form that such feedback takes has an influence on children's confidence, mental flexibility, self-control and therefore behaviour. This underlines the crucial importance of reflective practice for educators aiming to support positive behaviour in educational settings.

The term reflection within the current literature is often used to describe a variety of practices, from simply thinking of one's own plans to considering the social, ethical, and even political implication this thinking has on actual practice.[2] The word reflection carries with it the idea of looking back which can lead one to consider that reflection is something that happens after the event. We plan an activity and carry it out and we review and reflect on it later. However, reflective practice is richer when it is considered in the context of being present in the moment, an inclination towards careful consideration of what exactly is happening in the moment, a reflection in process. This is a deep level of reflection, which requires an awareness and engagement with the moment rather than wondering how this moment will impact on some distant outcome. It suggests an interest in the potential of this moment for you and those children you are working with.

There are many levels and types of reflections in the growth of reflective practice. Some definitions of reflective practice focuses on the connection between practice and identified learning goals and outcomes, through reviewing and analysis of one's own actions, decisions or choice of materials. Other definitions characterise reflective practice as a lifelong attempt involving a longer and more lasting commitment to the ongoing learning and continuous improvement of the quality of one's professional practice (York-Barr, Sommers, Ghere and Montie, 2006). Still other definitions consider reflective practice as requiring one to move beyond a focus on isolated events to consider the broader context including the personal, pedagogical, societal as well as ethical contexts associated with professional work (Larrivee, 2005).

There is general agreement that reflection can be considered on the following three levels:

The *surface level* is the level that focuses on the practice skills, actions and roles, generally looking at each teaching episode as an isolated event. The focus is often on the educator reflecting on approaches and techniques used to reach particular goals.

The *pedagogical level* is a more advanced level where the educator considers the theory and rationale for current practice. At this level the educator is expected to be working towards understanding the theory behind a particular practice and applying these theories to their practice.

The *critical level* represents the higher order where educators examine the social, ethical and political consequences of their educational processes and practices. At this level, they also inspect both their professional and personal convictions and how they impact directly, and indirectly, on children.

Larrivee (2005) recognises that new educators and students in training may be at a pre-reflective stage, requiring guidance in developing the skill of reflective practice. He notes that educators who are truly self-reflective examine how expectations and assumptions, family influences and cultural conditioning impact on children and their learning and behaviour. They also recognise that there are tensions between theory, policy and practice, which they need to reconcile. This level of reflection moves practitioners to look not only at their own practices but also at the social implications of these practices.

A reflective educator is one who regularly reviews her practice with regard to children's behaviour, asking why am I doing this, of what value is it to the child, the group, my colleagues, parents, community. Such reflection shows an understanding that part of working professionally in education is to be willing to recognise that there is always something more to learn about children's behaviour, child development, learning environments, education in general.

SOCIAL JUSTICE, TRANSFORMATION OR REPRODUCTION

This dynamic understanding of behaviour in context leads to another key point that strikes us in exploring behaviour through a theoretical lens: the potential for approaches to behaviour in educational settings to act as agents of either transformation or reproduction of existing social inequalities. Chapter 8 explored the potential for dominant cultures to be replicated through the mechanism of behavioural sanctions and teacher expectations. The reality of development, behaviour and education for individual children, parents, teachers and schools is complex and contextual and, as a result, behavioural interventions must consider diversity and its potential impact on capacity to benefit from them. On the other hand, behavioural interventions that look solely at individual characteristics to explain why they succeed or not can run the risk of the development of deficit perspective, one that sees the problem as located within the individual and, as a result 'blames the victim' rather than considering the many other factors of influence. Expecting all children, parents and families to behave in the same way or hold the same values, beliefs and capacities regardless of background or personal circumstances may be not only futile but damaging. The onus is on educational settings to be proactive on these issues, because previous experiences of education can leave some children and adults vulnerable to marginalisation and intimidation. Through creating strong 'linkages' across educational settings, home and schools, educators can take account of the needs of diverse children and families to ensure the creation of an educational context where everyone feels welcome. Drawing on the 'funds of knowledge' that children and their families bring with them to an educational setting can enrich the context within which learning occurs, and improve behaviour by avoiding the 'cultural dissonance' highlighted in Chapter 8.

However, even socially aware educators may become pessimistic about their ability to support the children with whom they work in the face of many apparently competing pressures. They may become overwhelmed by the idea of multiple influences on a child's behaviour, and wonder, with all that is out of their control, whether they can ever impact on a child's understanding of how to behave positively, and more broadly still the course a child's life will take. When educators feel this way, there is a danger that they will disengage from their responsibility to support children and avoid doing anything too novel or innovative, or speak up for a child whose behaviour may be linked to unmet need, because it is safer to just do what is always done. The adults most responsible for protecting children and ensuring their well-being and development could fail to meet those responsibilities through a sense that either 'nothing can be done' or 'it's not my job to do it'.

The impact of protective forces such as strong, supportive relationships and communication with an important adult, on the development of resilience in children is even greater in 'at-risk' contexts (Hayes et al., 2017). To return to previous points if educators are practicing reflectively and are involved in caring, mutually supportive relationships with children, then they are more likely to be empowered to overcome the inertia and fear inherent in working within systems, and act in the child's best interest, regardless of institutional norms. Equally, if children are on the receiving end of caring, mutually supportive relationships, they are more likely to be empowered to object to unjust disciplinary practices experienced. Relationships have the power to overcome inertia and act as a catalyst for change, even in difficult circumstances. The educational philosopher Paulo Freire refers to the changes this can lead to as 'transformation'. This belief in the transformative potential of education for profound change can begin with the provision and support for quality early years practice, something early childhood educators have to fight for in societies where primary education is privileged in terms of funding and status. In this way the adults who care most about children, including their parents and their educators, can work together to ensure that early educational experiences provide rich day-to-day experiences and a foundation for children's future academic, social and emotional well-being, including positive behaviour, now and in their future.

CONCLUSION: SUPPORTING POSITIVE BEHAVIOUR: A MULTI-THEORETICAL PERSPECTIVE

A key message of this book for educators is that no one theoretical perspective has all the answers for understanding children's behaviour in early years and primary education. Equally, we argue that any 'how-to' manual that claims to be able to tell an educator what to do in every situation is making a false claim, simply because, like adults, children are complex human beings, learning, developing and behaving in the midst of their relationships with other complex human beings, in cultures and societies over time. Nevertheless, there may be some 'non-negotiables' that you may like to identify for yourself with regards to your behaviour-based interactions with children, for example, 'in supporting positive behaviour in my educational setting I will always try to consider the child's perspective as well as my own', or 'in supporting positive behaviour in my educational setting I will never use humiliation as a disciplinary tool'.

FINAL TASK

My manifesto for behaviour:
In supporting positive behaviour in my educational setting I will always …
In supporting positive behaviour in my educational setting I will never …

RELATIONSHIPS, RECIPROCITY AND REFLECTIVE PRACTICE: THE NEW '3R'S' FOR POSITIVE BEHAVIOUR IN PRIMARY AND EARLY CHILDHOOD EDUCATION

In years gone by, the '3R's' that were considered crucial for education were 'reading', 'riting' and 'rithmetic'. Our multi-theoretical perspective on children's behaviour has brought us to the realisation that the new '3R's' that really matter for children and their educators in primary and early childhood education are relationships, reciprocity and reflective practice. As Bronfenbrenner famously put it, 'In short, somebody has to be crazy about that kid' (Bronfenbrenner, 2005, p. 262).

NOTES

1 This section draws on the work of the authors in Hayes et al., 2017.
2 This section draws on Hayes (2013).

References

Abramson, C. I. (2013). Problems of teaching the behaviorist perspective in the cognitive revolution. *Behavioral Science*, *3*(1), 55–71.

Ainsworth, M. D. S., Blehar, M., Waters, E. and Wall, S. (1978). *Patterns of Attachment*. Hillsdale, NJ: Erlbaum.

Alanen, L., Brooker, L. and Mayall, B. (Eds.). (2015). *Childhood with Bourdieu*. Basingstoke, UK: Palgrave Macmillan.

Alsaker, F. D. (2004). The Bernese program against victimization in kindergarten and elementary school (Be-Prox). In P. K. Smith, D. Pepler and K. Rigby (Eds.), *Bullying in Schools: How Successful Can Interventions Be?* (pp. 289–306). Cambridge: Cambridge University Press.

Alsaker, F. D. and Valkanover, S. (2001). Early diagnosis and prevention of victimization in kindergarten. In J. Junoven and S. Graham (Eds.), *Peer Harassment in School: The Plight of the Vulnerable and Victimized* (pp. 175–195). New York: Guilford.

Alsaker, F. D. and Valkanover, S. (2012). The Bernese program against victimization in kindergarten and elementary school. *New Directions for Youth Development*, *2012*(133), 15–28.

American Psychologist (2012). Dan Olweus: Award for distinguished contributions to research in public policy. *American Psychologist*, *67*(8), 673–674.

Anning, A., Cullen, J. and Fleer, M. (Eds.). (2009). *Early Childhood Education: Society and Culture* (pp. 80–90). London: Sage.

Applefield, J. M., Huber, R. and Moallem, M. (2000). Constructivism in theory and practice: Toward a better understanding. *The High School Journal*, *84*(2), 35–53.

Arseneault, L., Walsh, E., Trzesniewski, K., Newcombe, R., Caspi, A. and Moffitt, T. (2006). Bullying victimization uniquely contributes to adjustment problems in young children: A nationally representative cohort study. *Pediatrics*, *118*(1), 130–138.

Askay, R. and Farquhar, J. (2011). *Of Philosophers and Madmen: A Disclosure of Martin Heidegger, Medard Boss and Sigmund Freud*. New York: Brill.

ACAT (Association for Cognitive Analytic Therapy). (n.d.). *What Is CAT Understanding? How Cognitive Analytic Therapy Can Help Teams and Groups*. Dorchester: ACAT Ltd.

Balbernie, R. (2007). *What About the Children? Cortisol and the Early Years*. Available at www.whataboutthechildren.org.uk/downloads/research-summaries-2006-to-2010/summary_watch_2007_cortisol.pdf

Baldry, A. C. (2003). Bullying in schools and exposure to domestic violence. *Child Abuse & Neglect*, *27*(7), 713–732.

Balsam, R. (2013). Freud, females, childbirth and dissidence: Margarete Hillferding, Karen Horney and Otto Rank. *Psychoanalytic Review*, *100*(5), 695–716.

Bandura, A. (1977). Self-efficacy: Toward a unifying theory of behavioral change. *Psychological Review*, *84*(2), 191.

Bandura, A. (1986). *Social Foundations of Thought and Action: A Social Cognitive Theory*. Englewood Cliffs, NJ: Prentice-Hall.

Bartlett, S. and Burton, D. (2012). *Introduction to Education Studies*. London: Sage.

Bauman, S. and Del Rio, A. (2006). Pre-service teachers' responses to bullying scenarios: Comparing physical, verbal, and relational bullying. *Journal of Educational Psychology*, *98*, 219–231.

Baumrind, D. (1971). Current patterns of parental authority. *Developmental Psychology Monographs*, *4*(1), 1–103.

Baumrind, D. (1996). The discipline controversy revisited. *Family Relations: Interdisciplinary Journal of Applied Family Studies*, *45*(4), 405–414.

Belsky, J. (1984). The determinants of parenting: A process model. *Child Development*, *55*(1), 83–96.

Belsky, J. (1988). The 'effects' of infant day care reconsidered. *Early Childhood Research Quarterly*, *3*(3), 235–272.

Berk, L. E. (2008; 2009; 2015). *Child Development*. New York: Pearson.

Boroditsky, L. (2018). Language and the construction of time through space. *Trends in Neurosciences*, *41*(10), 651–653.

Borrell-Carrió, F., Suchman, A. L. and Epstein, R. M. (2012). The biopsychosocial model 25 years later: Principles, practice and scientific inquiry. *Annals of Family Medicine*, *2*(6), 576–582.

Bourdieu, P. (1984). *Distinction*. London: Routledge and Kegan Paul.

Bourdieu, P. (1985). The genesis of the concepts of habitus and field. *Sociocriticism*, *2*(2), 11–24.

Bourdieu, P. (1990). *Sociology in Question*. Cambridge: Polity Press.

Bourdieu, P. (1991). *Language and Symbolic Power*. Cambridge, MA: Harvard University Press.

Bourdieu, P. (1996). Understanding. *Theory, Culture & Society*, *13*(2), 17–37.

Bourdieu, P. (1997). The forms of capital. In A. H. Halsey, H. Lauder, P. Brown and A. S. Wells (Eds.), *Education, Culture, Economy and Society* (pp. 46–58). Oxford: Oxford University Press.

Bourdieu, P. (2000). *Pascalian Meditations*. Stanford, CA: Stanford University Press.

Bourdieu, P. and Passeron, J. C. (1977). *Reproduction in Education, Society and Culture*. London: Sage.

Bower, M. E. and Knutson, J. F. (1996). Attitudes toward physical discipline as a function of disciplinary history and self-labeling as physically abused. *Child Abuse & Neglect*, *20*(8), 689–699.

Bowlby, J. (1944). Forty-four juvenile thieves: Their characters and home-life. Edinburgh: Balliere, Tindall and Cox.

Bowlby, J. (1969). *Attachment and Loss Vol 1, Attachment*. New York: Basic Books.

Bowlby, J. (1973). *Attachment and Loss Vol 2, Separation, Anxiety and Anger*. New York: Basic Books.

Bowlby, J. (1980). *Attachment and Loss Vol 3, Loss*. New York: Basic Books.

Bowlby, J. (1988). *Attachment and Loss Vol 4, A Secure Base: Clinical Applications of Attachment Theory*. London: Routledge.

Bowlby, R. (2007). Babies and toddlers in non-parental daycare can avoid stress and anxiety if they develop a lasting secondary attachment bond with one carer who is consistently accessible to them. *Attachment and Human Development*, *9*(4), 307–319.

Bowman-Perrott, L., Burke, M. D., de Marin, S., Zhang, N. and Davis, H. (2015). A meta-analysis of single-case research on behavior contracts: Effects on behavioral and academic outcomes among children and youth. *Behavior Modification*, *39*(2), 247–269.

Boyer, W. (2016). Person-centered therapy: A philosophy to support early childhood education. *Early Childhood Education Journal*, *44*, 343–348.

Brennan, C. (2012). Learning to play and playing to learn. In M. Mhic Mhathúna and M. Taylor (Eds.), *Early Childhood Education and Care: An Introduction for Students in Ireland* (pp. 161–167). Dublin: Gill and Macmillan.

Brewster, S. (2004). Insights from a social model of literacy and disability. *Literacy*, *38*(1), 46–51.

Brohl, K. (2007). *Working with Traumatized Children: A Handbook for Healing*. Washington, DC: CWLA Press.

Bronfenbrenner, U. (1979). *The Ecology of Human Development: Experiments by Nature and Design*. Cambridge, MA: Harvard University Press.

Bronfenbrenner, U. (1989). The developing ecology of human development: Paradigm lost or paradigm regained. Proceedings from *Biennial meeting of the Society for Research in Child Development*, Kansas City, MO.

Bronfenbrenner, U. (1995a). The bioecological model from a life course perspective: Reflections of a participant observer. In P. Moen, G. H. Elder, Jr. and K. Luscher (Eds.), *Examining Lives in Context: Perspectives on the Ecology of Human Development* (pp. 599–618). Washington, DC: American Psychological Association.

Bronfenbrenner, U. (1995b). Developmental ecology through space and time: A future perspective. In P. Moen, G. H. Elder, Jr. and K. Luscher (Eds.), *Examining Lives in Context: Perspectives on the Ecology of Human Development* (pp. 619–647). Washington, DC: American Psychological Association.

Bronfenbrenner, U. (Ed.). (2005). *Making Human Beings Human: Bioecological Perspectives on Human Development*. London: Sage.

Bronfenbrenner, U. and Ceci, S. J. (1994). Nature–nurture reconceptualized: A bioecological model. *Psychological Review*, *101*, 568–586.

Bronfenbrenner, U. and Morris, P. A. (2006). The bioecological model of human development. In R. M. Lerner and W. E. Damon (Eds.), *Handbook of Child Psychology:* Vol 1, *Theoretical Models of Human Development* (pp. 793–828). Chichester, UK: John Wiley and Sons.

Bronowski, J. (1973). *The Ascent of Man*. New York: Little Brown.

Brooker, L. (2008). *Supporting Transitions in the Early Years*. Maidenhead, UK: McGraw-Hill.

Brooker, L. (2015). Cultural capital in the preschool years. In L. Alanen, L. Brooker and B. Mayall (Eds.), *Childhood with Bourdieu* (pp. 13–33). Basingstoke, UK: Palgrave Macmillan.

Brophy, J. (2006). History of research on classroom management. In C. M. Evertson and C. S. Weinstein (Eds.), *Handbook of Classroom Management: Research, Practice, and Contemporary Issues* (pp. 17–46). Mahwah, NJ: Lawrence Erlbaum Associates.

Brophy, J. E. and Good, T. L. (1986). Teacher behaviour and student achievement. In M. W. Wittrock (Eds.), *Handbook of Research on Teaching* (3rd ed., pp. 328–375). New York: Macmillan.

Bruner, J. S. (1996). *The Culture of Education*. Cambridge, MA: Harvard University Press.

Bub, K. L., Buckhalt, J. A. and El-Sheikh, M. (2011). Children's sleep and cognitive performance: A cross-domain analysis of change over time. *Developmental Psychology*, *47*(6), 1504.

Burck, C. (2005). *Multilingual Living: Explorations of Language and Subjectivity*. Basingstoke, UK: Palgrave Macmillan.

Caravita, S. C. S. and Cillessen, A. H. N. (2012). Agentic or communal? Associations between interpersonal goals, popularity, and bullying in middle childhood and early adolescence. *Social Development*, *21*(2), 376–395.

CDC (Center on the Developing Child at Harvard University) (2007). *A Science-Based Framework for Early Childhood Policy: Using Evidence to Improve Outcomes in Learning, Behavior, and Health for Vulnerable Children*. Available at www.developingchild.harvard.edu

CDC (Center on the Developing Child at Harvard University) (2017). *5 Steps for Brain-Building Serve and Return*. Available at https://46y5eh11fhgw3ve3ytpwxt9r-wpengine.netdna-ssl.com/wp-content/uploads/2017/06/HCDC_ServeReturn_for_Parents_Caregivers_2019.pdf

Cepeda, N. J., Kramer, A. F. and Gonzalez de Sather, J. C. (2001). Changes in executive control across the life span: Examination of task-switching performance. *Developmental Psychology, 37*, 715–730.

Chao, R. (2000). The parenting of immigrant Chinese and European American mothers: Relations between parenting styles, socialization goals, and parental practices. *Journal of Applied Developmental Psychology, 21*, 233–248.

Chao, R. (2001). Extending research on the consequences of parenting style for Chinese Americans and European Americans. *Child Development, 72*, 1832–1843.

Chatzitheochari, S., Parsons, S. and Platt, L. (2016). Doubly disadvantaged? Bullying experiences among disabled children and young people in England. *Sociology, 50*(4), 695–713.

Cherry, K. (2018). *How Genes Influence Child Development*. Available at www.verywell mind.com/genes-and-development-2795114

Christensen, P. and James, A. (2000). *Research with Children: Perspectives and Practices*. London: Falmer Press.

Clark, A. and Moss, P. (2011). *Listening to Young Children: The Mosaic Approach* (2nd ed.). London: National Children's Bureau.

Cochran, J., Cochran, N., Nordling, W., McAdam, A. and Miller, D. (2010). Two case studies of childcentered play therapy for child referred with highly disruptive behavior. *International Journal of Play Therapy, 19*, 130–143.

Cohen, H. L. and Filipczak, J. (1971). *A New Learning Environment*. San Francisco: Jossey-Bass.

Cohen, H., Filipczak, J. and Bis, J. (1965). *Case Project: Contingencies Application for Special Education. Progress Report*. Washington, DC: U.S. Department of Health, Education, and Welfare.

Committee for Children. (2005). *Steps to Respect: Program Guide*. Seattle, WA: Author.

Committee for Children. (2014). *Second Step: Social-Emotional Skills for Early Learning*. Retrieved from www.secondstep.org/Portals/0/EL/Research/EL_Review_Research.pdf

Committee for Children (2015). *Second Step: A Violence Prevention Curriculum. National Institute of Justice's CrimeSolutions.gov*. Retrieved from www.crimesolutions.gov/Program Details.aspx?ID=221

Cole, P. M., Tan, P. Z., Hall, S. E., Zhang, Y., Crnic, K. A., Blair, C. B. and Li, R. (2011). Developmental changes in anger expression and attention focus: Learning to wait. *Developmental Psychology, 47*(4), 1078–1089.

Cooper, P. (2006). *Promoting Positive Pupil Engagement: Educating Pupils with Social, Emotional and Behavioural Difficulties*. Malta: Agenda.

Cooper, P., Bilton, K. and Kakos, M. (2012). The importance of a biopsychosocial approach to interventions for students with social emotional and behavioural difficulties. In T. Cole, H. Daniels and J. Visser (Eds.), *Handbook of Behavioural, Social and Emotional Difficulties* (pp. 89-95). London: Routledge.

Cremin, H. (2007). *Peer Mediation: Citizenship and Social Inclusion Revisited*. Maidenhead, UK: McGraw-Hill, Open University Press.

Crouch, S. R., Waters, E., McNair, R., Power, J. and Davis, E. (2014). Parent-reported measures of child health and well-being in same-sex parent families: A cross-sectional survey. *BMC Public Health, 14*, 635–647.

Cullen, J. (2001). An introduction to understanding learning. In V. Carpenter, H. Dixon, E. Rata and C. Rawlinson (Eds.), *Theory in Practice for Educators* (pp. 47–71). Auckland, NZ: Dunmore Press.

Cummins, J. (2005). A proposal for action: Strategies for recognizing heritage language competence as a learning resource within the mainstream classroom. *Modern Language Journal, 89*(4), 585–592.

Cummins, J., Bismilla, V., Chow, P., Cohen, S., Giampapa, F., Leoni, L., Sandhu, P. and Sastri, P. (2005). Affirming identity in multilingual classrooms. *Educational Leadership, 63*(1), 38–43.

Curtis, D. (2001). Strategies for enhancing children's use of the environment. *Child Care Information Exchange, 142*, 42–45.

Dahlberg, G., Moss, P. and Pence, A. (2013). *Beyond Quality in Early Childhood Education and Care: Languages of Evaluation* (2nd ed.). London: Routledge.

Davidson, M. C., Amso, D., Anderson, L. C. and Diamond, A. (2006). Development of cognitive control and executive functions from 4 to 13 years: Evidence from manipulations of memory, inhibition, and task switching. *Neuropsychologia, 44*, 2037–2078.

Dawes, M., Chen, C.-C., Farmer, T. W. and Hamm, J. V. (2017). Self- and peer-identified victims in late childhood: Differences in perceptions of the school ecology. *Journal of Youth and Adolescence, 46*, 2273–2288.

De Bellis, M. D. (2005). The psychobiology of neglect. *Child Maltreatment, 10*(2), 150–172.

Derman-Sparks, L. (1989). *Anti-Bias Curriculum: Tools for Empowering Young Children.* Washington, DC: National Association for the Education of Young Children.

Derrington, C. (2007). Fight, flight and playing white: An examination of coping strategies adopted by gypsy traveller adolescents in English secondary schools. *International Journal of Educational Research, 46*(6), 357–367.

DES (Department of Education and Skills). (1993). *Guidelines on Countering Bullying Behaviour in Primary and Post Primary Schools.* Dublin: DES.

DES (Department of Education and Skills). (2013). *Anti-Bullying Procedures for Primary and Post Primary Schools.* Dublin: DES.

DfE (Department for Education) (2013). *Preventing and Tackling Bullying: Advice for Head-teachers, Staff and Governing Bodies.* Available at www.education.gov.uk

Diamond, A. (2013). Executive functions. *Annual Review of Psychology, 64*, 135–168.

Diamond, A. (2016). Why improving and assessing executive functions early in life is critical. In J. A. Griffin, P. McCardle and L. S. Freund (Eds.), *Executive Function in Preschool-Age Children: Integrating Measurement, Neurodevelopment and Translational Research* (pp. 11–43). Washington, DC: American Psychological Association.

Downes, P. and Maunsell, C. (2007). *Count Us In: Tackling Early School Leaving in South West Inner City Dublin – An Integrated Response.* Dublin: The South Inner City Community Development Association (SICCDA) and South Inner City Local Drugs Task Force.

Downey, D. B. and Pribesh, S. (2004). When race matters: Teachers' evaluations of students' classroom behavior. *Sociology of Education, 77*(4), 267–282.

Doyle, W. (2009). A reflection on person-centered classroom management. *Theory into Practice, Spring 2009, A Person-Centered Approach to Classroom Management, 48*(2), 156–159.

Dummer, S. R. (2010). Peer mediation: What school counselors need to know (Unpublished Master's thesis). University of Wisconsin–Stout, Menomonie, WI. Available at https://bit.ly/2vWV9Zt

Dunphy, E. (2012). Perspectives on early learning. In M. Mhic Mhathúna and M. Taylor (Eds.), *Early Childhood Education and Care: An Introduction for Students in Ireland* (pp. 203–213). Dublin: Gill and Macmillan.

Duschinsky, R., Van Ijzendoorn, M., Foster, S., Reijman, S. and Lionetti, F. (2018). Attachment histories and futures: Reply to Vicedo's 'putting attachment in its place'. *European Journal of Developmental Psychology*, 1–9.

Edwards, C. P., Gandini, L. and Forman, G. E. (Eds.). (1998). *The Hundred Languages of Children: The Reggio Emilia Approach – Advanced Reflections.* Westport, CT: Greenwood Publishing Group.

Edwards, J. (2009). *Language and Identity.* Cambridge: Cambridge University Press.

Ellis, R. J. (2012). *The Study of Second Language Acquisition.* New York: Oxford University Press.

Engel, G. L. (1977). The need for a new medical model: A challenge for biomedicine. *Science, 196*(4286), 129–136.

Erickson, M. F., Sroufe, L. A. and Egeland, B. (1985). The relationship between quality of attachment and behavior problems in preschool in a high-risk sample. *Monographs of the Society for Research in Child Development*, 50(1–2), 147–166.

Eriksson, S. (2013). The same but different: Negotiating cultural identities by migrant children in Irish mainstream classrooms. *Irish Journal of Applied Social Studies*, 13(1), 38–52.

Ertmer, P. A. and Newby, T. J. (2013). Behaviorism, cognitivism, constructivism: Comparing critical features from an instructional design perspective. *Performance Improvement Quarterly*, 26(2), 43–71.

Eurostat (2019). *Children at Risk of Poverty or Social Exclusion*. Available at https://ec.europa.eu/eurostat/statistics-explained/index.php/Children_at_risk_of_poverty_or_social_exclusion

Farrell, S. (2005). *Peer Mediation in Schools: An Update Report on a Pilot Project*. Dublin: Mediation Bureau.

Feeney, J. A. and Noller, P. (1990). Attachment style as a predictor of adult romantic relationships. *Journal of Personality and Social Psychology*, 58(2), 281.

Felix, E. D. and Greif Green, J. (2010). Popular girls and brawny boys: The role of gender in bullying and victimization experiences. In S. R. Jimerson, S. M. Swearer and D. L. Espelage (Eds.), *Handbook of Bullying in Schools: An International Perspective* (pp. 173–186). London: Routledge.

Ferster, C. B. and Skinner, B. F. (1957). *Schedules of Reinforcement*. New York: Appleton-Century-Croft.

Flaherty, S.-J. (2012). *A Good Practice Guide for Breakfast Clubs*. Dublin: Healthy Food for All.

Fleer, M. (2003). Early childhood education as an evolving 'community of practice' or as lived 'social reproduction': Researching the 'taken-for-granted'. *Contemporary Issues in Early Childhood*, 4(1), 64–79.

Foody, M., Murphy, H., Downes, P. and O'Higgins Norman, J. (2018). Anti-bullying procedures for schools in Ireland: Principals' responses and perceptions. *Pastoral Care in Education*, 36(2), 126–140.

Freiberg, H. J. and Lamb, S. M. (2009). Dimensions of person-centered classroom management. *Theory into Practice*, 48(2), 99–105.

Freud, S. (1901). *The Psychopathology of Everyday Life*. London: Hogarth.

Freud, S. (1905). *Dora: An Analysis of a Case of Hysteria*. New York: Simon & Schuster, Inc.

Freud, S. (1955). *Collected Works*. New York: Hogarth.

Fröjd, S., Saaristo, V. and Ståhl, T. (2013). Monitoring bullying behaviours may not enhance principal's awareness of the prevalence. *School Leadership & Management*, 34(5), 470–480.

Gage, N. L. and Berliner, D. C. (1998). *Educational Psychology*. Boston, MA: Houghton Mifflin.

Garon, N., Bryson, S. E. and Smith, I. M. (2008). Executive function in preschoolers: A review using an integrative framework. *Psychological Bulletin*, 134(1), 31.

Garrett, T. (2008). Student-centered and teacher-centered classroom management: A case study of three elementary teachers. *Journal of Classroom Interaction*, 43(1), 34–47.

Gatongi, F. (2007). Person-centred approach in schools: Is it the answer to disruptive behaviour in our classrooms? *Counselling Psychology Quarterly*, 20(2), 205–211.

Gaylor, E. and Spiker, D. (2012). Home visiting programs and their impact on young children's school readiness. In R. E. Tremblay, R. G. Barr and Peters, R. de V. (Eds.), *Encyclopedia on Early Childhood Education* (pp. 1-8). Montreal: CEECD and SKC-ECD.

Geddes, H. (2006). *Attachment in the Classroom: The Links between Children's Early Experience, Emotional Well-being and Performance in School*. New York: Worth.

Gerhardt, S. (2004). *Why Love Matters: How Affection Shapes a Baby's Brain*. London: Routledge.

Glock, S. (2016). Does ethnicity matter? The impact of stereotypical expectations on in-service teachers' judgments of students. *Social Psychology of Education*, 19(3), 493–509.

Good, T. L. (1987). Two decades of research on teacher expectations: Findings and future directions. *Journal of Teacher Education, 38*(4), 32–47.

Good, T. L. (1993). Teacher expectations. In L. Anderson (Ed.), *International Encyclopedia of Education* (pp. 140–153) (2nd ed.). Oxford: Pergamon.

Graham, I. (2012). *What's New? Supporting Children through Transitions in Their Early Years.* Dublin: Barnardo's.

Greene, S. and Hill, M. (2005). Researching children's experience: Methods and methodological issues. In S. Green and D. Hogan (Eds.), *Researching Children's Experience: Approaches and Methods* (pp. 1–21). London, Thousand Oaks, CA and New Delhi: Sage.

Greene, S. and Moane, G. (2000). Growing up Irish: Changing children in a changing society. *The Irish Journal of Psychology, 21*(3–4), 122–137.

Gregory, A., Cornell, D., Fan, X., Sheras, P., Shih, T.-H. and Huang, F. (2010). Authoritative school discipline: High school practices associated with lower bullying and victimization. *Journal of Educational Psychology, 102*(2), 483–496.

Gregory, A. and Mosley, P. M. (2004). The discipline gap: Teachers' views on the over-representation of African American students in the discipline system. *Equity & Excellence in Education, 37,* 18–30.

Gregory, E. and Ruby, M. (2011). The 'insider/outsider'dilemma of ethnography: Working with young children and their families in cross-cultural contexts. *Journal of Early Childhood Research, 9*(2), 162–174.

Griffore, R. J. and Phenice, L. A. (2016). Proximal processes and causality in human development. *European Journal of Educational and Development Psychology, 4*(1), 10–16.

Guerrettaz, A. M. and Johnston, B. (2013). Materials in the classroom ecology. *The Modern Language Journal, 97,* 779–796.

Gunduz, N., Uzunboylu, H. and Ozcan, D. (2017). Developing and testing a scale to assess teachers' attitudes toward peer mediation of student disputes. *Social Behavior and Personality, 45*(10), 1745–1760.

Hachfeld, A., Schroeder, S., Anders, Y., Hahn, A. and Kunter, M. (2012). Multikulturelle Überzeugungen: Herkunft oder Überzeugung? Welche Rollen spielen der Migrationshintergrund und multikulturelle Überzeugungen für das Unterrichten von Kindern mit Migrationshintergrund? (Cultural background or cultural beliefs? What role do immigration cackground and multicultural beliefs play for teaching children with immigrant backgrounds?). *Zeitschrift für Pädagogische Psychologie, 26,* 101–120.

Halpenny, A. M., Greene, S. and Hogan, D. (2008). Children's perspectives on coping and support following parental separation. *Child Care in Practice, 14*(3), 311–325.

Halpenny, A. M., Nixon, E. and Watson, D. (2010). *Summary Report on Parents' and Children's Perspectives on Parenting Styles and Discipline in Ireland. Reports. 13.* Available at https://arrow.dit.ie/aaschsslrep/13

Hamm, J. V., Farmer, T. W., Dadisman, K., Gravelle, M. and Murray, A. R. (2011). Teachers' attunement to students' peer group affiliations as a source of improved student experiences of the school social: Affective context following the middle school transition. *Journal of Applied Developmental Psychology, 32*(5), 267–277.

Hayes, N. (2004). Towards a nurturing pedagogy: Reconceptualising care and education in the early years. In N. Hayes and M. Kernan (Eds.), *Transformations: Theory and Practice. Proceedings of the Annual OMEP Conference 2003,* University College Cork. (pp. 140–152). Cork: OMEP.

Hayes, N. (2013). *Early Years Practice: Getting It Right from the Start.* Dublin: Gill and Macmillan.

Hayes, N. (2018). We are all in this together: Inclusive early childhood education. In M. Twomey and C. Carroll (Eds.), *Seen and Heard: Exploring Participation, Engagement and Voice for Children with Disabilities* (pp. 365–389). London: Peter Lang.

Hayes, N. and Kernan, M. (2008). *Engaging Young Children: A Nurturing Pedagogy.* Dublin: Gill and Macmillan.

Hayes, N., O'Toole, L. and Halpenny, A. (2017). *Introducing Bronfenbrenner: A Guide for Practitioners and Students in Early Years Education*. London: Routledge.

Hedges, H. (2010). Whose goals and interests? In L. Brooker and S. Edwards (Eds.), *Engaging Play* (pp. 25–38). Maidenhead, UK: Open University Press.

Hedges, H. (2011). Rethinking Sponge Bob and Ninja Turtles: Popular culture as funds of knowledge for curriculum co-construction. *Australasian Journal of Early Childhood*, 36(1), 25–29.

Hedges, H. (2014). Children's content learning in play provision: Competing tensions and future possibilities. In L. Brooker, M. Blaise and S. Edwards (Eds.), *The Sage Handbook of Play and Learning in Early Childhood* (pp. 192–203). London: Sage.

Hegarty, T. (2007). Towards a narrative practice: Conversations in a city centre school. In P. Downes and A. L. Gilligan (Eds.), *Beyond Educational Disadvantage* (pp. 441–450). Dublin: Institute of Public Administration.

Helgeland, A. and Lund, I. (2017). Children's voices on bullying in kindergarten. *Early Childhood Education Journal*, 45, 133–141.

Hey, V. (1997). Northern accent and southern comfort: Subjectivity and social class. In P. Mahony and C. Zmrocrek (Eds.), *Class Matters: Working Class Women's Perspectives on Social Class* (pp. 140–151). London: Taylor and Francis Hill.

Hilgard, E. R. (1996). History of educational psychology. In D. C. Berliner and R. C. Calfee (Eds.), *Handbook of Educational Psychology* (pp. 990–1004). New York: Simon and Schuster McMillan.

Hogan, D. (2009). Researching 'the child' in developmental psychology. In S. Greene and D. Hogan (Eds.), *Researching Children's Experience* (pp. 22–42). London: Sage.

Hornby, G. and Lafaele, R. (2011). Barriers to parental involvement in education: An explanatory model. *Educational Review*, 3(1), 37–52.

Humphrey, L. (2013). *Preschool bullying: Does it exist, what does it look like, and what can be done?* (Paper No. 192) (MSW thesis). St Catherine University, St Paul, MN. Available at http://sophia.stkate.edu/msw_papers/192

Institute of Medicine. (2013). *Educating the Student Body: Taking Physical Activity and Physical Education to School*. Washington, DC: The National Academies Press.

James, A., Jenks, C. and Prout, A. (1998). *Theorizing Childhood*. New York: Teachers' College Press.

James, A. and Prout, A. (1990). *Contemporary Issues in the Sociological Study of Childhood*. Abingdon, UK: Routledge Falmer.

Jansen, P. W., Zwirs, B., Verlinden, M., Mieloo, C. L., Jaddoe, V. W. V., Hofman, A., Verhulst, A. C., Jansen, W., van Ijzendoorn, M. H. and Tiemeier, H. (2017). Observed and parent-reported conscience in childhood: Relations with bullying involvement in early primary school. *Social Development*, 26, 965–980.

Jimerson, S. R., Swearer, S. M. and Espelage, D. L. (Eds.). (2010). *Handbook of Bullying in Schools: An International Perspective*. London: Routledge.

Jones, S. M., Bailey, R., Barnes, S. P. and Partee, A. (2016). *Executive Function Mapping Project: Untangling the Terms and Skills Related to Executive Function and Self-Regulation in Early Childhood* (OPRE Report # 2016-88). Washington, DC: Office of Planning, Research and Evaluation, Administration for Children and Families, U.S. Department of Health and Human Services.

Kelly, C., Gavin, A., Molcho, M. and Nic Gabhainn, S. (2012) *The Irish Health Behaviour in School-Aged Children (HBSC) Study 2010*. Galway: Health Promotion Research Centre, National University of Ireland. Available at www.nuigalway.ie/hbsc

Kennan, D., Brady, B. and Forkan, C. (2019). Space, voice, audience and influence: The Lundy model of participation (2007) in child welfare practice. *Practice*, 31(3), 205–218.

Kernan, M. (2007). *Aistear: Play as a Context for Learning and Development*. Dublin: NCCA.

Kernan, M. (2015). Learning environments that work: Softening the boundaries. Paper prepared for the symposium *Early Educational Alignment: Reflecting on Context, Curriculum and Pedagogy*. Dublin: TCD/NCCA. Available at www.ecalignment.ie

Kernan, M. and Devine, D. (2010). Being confined within? Constructions of the good childhood and outdoor play in early childhood education and care settings in Ireland. *Children and Society*, 24(5), 371–385.

Khan, N. A. and Hillman, C. H. (2014). The relation of childhood physical activity and aerobic fitness to brain function and cognition: A review. *Pediatric Exercise Science*, 26(2), 138–146.

Kiely, J., O'Toole, L., Haals Brosnan, M., O'Brien, E. Z., O'Keeffe, C. and Dunne, C. M. (2019). *Parental Involvement, Engagement and Partnership in Their Children's Learning during the Primary School Years: Final Report*. Dublin: National Council for Curriculum and Assessment/National Parents Council.

King, P. and Kitchener, K. (2002). The reflective judgement model: Twenty years of research on epistemic cognition. In B. Hofer and P. Pintrich (Eds.), *Personal Epistemology: The Psychology of Beliefs about Knowledge and Knowing* (pp. 37–61). London: Routledge.

King, P. M. and Kitchener, K. S. (1994). *Developing Reflective Judgment: Understanding and Promoting Intellectual Growth and Critical Thinking in Adolescents and Adults*. Jossey-Bass Higher and Adult Education Series and Jossey-Bass Social and Behavioral Science Series. San Francisco: Jossey-Bass.

Kirves, L. and Sajaniemi, N. (2012). Bullying in early educational settings. *Early Child Development and Care*, 182(3–4), 383–400.

Kiser, B. (2015). Body of knowledge. *Nature*, 523, 286–287.

Kraftsoff, S. and Quinn, S. (2009). Exploratory study investigating the opinions of Russian-speaking parents on maintaining their children's use of the Russian language. *Irish Journal of Applied Social Studies*, 9(1), 65–80.

Krishnan, V. (2010). Early child development: A conceptual model. *Paper presented at the Early Childhood Council Annual Conference 2010, 'Valuing Care', Christchurch Convention Centre, Christchurch*, New Zealand, 7–9 May 2010.

Ladino, L. D., Rizvi, S. and Téllez-Zenteno, J. F. (2018). The Montreal procedure: The legacy of the great Wilder Penfield. *Epilepsy and Behaviour, 83*, 151–161.

Larrivee, B. (2005). *Authentic Classroom Management: Creating a Learning Community and Building Reflective Practice*. Boston, MA: Allyn & Bacon.

Larzelere, R. E., Morris, A. S. E. and Harrist, A. W. (2013). *Authoritative Parenting: Synthesizing Nurturance and Discipline for Optimal Child Development*. Washington, DC: American Psychological Association.

Laursen, E. K. (2003). Principle-centred discipline. *Reclaiming Children and Youth, 12*(2), 78–82.

Lindsay, C. A. and Hart, C. M. (2017). Exposure to same-race teachers and student disciplinary outcomes for black students in North Carolina. *Educational Evaluation and Policy Analysis, 39*(3), 485–510.

Lipoff (2012). *Behaviourism and the developing child*. Accessible at www.funderstanding.com/educators/behaviorism-and-the-developing-child/

Lockhart, S. (2010). Play: An important tool for cognitive development. *Extensions*, 24(3), 1–8.

Lortie, D. (1975). *Schoolteacher: A Sociological Study*. Chicago: University of Chicago Press.

Low, S., Frey, K. S. and Brockman, C. J. (2010). Gossip on the playground: Changes associated with universal intervention, retaliation beliefs, and supportive friends. *School Psychology Review*, 39(4), 536–551.

Lund, I. (2015). Dropping out or holding on? Dropping out as a sign of the difficulties experienced by adolescents with social, emotional and behavioral difficulties (SEBD) in the transition to upper secondary school. In D. Lansing Cameron and R. Thygesen (Eds.), *Transitions in the Field of Special Education: Theoretical Perspectives and Implications for Practice* (pp. 205–217). Kristiansand, Norway: Waxmann Verlag.

Lundy, L. (2007). 'Voice'is not enough: Conceptualising Article 12 of the United Nations Convention on the Rights of the Child. *British Educational Research Journal*, *33*(6), 927–942.

Machowska-Kosciak, M. (2019). Language and emotions: A follow-up study of 'moral allegiances' – the case of Wiktoria. *TEANGA, the Journal of the Irish Association for Applied Linguistics*, *10*, 172–185.

MacRuairc, G. M. (2009). 'Dip, dip, sky blue, who's it? NOT YOU': Children's experiences of standardised testing – A socio-cultural analysis. *Irish Educational Studies*, *28*(1), 47–66.

Main, M. and Solomon, J. (1986). Discovery of an insecure-disorganized/disoriented attachment pattern. In T. B. Brazelton and M. W. Yogman (Eds.), *Affective Development in Infancy* (pp. 95–124). Westport, CT: Ablex Publishing.

Malaguzzi, L. (1993). *History, Ideas, and Basic Philosophy: The Hundred Languages of Children – The Reggio Emilia Approach to Early Childhood Education*. NJ: Ablex Publishing Corporation.

Maslach, C. and Leiter, M. P. (2017). Understanding burnout: New models. In C. L. Cooper and J. Campbell Quick (Eds.), *The Handbook of Stress and Health: A Guide to Research and Practice* (pp. 36–56). Hoboken, NJ: John Wiley and Sons.

Mayall, B. (2002). *Towards a Sociology for Childhood: Thinking from Children's Lives*. Maidenhead, UK: Open University Press.

Melhuish, E., Phan, M., Syvla, K., Sammons, P. and Siraj-Blatchford, I. (2008). Effects of the home learning environment and preschool center experience upon literacy and numeracy development in early primary school. *Journal of Social Issues*, *64*(1), 95–114.

Milgram, S. (1965). Some conditions of obedience and disobedience to authority. *Human Relations*, *18*(1), 57–76.

Miller, G. A., Galanter, E. and Pribram, K. H. (1960). *Plans and the Structure of Behavior*. New York: Holt.

Minton, S. J. (2010). Students' experiences of aggressive behaviour and bully/victim problems in Irish schools. *Irish Educational Studies*, *29*(2), 131–152.

Minton, S. J., Dahl, T., O'Moore, A. M. and Tuck, D. (2008). An exploratory survey of the experiences of homophobic bullying among lesbian, gay, bisexual and transgendered young people in Ireland. *Irish Educational Studies*, *27*(2), 177–191.

Mischel, W. (1971). *Introduction to Personality*. New York: Holt, Rinehart and Winston.

Mitchell, L. (2011). Enquiring teachers and democratic politics: Transformations in New Zealand's early childhood education landscape. *Early Years*, *31*(3), 1–12.

Miyake, A. and Friedman, N. P. (2012). The nature and organization of individual differences in executive functions: Four general conclusions. *Current Directions in Psychological Science*, *21*(1), 8–14.

Morris, A. S., Silk, J. S., Steinberg, L., Sessa, F. M., Avenevoli, S. and Essex, M. J. (2002). Temperamental vulnerability and negative parenting as interacting predictors of child adjustment. *Journal of Marriage and Family*, *64*, 461–471.

Morrison, B. (2007). *Restoring Safe School Communities: A Whole School Response to Bullying, Violence and Alienation*. Sydney: The Federation Press.

Mosley, J. and Sonnet, H. (2006). *101 Games for Better Behaviour*. Cambridge: LDA.

Moss, P. (2007). Bringing politics into the nursery: Early childhood education as a democratic practice. *European Early Childhood Education Research Journal*, *15*(1), 5–20.

Moss, P. (2008). What future for the relationship between early childhood education and care and compulsory schooling? *Research in Comparative and International Education*, *3*(3), 224–234.

Moss, P. (2011). *Democracy as First Practice in Early Childhood Education and Care*. In R. E. Tremblay, R. G. Barr and Peters, R. de V. (Eds.), *Encyclopedia on Early Childhood Education* [online]. Montreal: Centre of Excellence for Early Childhood Development.

Mulkerrins, D. (2007). The transformational potential of the home school community liaison scheme. In P. Downes and A. L. Gilligan (Eds.), *Beyond Educational Disadvantage* (pp. 133–143). Dublin: IPA.

Murdoch, D. and Barker, P. (1991). *Basic Behaviour Therapy*. Hoboken, NJ: Wiley-Blackwell.

Murray, C. and O'Doherty, A. (2001). *Éist: Respecting Diversity in Early Childhood Care, Education and Training*. Dublin: Pavee Point.

Murray, C. and Urban, M. (2012). *Diversity and Equality in Early Childhood: An Irish Perspective*. Dublin: Gill & Macmillan.

NCCA. (2009). *Aistear: The Early Childhood Curriculum Framework*. Dublin: National Council for Curriculum Assessment.

NEPS (National Educational Psychological Service). (2007). *Behavioural Emotional and Social Difficulties: A Continuum of Support*. Dublin: NEPS.

New Zealand. (1996). *Te Whāriki: Early Childhood Curriculum*. Wellington, NZ: Learning Media Ltd.

Nic Gabhainn, S. and Sixsmith, J. (2006). Children photographing well-being: Facilitating participation in research. *Children & Society, 20*(4), 249–259.

Nowak-Łojewska, A., O'Toole, L., Regan, C. and Ferreira, M. (2019). 'To learn with' in the view of the holistic, relational and inclusive education. *Kwatalnik Pedagogiczny/Issues in Early Education, 251*(1), 151–162.

Ntelioglou, B. Y., Fannin, J., Montanera, M. and Cummins, J. (2014). A multilingual and multimodal approach to literacy teaching and learning in urban education: A collaborative inquiry project in an inner city elementary school. *Frontiers in Psychology, 5*, 533–543.

O'Brien, J. (2018). *Better Behaviour: A Guide for Teachers*. London: Sage.

O'Connor, A. (2013). *Understanding Transitions in the Early Years: Supporting Change through Attachment and Resilience*. Oxford: Routledge.

O'Kane, M. (2015). Multiple transitions. Paper prepared for the symposium *Early Educational Alignment: Reflecting on Context, Curriculum and Pedagogy*, 15 October, 2015, Trinity College, Dublin, Ireland. Available at www.ecalignment.ie

O'Moore, A. M., Kirkham, C. and Smith, M. (1997). Bullying behaviour in Irish schools: A nationwide study. *Irish Journal of Psychology, 18*, 141–146.

O'Moore, M. (2010). *Understanding School Bullying*. Dublin: Veritas.

O'Shaughnessy, T., Lane, K. L., Gresham, E. M. and Beebe-Frankenberger, M. (2003). Children placed at risk for learning and behavioral difficulties: Implementing a school-wide system of early identification and prevention. *Remedial and Special Education, 24*, 27–35.

O'Toole, L. (2015). Student-centred teaching in initial teacher education. *International Journal for Cross-Disciplinary Subjects in Education (IJCDSE), 6*(1), 2111–2119.

O'Toole, L. (2016). *A Bio-Ecological Perspective on Educational Transition: Experiences of Children, Parents and Teachers* (Unpublished Doctoral dissertation). Dublin Institute of Technology, Dublin, Ireland.

O'Toole, L., Hayes, N. and Mhic Mhathúna, M. (2014). A bio-ecological perspective on educational transitions. *Procedia-Social and Behavioural Sciences, 140*, 121–127.

O'Toole, L., Kiely, J., McGillacuddy, D., O'Brien, E. Z. and O'Keeffe, C. (2019). *Parental Involvement, Engagement and Partnership in their Children's Education during the Primary School Years*. Dublin: National Council for Curriculum and Assessment/National Parents' Council. Available at www.npc.ie/publications/books

Olson, D. R. and Bruner, J. S. (1996). Folk psychology and folk pedagogy. In D. R. Olson and N. Torrance (Eds.). *The Handbook of Education and Human Development* (pp. 9–27). Hoboken, NJ: Blackwell.

Olweus, D. (1978). *Aggression in the Schools: Bullies and Whipping Boys*. London: Hemisphere.

Olweus, D. (1993). *Bullying at School: What We Know and What We Can Do*. Cambridge, MA: Blackwell.

Olweus, D. (1997). Bullying/victim problems in school: Facts and intervention. *European Journal of Psychology of Education, 12*(4), 495–510.

Olweus, D. (2000). Bullying. *Encyclopedia of Psychology, 1*, 487–489.

Olweus, D. (2005). A useful evaluation design, and effects of the Olweus Bullying Prevention Program. *Psychology, Crime & Law*, 11(4), 389–402.

Olweus, D. and Limber, S. (1999). Bullying prevention program. In D. Elliott (Ed.), *Blueprints for Violence Prevention* (pp. 29–35). Boulder: Institute of Behavioral Science, Regents of the University of Colorado.

Pavlov, I. P. (1927). *Conditional Reflexes: An Investigation of the Physiological Activity of the Cerebral Cortex*. Oxford: Oxford University Press.

Perry, G. (2012). *Behind the Shock Machine: The Untold Story of the Notorious Milgram Psychology Experiments*. London: Scribe.

Postholm, M. B. (2013). Classroom management: What does research tell us? *European Educational Research Journal*, 12(3), 389–402.

Prochner, L. and Hwang, Y. (2008). 'Cry and you cry alone': Timeout in early childhood settings. *Childhood*, 15(4), 517–534.

Psalti, A. (2017). Greek in-service and preservice teachers' views about bullying in early childhood settings. *Journal of School Violence*, 16(4), 386–398.

Purdy, N. and Smith, P. K. (2016). A content analysis of school anti-bullying policies in Northern Ireland. *Educational Psychology in Practice*, 32(3), 281–295.

Raizada, R. D. and Kishiyama, M. M. (2010). Effects of socioeconomic status on brain development, and how cognitive neuroscience may contribute to levelling the playing field. *Frontiers in Human Neuroscience*, 4, 1–11.

Reay, D. (1995). Using habitus to look at 'race' and class in primary school classrooms. In M. Griffiths and B. Troyna (Eds.), *Anti-racism, Culture and Social Justice in Education* (pp. 115–132). Stoke-on-Trent, UK: Trentham Books.

Reay, D. (2010). 'It's all becoming a habitus': Beyond the habitual use of habitus in educational research. *British Journal of Sociology of Education*, 25(4), 431–444.

Regan, C. (2019). Relational approaches to early childhood education: CAT mapping and reflective practice. *Paper presented at the 8th International CAT Conference*, Ferrara, Italy, 27–29 June, 2019.

Rich, A. (1986). *Blood, Bread, and Poetry: Selected Prose, 1979–1985*. New York: W. W. Norton.

Riley, P. (2011). *Attachment Theory and the Teacher–Student Relationship*. London: Routledge.

Ring, E., Mhic Mhathúna, M., Moloney, M., Hayes, N., Breatnach, D., Stafford, P., Carswell, D., Keegan, S., Kelleher, C., McCafferty, D., O'Keefe, A., Leavy, A., Madden, R. and Ozonyia, M. (2015). *An Examination of Concepts of School Readiness among Parents and Educators in Ireland*. Dublin: Department of Children and Youth Affairs. Available at www.dcya.ie

Roache, J. and Lewis, R. (2011). The carrot, the stick, or the relationship: What are the effective disciplinary strategies? *European Journal of Teacher Education*, 34(2), 233–248.

Robinson, K. and Harris, A. L. (2014). *The Broken Compass*. Cambridge, MA: Harvard University Press.

Rogers, C. R. (1974). Questions I would ask myself if I were a teacher. *Education*, 95(2), 134–139.

Rogers, C. R. (1995). *Client-Centered Therapy: Its Current Practice, Implications and Theory*. London: Constable.

Rogoff, B. (2003). *The Cultural Nature of Human Development*. New York: Oxford University Press.

Rose, E., Weinert, S. and Ebert, S. (2018). The roles of receptive and productive language in children's socioemotional development. *Social Development*, 27(4), 777–792.

Rosenthal, R. and Jacobson, L. (1968). Pygmalion in the classroom. *The Urban Review*, 3(1), 16–20.

Rubie-Davies, C. (2010). Teacher expectations and perceptions of student attributes: Is there a relationship? *British Journal of Educational Psychology*, 80, 121–135.

Ryle, A. (1998). Transferences and countertransferences: The cognitive analytic therapy perspective. *British Journal of Psychotherapy*, *14*(3), 303–309.

Ryle, A. and Kerr, I. B. (2002). *Introducing Cognitive Analytic Therapy: Principles and Practice*. Chichester, UK: John Wiley & Sons.

Saracho, O. (2017). Bullying prevention strategies in early childhood education. *Early Childhood Education Journal*, *45*, 453–460.

Saudino, K. J. (2005). Behavioral genetics and child temperament. *Journal of Development and Behavioral Pediatrics*, *26*(3), 214–223.

Schnall, P. L., Dobson, M. and Landsbergis, P. (2017). Work, stress and cardiovascular disease. In C. L. Cooper and J. Campbell Quick (Eds.), *The Handbook of Stress and Health: A Guide to Research and Practice* (pp. 99–124). Hoboken, NJ: John Wiley and Sons.

Sektnan, M., McClelland, M. M., Acock, A. and Morrison, F. J. (2010). Relations between early family risk, children's behavioral regulation, and academic achievement. *Early Childhood Research Quarterly*, *25*, 464–479.

Sergiovanni, T. J. (2005). *Strengthening the Heartbeat: Leading and Learning Together in Schools*. New York: John Wiley and Sons.

Sims-Schouten, W. (2015). Bullying in early childhood and the construction of young children as premoral agents: Implications for practice. *Pastoral Care in Education*, *33*(4), 234–245.

Siraj, I. and Mayo, A. (2014). *Social Class and Educational Inequality: The Impact of Parents and School*. Cambridge: Cambridge University Press.

Siraj-Blatchford, I. and Clarke, P. (2000). *Supporting Identity, Diversity and Language in the Early Years*. Buckingham, UK: Open University Press.

Skinner, B. F. (1938). *The Behavior of Organisms*. New York: Appleton-Century-Crofts.

Skinner, B. F. (1953). *Science and Human Behavior*. New York: Simon and Schuster.

Skinner, B. F. (1968). *The Technology of Teaching*. New York: Appleton-Century-Crofts.

Skinner, B. F. (1972). *Beyond Freedom and Dignity*. New York: Knopf.

Small, P., Neilsen-Hewett, C. and Sweller, N. (2013). Individual and contextual factors shaping teachers' attitudes and responses to bullying among young children: Is education important? *Asia-Pacific Journal of Research in Early Childhood Education*, *7*, 69–101.

Smidt, S. (2012). *Introducing Malaguzzi: Exploring the Life and Work of Reggio Emilia's Founding Father*. London: Routledge.

Smidt, S. (2013). *Introducing Vygotsky: A Guide for Practitioners and Students in Early Years Education*. London: Routledge.

Smith, J. D., Woodhouse, S. S., Clark, C. A. and Skowron, E. A. (2016). Attachment status and mother–Preschooler parasympathetic response to the strange situation procedure. *Biological Psychology*, *114*, 39–48.

Sorin, R. and Galloway, G. (2006). Constructs of childhood: Constructs of self. *Children Australia*, *31*(2), 12–21.

Spooner, F. and Browder, D. M. (2003). Scientifically based research in education and students with low incidence disabilities. *Research and Practice for Persons with Severe Disabilities*, *28*(3), 117–125.

Spyrou, S. (2011). The limits of children's voices: From authenticity to critical, reflexive representation. *Childhood*, *18*(2), 1–15.

Sroufe, A. (2005). Attachment and development: A prospective, longitudinal study from birth to adulthood. *Attachment and Human Development*, *7*(4), 349–367.

St George, A. (1983). Teacher expectations and perceptions of Polynesian and Pakeha pupils and the relationship to classroom behaviour and school achievement. *British Journal of Educational Psychology*, *53*, 48–59.

Stewart, M. (2012). Understanding learning: Theories and critique. In L. Hunt and D. Chalmers (Eds.), *University Teaching in Focus: A Learning-centred Approach* (pp. 3–20). London: Routledge.

Storr, A. (2001). *Freud: A Very Short Introduction*. Oxford: OUP.

Stronge, J. H., Ward, T. J., and Grant, L. W. (2011). What makes good teachers good? A cross-case analysis of the connection between teacher effectiveness and student achievement. *Journal of teacher Education*, 62(4), 339–355.

Strong-Wilson, T. and Ellis, J. (2007). Children and place: Reggio Emilia's environment as third teacher. *Theory into practice*, 46(1), 40–47.

Sussman, D. (2005). Defining torture. *Case Western Reserve Journal of International Law*, 37, 225–230.

Swain, M., Kinnear, P. and Steinman, L. (2015). *Sociocultural Theory in Second Language Education: An Introduction through Narratives*. Bristol: Multilingual matters.

Sylva, K., Melhuish, E., Sammons, P., Siraj-Blatchford, I. and Taggart, B. (2010). *Early Childhood Matters: Evidence from the Effective Preschool and Primary Education Project*. Abingdon, UK: Routledge.

Sylva, K., Melhuish, E. C., Sammons, P., Siraj, I. and Taggart, B. (2004). *The Effective Provision of Pre-School Education (EPPE) Project: Technical Paper 12 – the Final Report – Effective Pre-School Education*. London: DfES/Institute of Education, University of London.

Szapocznik, J., Kurtines, W. and Fernandez, T. (1980). Bicultural involvement and adjustment in Hispanic American youths. *International Journal of Intercultural Relations*, 4(3–4), (353–365).

Taylor, P., Rietzschel, J., Danquah, A. and Berry, K. (2015). Changes in attachment representations during psychological therapy. *Psychotherapy Research*, 25(2), 222–238.

Tennant, M. (2002). *Psychology and Adult Learning*. London: Routledge.

Thomas, A. and Chess, S. (1977). *Temperament and Development*. Oxford: Brunner/Mazel.

Toshalis, E. (2010). From disciplined to disciplinarian: The reproduction of symbolic violence in pre-service teacher education. *Journal of Curriculum Studies*, 42(2), 183–213.

Trevarthen, C. (2004). Brain development. In R. L. Gregory (Ed.), *Oxford Companion to the Mind* (2nd ed., pp. 116–127). Oxford, New York: Oxford University Press.

United Nations (1989). United Nations Convention on the Rights of the Child, adopted by the UN General Assembly, 20 November, 1989.

United Nations (2005). *General Comment No. 7 On Implementing Child Rights in Early Childhood*. Geneva: United Nations.

Van IJzendoorn, M. (1995). Adult attachment representations, parental responsiveness, and infant attachment: A meta-analysis on the predictive validity of the adult attachment interview. *Psychological Bulletin*, 117(3), 387–403.

Van Ijzendoorn, M. H. and Sagi-Schwartz, A. (2008). Cross-cultural patterns of attachment: Universal and contextual dimensions. In J. Cassidy and P. R. Shaver (Eds.), *Handbook of Attachment: Theory, Research and Clinical Applications* (pp. 880–905). New York: Guilford Press.

Vandenbroeck, M. (2018). Diversity in Early Childhood Services. In: R. E. Tremblay, R. G. Barr and Peters, R. de V. (Eds.), *Encyclopedia on Early Childhood Education* [online]. Montreal: Centre of Excellence for Early Childhood Development. Available at www.child-encyclopedia.com/documents/VandenbroeckANGxp1.pdf

Vlachou, M., Andreou, E., Botsoglou, K. and Didaskalou, E. (2011). Bully/victim problems among preschool children: A review of current research evidence. *Educational Psychology Review*, 23, 329–358.

Vygotsky, L. S. (1978). *Mind and Society: The Development of Higher Mental Processes*. Cambridge, MA: Harvard University Press.

Watson, J. B. (1924). *Behaviorism*. New Brunswick: Transaction.

Watson, J. B. and Rayner, R. (1920). Conditioned emotional reactions. *Journal of Experimental Psychology*, 3(1), 1.

Wertsch, J. (1985). *Vygotsky and the Social Formation of the Mind*. Cambridge, MA: Harvard University Press.

Wertsch, J. V. (2005). Making human beings human: Bioecological perspectives on human development. *The British Journal of Developmental Psychology, 23*, 143.

Whitbeck, L. B., Hoyt, D. R., Stubbon, J. D. and LaFromboise, T. (2001). Traditional culture and academic success among American Indian children in the upper Midwest. *Journal of American Indian Education, 40*(2), 48–60.

White, M., White, M. K., Wijaya, M. and Epston, D. (1990). *Narrative Means to Therapeutic Ends*. New York: W. W. Norton.

White, M. K. (2004). *Narrative Practice and Exotic Lives: Resurrecting Diversity in Everyday Life*. Adelaide: Dulwich Centre Publications.

Winslade, J. and Monk, G. (1999). *Narrative Counseling in Schools: Powerful and Brief*. Thousand Oaks, CA: Corwin Press.

Wood, D. (1988). *How Children Think and Learn*. Oxford: Blackwell.

Wood, E. (2013). Free choice and free play in early childhood education: Troubling the discourse. *International Journal of Early Years Education, 22*(1), 4–18.

Woodhead, M. (2006). *Changing Perspectives on Early Childhood: Theory, Research and Policy*. Paper commissioned for the *EFA Global Monitoring Report 2007, Strong Foundations: Early Childhood Care and Education*. Geneva: UNESCO.

Woolard, J. (2010). *Psychology for the Classroom: Behaviourism*. London: Routledge.

Wubbels, T. (2011). An international perspective on classroom management: What should prospective teachers learn? *Teaching Education, 22*(2), 113–131.

York-Barr, J., Sommers, W. A., Ghere, G. S. and Montie, J. K. (2006). *Reflective Practice to Improve Schools: An Action Guide for Educators* (2nd ed.). Thousand Oaks, CA: Corwin Press.

Zelenko, M., Kraemer, H., Huffman, L., Gschwendt, M., Pageler, N. and Steiner, H. (2005). Heart rate correlates of attachment status in young mothers and their infants. *Journal of the American Academy of Child & Adolescent Psychiatry, 44*(5), 470–476.

Zimbardo, P. G. (1971). *Stanford Prison Experiment*. Redwood City, CA: Stanford University Press.

Zimbardo, P. G., Maslach, C. and Haney, C. (2000). Reflections on the Stanford prison experiment: Genesis, transformations, consequences. In T. Blass (Ed.), *Obedience to Authority: Current Perspectives on the Milgram Paradigm* (pp.193–237). London: Lawrence Erlbaum Associates.

Index

Printed in Great Britain
by Amazon